P9-AFO-158

THE
COSTA RICA
TRAVELER

Getting Around
In Costa Rica

By Ellen Searby

Windham Bay Press
Occidental, California

First edition January 1985
Second edition January 1988
Third edition October1991

Also published by Windham Bay Press:
Alaska's Inside Passage Traveler, See More,Spend Less by Ellen Searby
The Vancouver Island Traveler, Guide to the Freshest, Friendliest Place on Earth, by Linda Daniel

Front Cover: Sta. Maira Lusia Urena with scarlet macaw at the Hotel Pico Blanco. Photo by Rolf von Richter.

Back Cover: Playa Manuel Antonio and Punta Catedral. Photo by Ellen Searby from Biesanz condos.

Black and white photos by Ellen Searby and Marion Stirrup
Maps by Ellen Searby and Henry Jori

ISBN 0-942297-04-0   Library of Congress Catalog Card No. 91-065217

Searby, Ellen.
   The Costa Rica traveler : getting around in Costa Rica / Ellen
Searby. -- 3rd ed. --
   p. cm.
   Includes bibliographical references and index.
   ISBN 0-942297-04-0

   1. Costa Rica--Description and travel--1981- --Guide-books.   I.
Title.

F1543.5   917.286'0453
                                        QBI90-351
              Key Title: Costa Rica Traveler
Windham Bay Press
Box 1198, Occidental, California 95465 U.S.A.
Copyright © 1991 by Ellen Searby. All rights reserved.
Printed in the U.S.A.

FOREWORD

Costa Rica has more choices of things to see and do with less distance between them than any other place I've been. In the space of 75 miles across its narrowest width, the land goes from sea level to over 12,000 feet and back to sea level. There are many landscapes and climates between, and the wide variety of plants and animals they support. Costa Rica would offer fine traveling even if this were all.

"We have so much to share," is a slogan of Costa Rica's tourism department, the Instituto Costarricense de Turismo (ICT). Costa Rica has nearly three million of the most friendly, helpful people in the world. A Canadian visitor wrote, "They treat you with a quiet dignity, like a guest in their home, instead of an invading tourist." Their pride in their country with its freedom and literacy, and their willingness to share it with the traveler, are a joy—and a lesson in humanity.

Before I vacationed in Costa Rica the first time, a U.S. friend des-cribed it as "the most hassle-free foreign travel you'll ever do." Even then with almost no Spanish except numbers, I found she was right. People helped any time they could think of a way to do so. They've met enough travelers to know what we want and have kept their con-siderate nature without becoming cynical. Meeting the Costa Ricans is as much a privilege as traveling in the beauty of their country.

OUR THIRD EDITION

In the years since *The Costa Rica Traveler* was first published, there have been many changes in Costa Rica. What has **not** changed is the friendly hospitality of the people and peace in their country. Costa Ricans have worked persistently for peace and economic stability in Central America. President Arias received the 1987 Nobel Peace Prize for his peace plan and efforts to bring peace with justice to the region.

Costa Rica has been discovered by travelers, nature lovers, TV crews, and airlines. Now those encouraging travel there must think of the type of travel and its effect on Costa Rica. Massive tourism is not a low impact industry, especially in a small space. Dispersed tourism, with emphasis on coming to enjoy natural attractions, whether ecological or active such as rafting and surfing, can help Costa Rica afford the protection of its natural scene instead of paving it (or burning it off for pasture). All of us need to think, be careful of our impact, and use self-control—government, resort developers and tour agencies, authors, and travelers.

While Costa Rica isn't built up like Waikiki or Cancun, you need hotel reservations in San Jose anytime and at beaches during holidays or high season. From mid-November through April, you should make reservations at least three months ahead. For December and Easter week, five months is better. If you're planning on renting a car, you should reserve it well ahead during high season. With reservations, you can easily avoid crowds, as there are beaches and parks with only one hotel nearby. If you have reserved there, you can enjoy the tranquility even on holidays! Meanwhile tourist facilities, roads, and tours, especially for nature-lovers, have increased. I inspected nearly 300 hotels and cabinas for this edition, some of them just opened. Many of you have written or told me your experiences with tourist services and asked for additional information in this edition. With no paid advertising in the book, I have felt free to comment on facilities as I found them. While Costa Rica is a real place in the real world of developing countries, everyone I have met has enjoyed his trip and many have returned for another visit or retirement.

Your suggestions and comments when you return are always welcome here. Facilities and tour agencies change managers after we inspect. Often it's an improvement, sometimes not. New hotels and cabinas are being built daily and can be mentioned in the Flash section in the next printing. Have a great trip!

USING THIS BOOK

Please check the Flash section at the back of this book for the latest important information we gathered just at presstime. This section is revised for each printing, without waiting for the next edition.

To call any Costa Rican telephone or fax number from the United States, dial 011-506 and then the number. The international country code for Costa Rica is 506. To call Costa Rican information from the United States, dial 00 for the international operator. Fax machines have multiplied greatly during the past few years in Costa Rica and are now invaluable for getting information and making reservations.

The 7.4 earthquake of April 22, 1991 rocked Costa Rica and raised its eastern shore as I prepared this edition. Since most of Costa Rica is undamaged and roads, bridges and other facilities are being repaired, I have left most text as it was, and will report in the Flash section on the condition of tourist facilities at each printing.

ACKNOWLEDGMENTS

I owe thanks to many people who helped me gather and update information for this edition. Without them I couldn't have done it.

Special thanks to LACSA, Costa Rica's airline. They helped me with this project, and their promotion has helped tourism in Costa Rica greatly. María Amalia Martí and Mayela Pacheco took time from their very busy schedules to help me and this book.

Within the Instituto Costarricense de Turismo (known in Costa Rica as the ICT and in the U.S. as the Costa Rican Tourist Board), Tania D'Ambrosio made appointments for me and answered questions or found those who could. Teresa Bejarano, director of marketing, and her staff helped in every way possible, and driver Jorge Chacon guided and interviewed with me.

The following capable and cheerful people made my field time much more effective with their suggestions, information, and assistance: John Aspinall, John and Maxine Bota, Amos Bien, Robert Chaverri, Fernando Cortes, Lillian DeSha, Patricia Duar, Richard and Dery Dyer of the *Tico Times*, Archie and Ed Fields, and their guide, Wendell Hudson, of Rio Colorado Lodge, Richard and Margot Frisius, Letty Grant, Michael Kaye, Jim Lewis and the staff of Costa Rica Expeditions, Bernardo Madriz of Servicio Parques Nacionales and the rangers and staffs of many parks and preserves, Roberto Morales, Maricarmen Oreamuno, Jerry Ruhlow, and Lee Weiler.

Naturalist-guide Carlos Gomez made many miles of back country memorable as he drove through rivers and floods, over mountain trails, and even out of a strikers' roadblock, with stops for rare birds and photos. Joyce Veazey professionally copy-edited my text (and may have to wait for the next edition to see me get all her improvements into it).

Any errors in the book are my responsibility, not theirs. Their explanation of their country and their culture was wonderful. May you enjoy Costa Rica as much as I do!

Henry Jori, my husband, drew maps, proofread copy, offered many useful suggestions, and gave moral support and encouragement while I worked on this project. My assistant, Shirley Weeks, put up with me while she compiled information, ran copies, and looked for whatever I couldn't find. Cyndi Reese, Ric Barnett, and Janis Wells covered for some of my computer illiteracy. Without them all, you'd never see this.

Seasons & Activities Table

SEASONS & ACTIVITIES	D	J	F	M	A	M	J	J	A	S	O	N
Rainy season, San Jose						•	•	•	•	•	•	•
Dry season, San Jose	•	•	•	•	•							
Rainy season, Guanacaste							•	•	•	•	•	•
Dry season, Guanacaste	•	•	•	•	•							
Rainy season, Limón	•	•				•	•	•	•	•	•	•
Dry season, Limón			•	•	•							
Independence Day										15		
Carnivals	SJ					Punt					Limón	
Horse Shows	SJ			SJ	Tilar							
Rodeos, Guanacaste		18	•						25			
Bullfights		18	•						25			
Tarpon, East Coast		•	•	•	•	•	•	•				
Snook, East Coast	•								•	•	•	•
Marlin, West Coast	•	•	•	•	•	•	•	•	•	•	•	•
Sailfish, West Coast	←		North			✕			South			→
Tortuguero												
Green Turtles, egglaying								•	•	•		
Green Turtles, hatching									•	•	•	
Guanacaste												
Leatherback, egg laying	•	•	•	•								•
Leatherback, hatching	•	•	•	•								
Ridley egg laying	•					•	•	•	•	•	•	•
Ridley hatching	•	•					•	•	•	•	•	•
Dove hunting, Guanacaste	•	•	•	•								•
Duck hunting, Guanacaste	•	•	•	•								•

TABLE OF CONTENTS

Jungle waterfall near Playa Montezuma.

COSTA RICA

If there is a tropical Camelot, peaceful Costa Rica is it. Despite turbulence in its neighbors, Costa Rica has the best working democracy in Latin America, the freest, most honest elections, and the highest literacy rate in the region. Beset with the same economic, social, and environmental problems that face other developing nations, Costa Rica is much farther along the road to solution than most others.

Costa Rica is tiny, about the size of West Virginia. You can fly into San Jose, the capital, up in the Central Valley, and decide whether you want to swim in the Atlantic or Pacific Ocean that afternoon!

WHY COME? MAJOR ATTRACTIONS

Costa Rica in its small space has many attractions that are major by any standard. Among them are:

Children surf at Dominical.

Beaches

Costa Rica has hundreds of beaches, most uncrowded. You may find yourself the only person on a beach five miles long! Do you prefer white, black, yellow, or red sand? Costa Rica has them all. Do you want to surf, snorkel, walk on a wild driftwood-littered beach, watch thousands of sea turtles come ashore to lay eggs in the sand, watch newly hatched baby turtles crawl down to the sea, swim or wade in calm water, gather agates and moonstones polished by waves, fish for tarpon, marlin, and other gamefish, walk palm-shaded paths along the shore watching for parrots, monkeys, egrets, and end the day enjoying one of the world's finest sunsets?

All Costa Rican beaches seem to have at least four or five of the above features. You can pick an area suited to your interests. I like being able to watch monkeys, birds, iguanas, and perhaps a sloth while I walk to the beach for a swim. Usually several nearby beaches have different attractions, adding variety to your vacation.

Do take seriously local advice on rip currents which exist at most beaches with surf. Beaches which always deserve respect for rips include Junquillal, Jacó, Esterillos, and First Beach at Manuel Antonio. Beaches sheltered by islands offshore or nearby headlands are usually safe. Costa Rica has many beaches where a two year-old can safely splash anytime.

Accommodations range from some of the world's finest hotels, through very comfortable, reasonably priced cabinas and motels, to basic cabinas and rooms, and, of course, camping out. They are described later in this book, according to location. More resorts now rent surf-boards and snorkeling gear as well as horses and bicycles. Even the most serious birding tours include beach trips.

Volcán Arenal erupts cinders, ash, and steam.

Volcanoes

Costa Rica's backbone north and east of San Jose is a chain of volcanoes extending down from Mexico through Central America. Costa Rica has 10, three of them active. You can ride public buses or bus tours from San Jose to the tops of Irazú, 11,260 ft., and Poás, 9,500 ft. Others are reached by hiking, horse, or jeep trail. Irazú erupted in 1963, showering San Jose with five inches of ash, causing millions of colones in damage to property, livestock, and the 1964 coffee crop, but enriching the Central Valley soil for years to come. On a clear morning you can see both the Atlantic and Pacific Oceans from its summit. In 1991 Irazú gave off steam and had frequent earthquakes.

Poás last erupted in 1978, but has a constantly varying steam cloud boiling up from the fumaroles in its crater. Recently it has sent up more sulfurous steam and the Park Service has sometimes closed the park due to the acid vapors. You'll notice the effect on plants and trees near the summit and on the metal parts of the visitor center. If the steam is blowing toward the overlook, you shouldn't stay there long.

Both volcanoes have overlooks at the edge of their craters with fantastic views of the banded rocks and ash that form their rims. Riding up these heights, you pass from warm to a very cool and cloudy tropical climate. Coffee plantations give way to dairy cattle and potato patches on terraces up the steep slopes. In the cloud forests at higher elevations, tree branches support communities of bromeliads, orchids, and other plants. Up here in the clouds, the forest and the ash-covered slopes near the craters are another world from the busy streets of San Jose.

Arenal, between Tilarán and Fortuna, is the only erupting volcano in Costa Rica at presstime. From the road near Lake Arenal you can hear rumbles and see red lava at night and ash clouds by day during its almost daily eruptions. Red-hot lava is thrown up into the air to shower and roll down the slopes. Action isn't guaranteed, however, and you could hear only a growl or be there when clouds cover the mountain. You'll have a better chance if you stay overnight instead of going just for a few hours. Climbing this volcano is dangerous and has cost lives.

Poás Crater from the overlook.

Guápiles Highway crosses Braulio Carrillo Nat'l. Park, a scenic drive in the cloud forest.

National Parks

Costa Rica has done an incredible thing for any nation, much less a struggling developing country—it has set aside 12% of its small space in a national park system, one of the world's most important. Another 15% of the nation is in forest reserves or other protected status, putting over one quarter of the country under some protection. As tropical forests are cut everywhere, these preserved areas are the only hope of saving many plant and animal species. There is at least one sample of every ecosystem in the country within the park system.

All the volcanic summits are within parks or biological preserves. Santa Rosa is a dry tropical forest, while Corcovado in the southwest is a rolling, wet lowland with as many bird species as the United States and Canada combined. Rare is the park that doesn't have at least 200 birds species and 100 animal species! Insect species are in the thousands and still being counted. Some parks preserve cultural or archeological features, such as prehistoric village sites.

There's something for most travelers in the parks. You can watch sea turtles come ashore to lay their eggs in the sand at Tortuguero and Santa Rosa and come back several months later to see newly hatched babies scramble down to the sea. At Caño Island and Cahuita you can snorkel on coral reefs. At Rincon de la Vieja you can walk up to thermal springs and "pailes," springs of boiling mud. In Santa Rosa's dry forest, undergrowth and vines are widely spaced and you have clear views of monkeys, coatimundis, peccaries, armadillos, and hundreds of birds. I saw all

Main archeological site at Guayabo Nat'l Monument.

of these on one walk there.

Costa Rica's limited park budget is going to the preservation of these precious habitats for wildlife, while most unprotected land is being cut over for lumber and to make cattle range. Funds aren't being spent for building plush facilities or even access roads in some cases. While you can drive up to some parks by bus, La Amistad, the largest, covering the Talamanca Range along the Panamanian border, may only be reached by dirt roads to the park boundaries on both east and west sides. There is not a single lodge or hotel within the parks. For the more remote parks, arrangements must be made with park headquarters in San Jose so the staff knows what help you'll need—space in a bunkroom, meals or use of cooking facilities, guide, possibly horses to rent if the rangers don't need them that day, etc.

If your time is limited and you want to see the maximum wildlife in remote parks, you may want to go on a nature tour led by biologists. Smithsonian, the National Audubon Society, Mountain Travel, and other adventure tour operators organize these. Within Costa Rica, there are several outfitters whose addresses are given in our Sources of Information section near the end of the book.

Young margay peers from a tree.

Birds and Wildlife

Costa Rica is home, seasonally, to one-tenth of the world's bird species, over 850 (the U. S. and Canada combined have about 350)! For such a small country, this seems impossible, but Costa Rica's 12,600 feet of altitude range, wet and dry zones, and strategic location in the overlap between North and South American bird ranges account for it. This nation's dedicated protection of those habitats may be all that keeps many of these species alive.

From trips to the zoo, you know that tropical birds are often brighter and more spectacular than most temperate birds, though nearly invisible brown twitters (my term which saves reaching for the bird book) are found in every forest. Chattering flocks of parrots and lorikeets fly overhead in early morning and evening. An early morning look in any hotel garden or city park is rewarding.

Costa Rica's pride is the resplendent quetzal, never found in zoos, but living in the high, cool forests of Monteverde and the Talamanca Mountains. With its red underside, iridescent green back and trailing green tail plumes, it is like no other! It is most easily seen on guided trips in March and April, when it is nesting and less cautious than usual—and the guide knows where the nests and food trees are.

15

Depending on location, season, and luck, you may see scarlet macaws, tanagers and orioles, toucans, and waterfowl of all kinds including roseate spoonbills and the rare jabiru stork. Estuaries and lagoons where small rivers reach the sea may have a dozen species visible at a time, very near the beach hotel you're staying in. Palo Verde National Park at the mouth of the Tempisque River is a great waterfowl haven that attracts naturalists from many nations.

A biologist from Cornell was studying hummingbirds at Monteverde. Knowing there were several pages of them in my bird book, I asked how many there were in her area. "Thirty species, but only eight common."

When you're watching birds or monkeys in the bush, it's very easy to forget the ground at your feet. *Don't.* In Rincon de la Vieja National Park, I saw my first Rey del Zopilote (king buzzard) in the wild. It's a huge, creamy-white bird with black on the wings and a red and orange head. I stepped off the horse I'd been riding, camera in hand, and got four shots before ants from the hill I was standing on reached and stung my neck! With that lack of care, I was lucky there wasn't a snake.

Guided tours are the easiest way to be sure of seeing certain birds, and may be the only practical way to get to Corcovado National Park, usually reached by charter flight. Recently nature tours have grown in numbers and variety, generally providing tours and guides in the national parks, biological reserves where they are often the only groups permitted, and on some private reserves.

I've added a new section in the "Planning Your Trip" chapter, "Nature Tours and Lodges" where you'll find descriptions and addresses to help

Wood stork soars over Palo Verde Nat'l. Park.

Three-toed sloth crawls across trail at Manuel Antonio.

you choose where you want to go. Especially if you want a multi-day tour, it's best to write the operators some months in advance and ask which adventure travel and nature tour organizations are sending them groups. With an expert guide, I watched one group identify over 150 bird species in four days, including the resplendent quetzal and the three-wattled bell bird.

For these trips or for looking on your own, you'll want binoculars, insect repellent, a shade hat, sunscreen, a day pack and canteen, a rain parka, and good walking shoes. Bird books printed outside Costa Rica are very expensive within the country, so it's worth bringing them with you. *Birds of Costa Rica* by Stiles and Skutch is in stores and our catalog at the back of this book or can be ordered from Cornell University Press, 124 Roberts Place, Ithaca, NY 14850-2426. 1-800-666-2211. 656 pages, great illustrations. $65 hb, $35 pb. They take credit cards. *The Butterflies of Costa Rica and Their Natural History* by DeVries is published by Princeton University Press. The pictures in both of these books are enough to bring any avid nature lover to Costa Rica.

Mammals and reptiles in Costa Rica are as diverse as the birds, but generally fewer and much harder to spot. Some are nocturnal and others live only in the tree canopy far above the ground. Many are endangered, due more to loss of habitat than overhunting, except in the case of sea turtles. Jaguars, ocelots, margays, howler, squirrel, spider and capuchin monkeys, sloths, deer, tapirs, peccaries, agoutis, coatimundis, foxes, coyotes, armadillos, and manatees are among the animals. You can see some of them in the zoo in San Jose. Iguanas, crocodiles, and caimans are common in some areas. Green turtles next on the Caribbean coast, primarily at Tortuguero, and leatherback and Pacific Ridley turtles nest on several Pacific beaches.

While many of these animals are not only shy but nocturnal, an early morning or early evening watch at a water hole, especially in drier Guanacaste, is a good way to see them. I've seen howler monkeys, storks, and deer in streams beside highway bridges (when someone else was driving). Even in national parks where they do exist, many are rarely seen. Good luck.

The Serpentarium in San Jose features Costa Rican snakes and frogs and maybe the only place you'll see them in the country. If you want to see the fer-de-lance, bushmaster, and coral snake up close, safely, this is your spot. It also has snakes from other areas including a 19 foot Asian python. Ave. 1, Calles 9/11. Phone 55-4210. Open seven days a week, 10 -7. Admission US$1. Feeding is Thursday morning before opening, but you can call ahead for an appointment.

"Poor Man's Umbrella" has leaves over 6 ft. across.

Prize winners at the Nationall Orchid Show.

The Butterfly Farm a few miles west of San Jose is the best place to many of Costa Rica's butterflies up close in a big walk-in enclosure full of tropical plants. Directions and information are in the San Jose chapter.

Flora

Costa Rica's flowers, flowering trees and shrubs, and an incredible variety of other tropical plants are a delight to anyone. February and March are the height of the blooming season for trees, including the red Poro tree used for living fence posts along roads.

The national flower is an orchid, the *guaria morada*, and there are nearly 1,200 known species of orchids in the country. At any season, some varieties are in bloom. Finding one beside a trail in the Monteverde forest was a thrill I won't forget. Collecting orchids is done only by government permit, and then you probably couldn't get them back into your home country. Bring a close-up lens and collect them on film! Gift shops offer the sealed vials of tissue-cultured orchid starter plants produced at CATIE, the research station near Turrialba. They have the *guaria morada* and another endangered species the station hopes to preserve. You can bring these home, but will need some expertise to raise them.

The annual orchid show in San Jose in mid-March has a fantastic variety of plants raised by local enthusiasts. Costa Rican residents can buy many varieties of orchid plants at the show.

Any time of year you can visit the Lankester orchid gardens, now run by the University of Costa Rica, near the road (1 km from the Paraiso bus) between Cartago and Paraiso, open 9 a.m. to 3 p.m. Admission charge. On its 649 acres of nature reserve, forest, paths, and greenhouses are 800 species of orchids as well as bromeliads, ferns, and other tropical plants. March and April are peak season, but some are in bloom any month.

Within the national parks and in other areas that haven't been deforested, you can enjoy magnificent tropical hardwood trees with huge trunks and spreading branches, often supporting colonies of bromeliads and other plants on branches and trunks. Even in yards everywhere you may find 6-foot examples of shrubs you struggle to grow in tiny pots at home. From landscaped hotel grounds and urban parks to primeval forests and coconut walks along the Caribbean, the variety and colors are thrilling, with surprises on every walk.

"The Jungle Train"

Known as the Northern or Atlantic Railway, this 100-mile narrow-gauge train, completed in 1890, was the key to development of Costa Rica. Until it was built, the country's only export, coffee, had to be hauled by oxcart and pack mule down mountain trails to Puntarenas on the west coast and and across Panama or around Cape Horn to market.

Six thousand people died building the railway. Malaria and yellow fever in the eastern lowlands were the main killers. The young American, Minor Keith, struggled with the project for nearly 20 years before it was done. When some miles of track were laid from the east coast and money was running short, Keith imported banana seedlings and started the plantations that became the United Fruit Company. Jamaican workers were brought in, as they were more resistant than others to malaria, and were given land along the track.

Their descendants still live on the Caribbean lowland. These people speak English, making this coast an easy place to travel for those with limited Spanish.

In 1990 a huge landslide covered the track between Cartago and Turrialba, and Costa Rica doesn't have the funds to repair and maintain that unstable section. You can still see a spectacular part of "the jungle

Reventazón River from the"jungle train".

train" route between Turrialba and Siquirres, following the rushing Reventazón River in passenger rail cars that presently run on Thursdays and Saturdays, leaving Turrialba at 1 p.m. Across the river rainforest extends for miles in forest reserves. Tour operators use reserved space on the train return you to San Jose by bus. Some tours stop in the Orósi Valley en route to Turrialba. Independent travelers may have a better chance of getting space on the train by boarding at Siquirres about 9 a.m. and riding it up to Turrialba (sit on left side going up).

The train was the *only* surface route from San Jose to the east coast until 1970 when the first road was built via Turrialba and Siquirres. Villagers along the track depended on the train to get to schools, hospitals and markets. Now, driving on the Guápiles Highway which opened in 1987 and reduced driving time to the coast to 2 1/2 hours, it's hard to believe how recently the capital and the coast have been closely connected.

Electric Train to West Coast

As thousands of cruise ship passengers have found, the electric narrow-gauge train from San Jose to Puntarenas is a delightful, scenic ride through farming country, along the gorge of the Barranca River, with stops at tiny villages not reached by highway or bus. While newer and not as historic as the Atlantic Railway, the Pacific Railway offers a beautiful four hour ride that is much more scenic than the bus trip from San Jose to Puntarenas.

At its many stops villagers get on to go or come from market in Orotina, the only large town you pass. Going west, if you are on the left side of the train, you look down into the Barranca gorge as the train skirts steep ridges, turns tightly around canyons, sways through tunnels, and stops at a small station with a few houses or a ranch every few minutes. After Orotina the valley widens and you are soon down in the lowlands following the river and then the shore with stops at Mata Limón, Caldera, Chacarita, and several other villages on the way into Puntarenas.

The train leaves from the Ferrocarril Pacifica station on Ave. 20 at Calle 2 at 1 p.m. daily (check with ICT or the station, 26-0011, about Sundays). Note that during Christmas shopping season it leaves at about 3 p.m. on the afternoon run and makes the last part of the trip in the dark. It leaves Puntarenas at 1 p.m., and offers an alternative when lines for the bus are hours long. Check the schedule as there have been changes. Fare is about $1.25, a real bargain for all that entertainment.

"Los Canales"—Inland Waterway

From Moín, a few miles north of Puerto Limón, a jungle waterway extends over 70 miles up the northeast coast to Barra Colorado. Eight rivers form lagoons behind jungle-covered sandbars as they reach the ocean. By digging canals to connect them, the Costa Ricans have built a continuous water highway where there are no land roads. Fishing boats, skiffs, dugout canoes, coconut barges, a government boat and tour boats ply the scenic highway. Traffic varies seasonally according to water depth (less in February and March), fishing and crop seasons.

The ride is spectacular! You glide along a passage sometimes less than 100 feet wide between banks lined with palms and jungle. Water hyacinths cover water near the shores. Turtles sun themselves on logs and an occasional caiman splashes into the water just as you get your camera focussed. You pass a family of howler monkeys in a treetop and later a trio of brown spider monkeys swinging effortlessly from one limb to another. A dozen white egrets take off from a tree ahead. A huge blue-green kingfisher swoops beside the boat. The boat driver points at a treetop and you peer but don't see anything move. Nothing does—it's a sloth hanging spread-eagled by the front and back feet on the same side. At least there's

Local "bus" to town.

no rush to get the picture. The tree's leaves move in the breeze, but the sloth doesn't.

Occasionally you pass a small farm or a thatched hut with a pig standing on the canal bank and a housewife washing clothes in the water. Standard yellow highway signs note the kilometers to villages at river intersections. At Parismina, Tortuguero, and Barra Colorado, there are fishing lodges where tarpon and snook fishermen fly in from San Jose for a few days to a week. Tortuguero is a village described in the Eastern region later in this book. If you're not on a tour going farther, you may want to stop over here. Just north of the village is the river mouth where waves break in the Caribbean. You turn left up another river channel and pass a hill on the right, the only one for miles. This is Tortuguero National Park, refuge for the green turtle, the manatee, and many other species. For more details, see the sections on that park. Soon you leave the river and follow a palm-lined canal straight for miles with poetic reflections in the dark bog water. Against the afternoon sky a silhouette crosses ahead—it looks like a bird attached to a canoe—a toucan! The first time you see one outside a cage is a real thrill. Great blue herons and small night herons wade near shore until you approach before flying off.

This ride ends at the village of Barra Colorado, the mouth of the Rio Colorado. Now, with peace restored in Nicaragua, you can continue on a tour boat (Rio Colorado Lodge and Costa Rica Expeditions run loop

Relaxing in a tour boat while watching for monkeys.

trips) up the Rio San Juan, which forms the Costa Rican border, up the beautiful Sarapiquí River to the village of Puerto Viejo and thence by road back to San Jose.

Presently your choices for the ride I've described are by tour boat, government launch or by making your own arrangements with freight boats. My first trip up this waterway was in a fast, narrow, and very unstable fish-hauling boat that made the round trip from Barra to Moín and back in a day. Night came very black with rain showers as the driver peered through a slit in the plastic before him and steered around logs I couldn't see, occasionally switching on a dim flashlight to shine at boats we met. No navigation lights on shore here—any flashing light was a firefly!

The government boat, the *Gran Delta*, runs several days a week (starting very early in the morning from Moín) when water depth permits. It has a schedule which you may be able to get from the ICT office under the Cultural Plaza in San Jose. I rode one time on the *Gran Delta*, and speed plus noise made wildlife photography impossible though it was a cheap way to reach Tortuguero for several days of more leisurely viewing. *Tortuguero Odysseys*, offers a round trip by boat to Tortuguero for about $60 per person, and will arrange overnights in budget rooms there if you want to stay over, (58-1940, 58-2705).

Poling dugout "cayuga" along the canal.

Cheapest and slowest are the "cocoboats" which haul coconuts to Moín and local shoppers back. Built like powered barges, they make the African Queen look quite seaworthy. If you're planning to ride a local boat, you need to be flexible and allow an extra day or two in case there aren't any boats leaving north or south the day you want to go. Charter flights can be arranged from the airport in San Jose and the fishing lodges at Tortuguero and Barra Colorado use them. SANSA flies to Barra several days a week, about $18, which you must pay to hold a reservation.

Tour boats are the most predictable way to go if your trip is scheduled. They also stop for wildlife photos. The guides are looking for animals and know where they are most likely. **Rio Colorado Lodge** at Barra Colorado runs several trips weekly from San Jose on their modern tour boat, with a short stop at Tortuguero, using a mini-bus between San Jose and Moín and charter flights between Barra and San Jose. You may do this loop in either direction, depending on their schedule. The tour takes 2 days, but you can stay extra days at the lodge or ride the bus to Limón, stay overnight, and join a tour there if you've booked it before leaving San Jose. **Costa Rica Expeditions** runs tours on the canales as far as Tortuguero to Tortuga Lodge, allowing time for canoeing up back channels of the river. **Isla de Pesca**, a fishing lodge at Barra Colorado, now has a tour boat running regularly to their lodge. The *Mawamba* travels the canales and does so quietly enough to allow seeing wildlife.

The 1991 earthquake raised the land up to four feet at Moín and left the canal unnavigable south of Parismina. While it's being dredged at presstime, tours are driving from Siquirres northeast to the Reventazón River and putting into boats there, meeting the canal at Parismina.

Tarpon leaps from the water near Barra Colorado. (Casa Mar photo)

Fishing in Costa Rica
(by Jerry Ruhlow, fishing columnist for the *Tico Times*)

Where else but Costa Rica can you get up in the morning and choose between fishing two oceans that offer the best angling in the world on sailfish, marlin, tarpon, snook and countless other species? Or enjoy some freshwater sport on a high mountain trout stream, a magnificent lake abounding in rainbow bass, or hundreds of miles of virgin rivers filled with snook and such exotic species as bobo and machaca, all only a one to three hour drive from the capital, San Jose?

Fishermen routinely raise 20 to 30 sailfish a day along with blue, black and striped marlin on the Pacific Coast, and some have scored all four species of billfish in a single day. In recent years, charter boats have caught and released an average or 500 marlin during the peak season from January through August and raised an average of 10 sails per boat each fishing day from April through mid-August. In 1991 a record Pacific blue marlin weighing 760 lb. was caught near Flamingo.

Costa Rica's four-day International Sailfish Tournament is widely recognized as the most productive of any billfish competition in the world.

Fishing for sailfish near Drake Bay.

During the 12th annual event in 1990, 72 anglers caught and released 540 sailfish and eight marlin on 20-pound-test line, a record success ratio of 1.90 fish per angler per day!

But billfish aren't all the Pacific Coast offers. Usually fishing no more than 30 to 40 minutes out, sportsmen score consistently on dorado, big snapper, tuna, jack crevalle, wahoo, rainbow runner, blue runner, amberjack, grouper, mackerel, trevally, bonito, and skipjack. World record for dorado is an 87-pounder caught in Costa Rica in 1976, but challengers are caught every year.

Other International Game Fish Association records caught in Costa Rica include all-tackle and/or line-test and fly fishing marks for Pacific dog snapper, rainbow runner, Pacific sailfish, roosterfish, big-eye tuna, big-eye trevally, cubera snapper, tarpon and snook.

About 50 charter boats are available along the West Coast, ranging from 23 feet to more than 50 feet, all equipped with tournament quality tackle.

The Pacific Coast is divided roughly into three fishing areas: the Guanacaste region to the north, the central coastal area around Quepos, and the Drake Bay-Golfito region to the south. Despite the short distance the peak months for each species vary between these regions.

Fishing is hot somewhere in Costa Rica for several species just about any month of the year. Like any place in the world, fishing varies in each area according to season, wind, weather, water temperature, moon phase, and other variables. But no place on earth offers a better chance of getting on a hot bite than does Costa Rica.

To the north, boats are available at Flamingo Beach, Playa de Coco, Potrero, Playa Hermosa, Tamarindo, Garza, Playa Carrillo, Tambor and Puntarenas.

Two charter boat services run out of Quepos on the central coast, and both operators also arrange multi-day trips to Drake Bay and Caño Island farther south. **Sportfishing Costa Rica**, phones, 33-9135, 33-3892, Fax, 23-6728. **Costa Rican Dreams**, phones, 39-3387, 77-0593, Fax, 39-3383.

A fishing lodge on the Osa Peninsula near Golfito and wilderness nature camps around Drake Bay also offer fishing trips.

On Costa Rica's Caribbean Coast, the target of most sportsmen is the acrobatic tarpon, possibly the most dramatic and exciting sport fish in the world. Tarpon are caught year round, but during the peak season, February through June, it's not unusual to raise 20 or more of the Silver Rockets every day, averaging 80 pounds, with plenty hitting the 100 pound mark or better.

Tarpon are caught just outside the river mouths, in coastal lagoons and rivers, and more recently in the lower San Juan River, bordering Nicaragua and reached by boats from Barra Colorado and the Sarapiquí River.

Besides tarpon, the fishing lodges along the Caribbean Coast are famous for snook fishing. Five current IGFA world records plus a fly fishing record for that species came from this area, including the aa-tackle 53 lb. 10 oz. snook caught in 1978.

November through January there's a light tackle bonanza as immense schools of a small variety of snook known as *calba* move into the area. Calba average around four pounds and are taken on jigs and bass plugs worked along the river banks. When the run is on, you will hook a fish on nearly every cast.

Two IGFA record cubera snappers and a jack crevalle world mark have been caught by tarpon anglers working just outside the mouths of rivers flowing into the Caribbean, an area with many barracuda, king-fish, giant groupers, sharks, tripletail, mackerel and other species.

This is largely a virgin fishing area that opened up for species other than tarpon in 1990 when Archie Fields's Rio Colorado Lodge replaced the 16-foot aluminum skiffs powered by 25 hp. motors traditionally used in the region with new 18-foot center consoles with 40 hp. motors. These boats can get outside the river mouths more often and work the offshore waters, where Atlantic sailfish, dorado and wahoo are now being caught.

In the estuaries around the river mouths and farther up the rivers and backwater lagoons of the Caribbean region, fishermen also find drum, catfish, gar and such exotic species as the rainbow bass (guapote), mojarra and machaca.

Waiting for tarpon in idyllic spot on the canal.

Three lodges are near the mouth of the Rio Colorado, the largest Costa Rican river that flows into the Caribbean. Others are at the mouths of the Tortuguero and Parismina Rivers farther south.

Hottest tarpon action is usually outside the river mouths where leaping schools sometimes spread for acres in every direction. But when wind and surf prevent the boats from getting outside, tarpon can usually be found in the rivers and back lagoons as well. There you fish amidst incredible tropical jungles, with overhead branches draped in wild orchids. You're likely to see monkeys, brilliantly colored parrots, macaws, toucans, herons and egrets, while caimans and turtles bask along the shore.

Big snook are most often caught by casting jigs and plugs from the beach near river mouths, but are also taken trolling along the shore just inside the rivers.

Freshwater fishermen find plenty of sport in Costa Rica. According to University of Costa Rica ichthyologist William Bussing, there are 127 species of freshwater fish in 33 families in Costa Rican waters, and some provide excellent sport and fine eating.

Rainbow trout averaging 11 inches are found in a dozen high altitude rivers, while the warmer lowland waters offer rainbow bass (guapote), mojarra, machaca, bobo, and vieja.

Lake Arenal, in the San Carlos Valley about a three hour drive from San Jose via good highway, is famous for its rainbow bass, a member of the *cichlid* family, fished as you would for largemouth bass. The season is from January through September. An informal tournament organized by local enthusiasts is held annually in April or May. (See the *Tico Times* for dates.)

Colored in subtle shades of turquoise, rose and purple with feathered ends to its caudal and dorsal fins and a distinctive hump on the mature male's head, the rainbow bass, or guapote, frequently run five to eight pounds with an 11 1/2 pounder holding the world record.

Located at the base of a highly active volcano surrounded by tropical jungle rich in wildlife, the beautiful 15 mile-long lake has two fishing lodges that offer overnight accommodations, guides and boat rentals. Hotels in Tilarán and Cañas are nearby, as are the hot springs at Tabacón.

Rivers feeding to the Caribbean also have plenty of guapote, and visitors to the lodges there often take a day off from tarpon fishing to go after the hard-hitting rainbow bass and other exotics farther up the jungle rivers.

Like all fishing, action will vary with the seasons. Most inland areas are hard to find on your own and may require a 4-wheel drive. Local tackle stores are helpful, and Costa Rica Sun Tours now offers one-day guided trips for freshwater angling. *J.R.*

Check Jerry Ruhlow's column in the *Tico Times* for the latest information on where fishing is hot, reports of recent tournaments, and notes on ones upcoming (some international and some *very* informal).

Facilities are increasing for fishermen, with new lodges, more charter boats, and a large corps of knowledgeable guides on both coasts. For scuba fishermen, equipment and air refills are now available at major resorts on the west coast as well as in San Jose. You will need an ocean fishing license which your lodge can get for you (they need your name, marital status, address, and passport number) or which you can get from the Ministerio de Agricultura y Ganaderia, Calle. 1, Ave. 1, San Jose, Costa Rica. Phone 23-0829.

Fishing lodges are listed by location in the second half of this book. For the East Coast, see Parismina, Tortuguero, and Barra Colorado. For the West Coast, see Golfito (and the wilderness lodges on the Osa Peninsula under Nature Lodges), Quepos, Puntarenas, Playas Naranjo and Tambor on the southern Nicoya Peninsula, and Playas Carrillo, Tamarindo, Flamingo, and Hermosa on the Northwest Coast.

For tarpon, Ruhlow recommends bringing a 6 1/2 foot medium action rod with a conventional or level wind reel that will take 200 yards of 20 lb. line, such as a Garcia 6500 or 7000. "Hot" lures vary from year to year, and lodges usually have the latest for sale. Ruhlow likes plastic tailed jigs such as Scampi or Sassy Shad, and Rapallas in colors or natural. Your lodge will send a recommended list when you book, and can rent equipment if you don't bring your own.

You should bring a wide-brimmed hat, long-sleeved shirts, long pants, and a good sunscreen. On the Caribbean coast and southern Pacific coast near Golfito, bring light rain wear all year. In San Jose you can buy tide tables and fishing tackle at La Casa del Pescador, Calle 2, Ave. 18/20.

Freshwater fishing is open November 1 to June 1. Permits for freshwater fishing, including river mouths and from the beach even in salt water, cost $10, and are available at the Banco Nacional de Costa Rica, Information Department, Ave. 1, Calle 2/4, behind the main post office, 9–3 p.m. M–F. Several areas offer trout fishing with fish originally planted, including the Chacon farm (71-1732) at San Gerardo de Dota, in the mountains near the Interamerican Highway.

Travel agents in the United States and elsewhere book package tours to the fishing lodges.

Tarpon fisherman and his catch at Rio Colorado Lodge.

Hunting

The days of unlimited sport hunting for jaguars and other exotic species are over in Costa Rica and most other places. As tropical forests everywhere are converted to crop or rangeland, the remaining habitat will not allow a surplus for hunting. Most species formerly hunted in Latin America are now threatened or endangered.

In Costa Rica there is legal hunting by permit for doves and ducks on the winter range—some of the same birds you see on spring and fall migrations in North America. The dryland rice fields of Guanacaste are hunted, from November through March. Hunters sometimes get 140 doves in a day, usually given to nearby villagers for food. Hunters stay in or near Nicoya. For package tours or information, write Archie Fields, owner of the **Rio Colorado Lodge**, who holds permits for the area (address and phone in Sources of Information).

Water Sports

Swimming—Besides the beaches and rivers, most major hotels and apartotels have pools. Sabana Park has an Olympic-size pool, as does the Cariari Country Club. The pools fed by Oja de Agua spring south of Juan Santamaria Airport, are colder but unchlorinated due to the large supply of fresh water. There are major swim meets and a well-organized junior racing program at Sabana Park and the Cariari Country Club.

Surfing—Costa Rica is being discovered, not for having the world's highest waves, but for having **long** and **very consistent** waves that make good riding. **Boca Barranca,** just south of Puntarenas is nearest San Jose, with long waves. **Jacó Beach** and **Playa Hermosa** (there are many Playa Hermosas in Costa Rica) a few miles south have hosted recent tournaments. Jacó has lower waves for novices though some rips, and lots of places give surfer discounts May-November. Playa Hermosa has bigger waves and is easy to get to from rooms at Jacó. **Playa Pavones**, south of Golfito, is famous for its almost endless waves. Barely discovered beaches line the northwest coast from Mal País to the Nicaraguan border. Inside Santa Rosa National Park, 13 km from the entrance by 4-wheel drive if the road is "passable", is **Witch's Rock** with famous tubular waves. Camping and water you should treat is nearby.

On the East Coast, **Playa Bonita**, north of Limón, is rough, rocky, and dangerous. The beaches south to Cahuita are undeveloped. **Puerto Viejo** has **Salsa Brava**, a break on the reef in front of town for experienced surfers only.

Costa Rican beaches have been rated according to pollution levels (bacterial counts), A, B, and C. A is the cleanest. Avoid the others.

Surfboards are rented at Jacó, Manuel Antonio, Playa Hermosa in Guanacaste, Limón and Cahuita. Surf shops in the San Jose are are in San Pedro near Banco Popular. (**Keola Surf Shop**, 25-6041, and **Mango Surf Shop**) and Los Yoses (**Tsunami**), the eastern suburbs.

Windsurfing—board sailing is also growing. For cool water and wind, almost sure to be at least 25 knots every afternoon, we recommend Lake Arenal. You'll want some cold protection, but the lake is 14 miles long and always windy! At the coast, Guanacaste's Playa Hermosa in the northwest, is popular.

Snorkeling near Caño Island.

Scuba and snorkeling—Costa Rica has good snorkeling on both coasts. Cahuita, south of Puerto Limón, has the only sizable coral reef on the Caribbean coast, complete with sunken Spanish ship. **Cahuita Tours** and **Moray's**, listed under Cahuita, rent gear and do tours. A few miles south, at Puerto Viejo, snorkeling is good in the bay in front of townand at Punta Uva, several miles south. On the west coast at Playa Hermosa, **Aqua Sports** rents equipment, including sailboards, and has boats and guides. They will take divers to offshore reefs and the Islas Murciélagos, one of the best diving areas in Costa Rica, accessible only by boat. **Diving Safaris** in San Jose runs trips to both coasts and has equipment.

I have found snorkeling good on rocky points near many beaches such as Playa Coco, but to get really clear water with 80 ft. or more visibility, you need to go offshore, away from farming and erosion. Off the northwest coast, the Islas Murciélagos, and off the Osa Peninsula in the southwest, Caño Island are such places. **Marenco**, **La Paloma**, and **Drake Bay**

Wilderness Lodge provide tours to the island. Drake Bay Wilderness Lodge loans snorkeling gear. (Descriptions under Nature Tours & Lodges.) **Phantom Isle Lodge** on a Drake Bay cove (not an island) emphasizes scuba, provides everything but regulators and bcd's, and offers packages, Range A+, to their rustic lodge with cabins on a steep, shady hill above the open air dining room. Appeals to young crowd. Also offers deep-sea fishing. Phone, 25-7682. U.S. reservations: Phantom Isle Tours, Box 559, Manvel, TX 77578. (713) 489-9156. Canada: (416) 479-2600.

The **best** diving in Costa Rica is at Coco Island, over 300 miles west of the mainland. It is a national park, with no facilities onshore. Fishing isn't allowed within 15 miles of the island. **Seaventures**, run by Calypso Tours, offers 10-day Coco Island charters. Phone, 55-3022, Fax 33-0401. **Costa Sol** runs the *Okeanos* on diving cruises to Coco, and the *Temptress* cruising down the southwest coast, phone 20-1679; in U.S. 800-348-2628. Anywhere you go on the coast, it's fun to have a snorkel and see what you can find. While resorts often rent snorkeling gear, and some hotels even loan it, you may want to bring a mask and snorkel.

Playa Hermosa on the northwest coast features a full range of water sports and equipment rented by **Aqua Sport**, 67-0050. If you call **Diving Safaris**, 24-0033, in San Jose, they could give you good tips for other areas and they run tours. **El Ocotal**, the deluxe fishing lodge south of Playa del Coco, has a dive shop, does tours, and rents gear including

Rafting on the Pacuare River.

cameras. Phone 67-0230, Fax 67-0083. (More details on the lodge in the regional section.)

Rafting—Costa Rica's rivers offer excellent whitewater on the General, Chirripo, Pacuare and Reventazón Rivers, and flat water floating to watch wildlife on the Corobicí and Bebedero Rivers. One-day and multi-day trips are offered. **Aventuras Naturales**, 25-3939. **Costa Rica Rafts**, a division of Costa Rica Expeditions, 57-0766. **Rios Tropicales**, 33-6455.

Kayaking—Whitewater kayak enthusiasts from many countries train in the rivers near Turrialba, and international competitions are held there. **Rios Tropicales** offers sea kayaking trips on the Gulf of Nicoya, camping out on secluded islands. Jungle kayaking trips on the Sarapiquí River and its tributaries are offered by **Rancho Leona** which also rents kayaks and offers rustic lodging at La Virgen de Sarapiquí. Package tours, Range A. Phone, 71-6312.

Sports

Costa Ricans are avid sportsmen and have built many facilities throughout the country. Some are basic. A few are luxurious. There are local and international tournaments in several sports, so you can be a spectator or participant according to your interests.

Soccer is Costa Rica's national sport, played everywhere.

Soccer (futbol)—almost every village with a bit of flat ground has a soccer field, often in front of the church. After work and on weekends, there's almost always play. Major games and tournaments are played in Sabana Park at the west end of San Jose. Newspaper sport sections always carry the latest soccer results.

Basketball—is also popular, with major games played at the national gymnasium in Sabana Park. There are baskets for practice in the park and in most villages.

Golf—Cariari Country Club, a few miles west of San Jose, has the only 18-hole golf course in Costa Rica, though others are planned. Designed by a major golf course architect, it's the site of international tournaments featuring many PGA pros. There are also 9-hole courses: at the Costa Rican Country Club in Escazú, at Los Reyes Country Club near Alajuela, at Tango Mar on the Nicoya Peninsula, and at El Castillo Country Club above Heredia. Most have equipment available.

Tennis—Several deluxe hotels have courts as do Sabana Park, the nearby Costa Rica Tennis Club, the Cariari Country Club (where the World Friendship Tournament is played in March and April), the Costa Rica Country Club, and the Los Reyes Country Club. The Costa Rica Tennis Club and Sabana Park courts are close to San Jose.

Criollo stallion shows his high-stepping trot.

Horseback riding—Costa Rica raises very fine jumpers and parade horses, notably Andalusian and Paso Fino horses with the soft gait prized by the Spaniards. The criollo, developed in Latin America, is a high-stepping parade and stock horse. On early mornings in the suburbs of Santa Ana and Escazú, you may see them in the streets. During Christmas week, there is the Horse Parade(Tope) in downtown San Jose with over 1000 of the country's finest. In mid-March, Bonanza, the national horse and cattle show, is a competition with classes for each breed, held at the grounds behind the Hotel Herradura.

Near San Jose, you can take instruction and ride at **Hipico La Carana**, about 15 miles west of the city, and at the **Cariari Country Club**. Jumping, equitation, and dressage are featured with expert instruction. Horseshows are frequent. Elsewhere you can rent country horses, and yours hotel may arrange it for you. Many of these horses have a very comfortable running walk (or "single-foot" as it's called in the U.S.). Note that on the coasts where it is often hot, riding early or late may be more fun than at midday.

Costa Rican-style bullfight for boys armed with cardboard batons.

Rodeos and Bullfights—Guanacaste is the cattle country of Costa Rica, with the festivals and sports that go with it. Rodeos and bullfights are frequent during the dry season from November to April, in Santa Cruz, Nicoya, Liberia and Tilarán. In Costa Rican bullfights, the bull chases men around the arena and the only injuries are to the people! During Christmas holidays, there are rodeos and bullfights in San Jose, including several Mexican-style bullfights then in which the bull is killed. Rodeos are sometimes held at the Cariari Country Club.

Bicycling—Bicycle touring and racing is a major sport in Costa Rica. The big event of the year is the "Vuelta a Costa Rica" in December, lasting 12 days and crisscrossing the mountain backbone of the country several times, from sea level to over 11,000 feet. It attracts cyclists from many countries, including the United States. The Recreational Cycling Association plans family outings which many join on Sundays.

A friend who has cycled long distances here says that drivers are more considerate of cyclists than he expected and give room when passing. He warns that one needs to be prepared for heat and great temperature changes with altitude. He carries liquids and a gas mask for long grades also used by diesel trucks and buses. Despite heat and fumes at times, he recommends cycling in Costa Rica though not in San Jose.

Bicycle tours are now offered, for one or more days. One takes you to the top of Poás for the mostly downhill run. There are tours in Guanacaste and from Limón to Cahuita and Puerto Viejo. You will feel the humidity, but a van accompanies the group and carries gear. Bicycles are furnished. **Costa Rica Mountain Biking,** phone 22-4380. **Horizontes,** phone, 22-2022, Fax 55-4513.

Other Sports—Wrestling, in the national gymnasium at Sabana Park, car and motorcycle racing at La Guácima near Alajuela, volleyball everywhere, baseball and Little League programs, and jogging for everyone on the paths at Sabana Park are a few of the other sports you can watch and participate in.

Theater and Museums

These are almost all in San Jose or its suburbs, though historical and archeological sites are scattered throughout the country.

The **National Theater** is Costa Rica's symbol of the people's interest in the arts as well as the national architectural treasure. A European opera company, led by singer Adelina Patti, came to Guatemala City in the late 1800's but didn't travel on to Costa Rica because there was no suitable place to perform. In response, the coffee growers agreed to pay a tax on coffee they exported to raise money for a theater. Construction started in 1890 and the building was finished in 1897.

Today it is one of the busiest buildings in the country, with performances or official functions 320 days a year. If your Spanish is good, enjoy one of the many plays presented by Costa Rican and touring foreign companies. With little or no Spanish, you can watch dance performances, opera, or the National Symphony. Check the schedule of upcoming events so you won't miss the ones you'd like during your stay. Tickets are amazingly inexpensive, many under $2.

The theater is patterned after European opera houses though on a smaller, more comfortable scale. The facade, overlooking a rose garden and a tree-shaded square, is Renaissance style, with figures representing Music, Fame, and Dance. Statues of Beethoven and Calderon de la Barca fill niches on either side of the entrance. The lobby inside has marble floors and columns. To your left is a refreshment area with coffee and great ice cream concoctions, its walls usually adorned with art exhibits. The grand staircase and foyer on the second floor feature Italian marble sculptures, paintings and a mural of Costa Rica's main exports. You can tour the building with or without a guide during the day, but shouldn't miss the experience of a performance. Ave. 2, Calle 3, adjacent to the Cultural Plaza and Gran Hotel Costa Rica.

The National Theater adjoins the south side of the Cultural Plaza and faces the same square as the Gran Hotel Costa Rica. Other smaller theaters are around the San Jose area and the University of Costa Rica campus. Check the English language *Tico Times,*weekly on Fridays, for performances, locations and for art exhibits in the city which change often. *Note:* In 1991 the Costa Rican government announced that serious earthquake damage in December 1990 would require at least a year to repair before the building could be reopened for performances.

Teatro Melico Salazar on Avenida 2.

The **National Museum** of Costa Rica is in the Bellavista Fortress, the former army barracks on Calle 17, Ave. 2/Ctl (see the San Jose section for an explanation of San Jose street addresses). Phone, 57-1433. Open Tues.–Sun., 10-5. Closed Mondays, holidays. Admission $.45. Students with identification free. The outside walls of this fortress still show bullet scars from the revolution of 1948, after which the army was abolished. The museum features an excellent exhibit of pre-Columbian artifacts, historical exhibits from the colonial period, and historical religious costumes and articles. All of Costa Rica's history and historical art are represented here in the massive stone buildings surrounding a garden.

The **Jade Museum** features prehistoric carvings of jade and stone, and some ceramic and gold articles, arranged according to their region and historical period. It's on the 11th floor of the INS (Institute for National Security) Building, Calle 9, Av. 7. Phone, 23-5800, Ext. 2581. Open Mon.–Fri., 9–3. Admission free.

Note that museum openings are usually early in Costa Rica, often 8:30 or 9 a.m. Closings may be at 3 or 4 p.m. Most museums are open on Sundays—sometimes admission free. Most, except for the Natural Science Museum, are closed Mondays.

The **Gold Museum** is near the ICT information center under the Cultural Plaza on Ave. Central. This collection, one of the finest in the world, contains over 2000 pre-Columbian gold artifacts. Its 24,000 troy ounces comprise the second largest collection in the Western Hemisphere. The artistic wealth as well as the gold make it well worth a visit. Many of the articles were obtained from private collections of burial and religious art. Tues.–Sun., 10–6. Phone, 23-0528, Ext. 282.

The **Museum of Costa Rican Art** occupies the former airport terminal building in Sabana Park on Calle 42 at the west end of Paseo Colon, Phone, 23-7155. Open Tues.–Sun., and holidays, 10–6. Closed Mondays. In this lovely Spanish-style building is a great collection of some of the most expressive art you'll ever see. Most is modern, but some sculptures are pre-Columbian. There are changing exhibits as well as the permanent collection.

The **Natural Science Museum** is in the Colegio La Salle, a school across from the south side of Sabana Park. Phone 32-1306. Open Mon.–Fri. 8 to 3 and Sat. 7:30-12. Small admission charge. All specimens (over 22,500) and scenes were prepared locally, though they feature species from around the world as well as Costa Rica.

The **Entomology Museum** at the Agruicultural School on the University of Costa Rica campus in San Pedro, east of San Jose. is the only insect museum in Central America. The butterflies alone are worth a trip. Phone 25-5555. Open Wed., Thurs., 1-6. Free. Note information on the new Butterfly Farm in the San Jose chapter.

Ripening coffee berries, Costa Rica's key crop.

COSTA RICA—THE NATION

Geography and Climate

With a land area of about 19,700 square miles, Costa Rica is the second smallest country in Central America, after El Salvador. Its rapidly growing population of nearly three million is the second smallest as well, after Panama. Costa Rica forms a land bridge with coasts on both the Atlantic and Pacific Oceans between Nicaragua and Panama.

The Atlantic Coast is a lowland, rather straight and with few good harbors, about 125 miles long. The Pacific Coast has two deep bays formed by the Nicoya and Osa Peninsulas, and is over 600 miles long. The ports of Puntarenas, with the new port at Caldera just to the south, and Golfito in the southwest corner of the country are in these bays. Many of the beaches we've mentioned line this coast.

Costa Rica has a mountainous backbone running the length of the country with just one very significant break, the Meseta Central or Central Valley. The northern mountains are a chain of volcanoes extending south from Nicaragua, including the Cordilleras Guanacaste, Tilarán and Central. Within this chain are active and dormant volcanoes, thermal springs, and many cinder cones. It's a very active zone with eruptions, earthquakes and steam clouds. South of the Meseta Central is the Talamanca Range topped by Cerro Chirripó, over 12,500 ft. high, continuing south into Panama.

The Meseta Central is by far the most important area of the country though it's only about 15 by 40 miles. This rolling area of rich volcanic soils has a spring climate all year thanks to its altitude of about 4,000 feet. Frost never happens and the main seasonal variation is rain. Temperatures vary widely according to altitude, with a few hundred feet making a real difference. Two-thirds of the people live here and it's one of the most heavily populated areas in Latin America.

People have described Costa Rica as "the Meseta Central and everywhere else." The bustling capital of San Jose, with 300,000 people, and the nearby towns of Heredia, Alajuela, Cartago and Turrialba, plus a swarm of smaller villages, are indeed the center of government, industry, agriculture, and most important, the outlook, of Costa Rica.

South of the Meseta Central, bordering the western flank of the Talamanca Mountains, is the Valle de General, with its principal town of San Isidro de General. While it is lower and warmer than the Meseta Central, it isn't as crowded, and many farmers have moved into the area recently since the Interamerican Highway and the new road down the west coast from Esparza have connected this area more closely to domestic and international trade. No roads cross the Talamancas and few lead far into them.

The Nicoya and Osa Peninsulas have central ranges of hills to 3,000 ft., with some of the Nicoya hills being quite steep. The western coastal plain is generally rolling rather than truly flat, and extends from the Panamanian border northward, widening to form the cattle and rice country of Guanacaste, to the Nicaraguan border. Similarly, the eastern plain widens from south to north, forming a wide northern and eastern lowland north of Puerto Limón. The lowlands have a limited population, mostly in agriculture, few large towns, but do have some larger fincas or plantations.

Costa Rica extends from 8 degrees to 11 degrees north of the Equator, so the sun is never far from overhead (it actually passes over during April and September). The length of daylight hours varies only slightly all year and the average daily temperature in a given location may vary only a few degrees throughout the year. In San Jose, the daily highs are in the 70's, Fahrenheit, almost all year. Alajuela, a few hundred feet lower, averages several degrees warmer, while Limón and Puntarenas at sea level are usually in the high 80's or 90's during "summer", December through April. March and April are the warmest months and can be hot, even in the capital. November through January are the coolest, with occasional wintry chills from northern storms. There is much greater variation, especially in the mountains, between day and night temperatures at the same place. You will usually want a sweater or jacket at night in San Jose, and I wore one on a rainy night in a leaky boat in the Tortuguero Canals at sea level.

Altitude rather than season really controls temperature here. Frosts do occur on Chirripó, and most land above 6500 ft. is in cloud forest, cool with fog or rain brought by the northeast trade winds. Mornings are often clear in the mountains, with clouds building in the afternoon.

Those of you who've joined the metric world will find the distances, altitudes and temperatures as given in Costa Rica easy. This U. S. resident has not yet learned to think metric and so will use miles, feet, and Fahrenheit, with apologies for any confusion.

Rainy and dry seasons and the amount of rainfall are controlled by the northeast trades, and the doldrums (a tropical zone of rising air which follows the sun north and south), and the mountain chain running through Costa Rica. The dry season in San Jose and the West is usually December into April (May in Guanacaste) while it runs from February to April on the Atlantic Coast. Though the east coast is wetter, some areas in the southwest get extra rain because of being aligned with passes which allow the moist winds through. Wettest are spots in the eastern mountains where one station reported rain on 359 days in one year! However, on the drier northwest coast, there are few rainy days even in the wet season, and the rain then is generally in late afternoon or night.

Even rainy season shouldn't stop you if you allow for it. On October mornings in San Jose, I enjoyed the clear moist air, Poás Volcano with its steam plume against the blue sky, and flocks of chattering parrots passing overhead. All morning and early afternoon stayed dry, though clouds gathered. By late afternoon almost every day, the sky burst. People still out unfolded the umbrellas they always carried. I liked sitting on the roofed porch watching the rain gauge fill and overflow.

Golfito in the southwest actually has a climate much like the Caribbean coast, due to wind direction and mountain shape. One December evening there even an umbrella didn't help much in the four inches of rain that fell in two hours, but it was warm and the rain cooled the town after a hot sunny day.

Costa Rican Holidays

January 1, New Year's Day

March 19, St. Joseph, patron saint of San Jose

Easter, Wednesday noon through Easter Sunday

April 11, Battle of Rivas

May 1, Labor Day

June, Corpus Christi

June 29, St. Peter and St. Paul

July 25, Guanacaste Day, celebrating its annexation.

August 2, Virgin of Los Angeles

August 15, Mother's Day

September 15, Independence Day

October 12, Columbus Day

December 8, Conception of the Virgin

December 24, 25, Christmas Eve and Christmas Day

While these are the official days, during Christmas holiday week between Christmas and New Year's, and during Easter Holy week, from Wednesday noon through Sunday, most of the country is shut down. Not only are banks and offices closed, but buses don't run on some days, meaning that you need to plan ahead where you will be, with reservations, and how you will get around. Rental cars are booked months in advance for Christmas and Easter weeks. If you want to see San Jose on foot, try Good Friday, when the only moving traffic is religious processions. Costa Ricans who can take vacation then do so, and the more accessible beaches are jammed. Columbus Day is the time of annual festival in Limón, and the August 2 holiday of the Virgin of Los Angeles is Cartago's biggest festival. Thousands of celebrants march from San Jose (and from all over Costa Rica) to Cartago!

History

Here is a brief outline of Costa Rican history, to give some perspective to what you will see. For more information and an excellent discussion of social and political conditions, you could read *The Costa Ricans* by Richard, Karen and Mavis Biesanz, who have lived in Costa Rica for years.

Before the Spaniards came, Costa Rica had several dozen independent tribes who apparently didn't form the empires that the Mayas, Aztecs, and Incas did to the north and south of them. Besides hunting and gathering, they farmed and had some permanent settlements which are now being studied. The sculptures and ceramic figures you can see in museums show that they had artists and had developed culture.

In 1502, Columbus landed at Cariari, now Puerto Limón, and stayed

44

for several days. The Indians showed his men some gold and he felt there was hope for more.

However, the small tribes hadn't accumulated the wealth that drew the Spaniards to the bigger empires. Warfare between the tribes and with the Spaniards plus the diseases brought by the white men to which the natives had no immunity nearly wiped out the native population.

The Spanish who came and settled found both coasts had a hot, humid climate and tropical diseases which many couldn't tolerate. The coasts were also raided by pirates of many countries, especially British, who sacked and burned whatever the settlers had. There were no easy routes to the interior, but eventually small farmers did settle up in the cool, healthful climate of the Meseta Central.

Unlike the other Spanish colonies, these settlers had no way to amass great wealth, no natives to enslave, and few to intermarry. The farmers remained almost pure Spanish and didn't develop the social classes or the mestizo majority that characterized most of New Spain. They were almost forgotten by Spain since they had little to trade and no wealth to send back to Europe. Even the access routes to their settlements mostly led up from the west coast instead of the east.

Cartago was the main town, started in 1563, but San Jose wasn't established until 1737, Heredia in 1717. The population, mostly poor and still struggling, hadn't grown enough to settle the whole valley, though they had brought some fine cattle and horses from Spain and continued to grow livestock and food crops.

In the late 1700's, coffee was introduced, and with the rich volcanic soils and near perfect climate, it was a winner! Land was given to those who would plant it for an export crop. Big and small farmers grew it, and the bigger landowners built *beneficios* to process the beans from everyone. Even though the coffee had to be carried by oxcart west to Puntarenas and thence around Cape Horn or across Panama, Costa Rica finally grew in population and wealth.

In 1821, the Spanish colonies declared independence from Spain. Various attempts were made to unify the former colonies in the Central American Federation which Costa Rica joined in 1824 and from which she withdrew in 1838. The lack of rapid communication, as well as differing interests, made a unified regional government very difficult, though economic and political treaties based on regional interest had been signed.

Coffee growth and trade led some families to become richer and more powerful than others, and Costa Rica was no longer a classless society. It was still a group of small towns and farms with little feeling of nationality. The town councils met separately and rivalries grew until San Jose won a battle with Cartago and the capital was moved to San Jose in 1823.

Democracy developed, with some setbacks according to the personalities of those who were elected chief of state, and then president after 1847. Some of the most autocratic leaders are remembered for starting schools and getting roads and railroads built. Juan Rafael Mora, president 1849-59, recruited an army of volunteers which marched from San Jose to Santa Rosa (now a national park) to surround and drive out pro-slavery American William Walker and his band of filibusters who were trying to establish a slavery empire in Central America. Walker and his band were driven back into Nicaragua and again defeated at the Battle of Rivas.

National hero, Juan Santamaria, was a youth from Alajuela who volunteered to torch the building Walker and his men occupied, knowing it was a suicide mission. Walker was later captured in Honduras, held by the British navy, and turned over to Honduran authorities who executed him. President Mora's proclamation of the right of the Costa Rican people to be free of foreign despots is respected by Costa Ricans as U.S. citizens respect the Declaration of Independence.

In 1889, for the first time, Costa Rica's election was not controlled by the party in power (more than a hundred years later, many other nations still haven't reached this point). Later administrations have passed laws establishing national health insurance, labor rights, and property rights.

The last internal military strife was in 1948 when the party in power tried to use the army to remain so after losing an election. A volunteer group led by Jose Figueres took Cartago, and after widespread violence and bloodshed that killed 2000 people, a cease-fire was arranged. Costa Ricans were determined this should never happen again. Among the changes Figueres and his followers enacted were limits on the length of presidential terms and elimination of the army. A well-armed and trained national guard serves as the country's police force. Its control is turned over to the election tribunal before national elections to remove it from politics and guarantee free elections.

Costa Rica celebrated the fortieth anniversary of the constitution in 1988, justifiably proud of 40 years of free elections, democracy, and survival without an army in Latin America! President Oscar Arias proposed a peace plan for Central America which was adopted, with modifications by all the Central American governments in August 1987. For his effort he was awarded the Nobel Peace Prize in 1987. Costa Rica's contribution to peace and democracy is very big for so small a nation.

In recent years, the population, size of bureaucracy, and foreign debt have grown rapidly. With almost all exports in the form of raw agricultural products, Costa Rica is at the mercy of the world prices for them and for the oil it needs. The International Monetary Fund places stringent conditions on economic policy in an effort to control the foreign debt. Costa Rica is spending most of its income from foreign trade to pay the interest on that debt, a heavy burden on a country with many other needs. If you check prices in stores you'll quickly discover the difference between products from Central America and those imported.

The turmoil in the Central American countries to the north and the resulting refugee flow into Costa Rica added tension. Nicaragua's election and change of government haven't solved its problems, but many Nicaraguans have returned to their country.

Despite urgent economic problems, including an inflation rate of 25% in 1991, Costa Ricans are well aware that they have advantages in education, personal freedom, and the possibility for personal progress that few in Latin America have. Many other countries now provide research funds, economic aid, and increased trade.

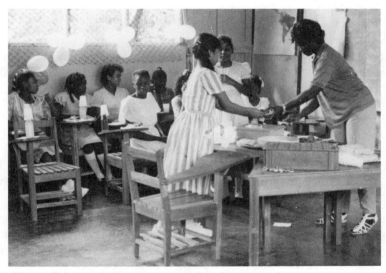

Class at Cahuita school enjoys party on last day of school.

Social Conditions

"Tell them Costa Rica is different," everyone said, from truck drivers to government department heads. They're right. Where else can you see this from 20,000 feet? Fly over El Salvador and you'll see big fields with a cluster of small houses and one big house. Fly over Costa Rica and you'll see many small fields and villages with houses that look similar from that distance, especially in the Meseta Central. Plantations owned by the banana companies and some of the cattle fincas in Guanacaste are an exception, but not as prevalent as in other Latin American countries.

A walk through San Jose will show you that there are rich and poor here, but most people are middle class. Costa Rica has the largest proportion of middle class in Latin America. That, its high literacy rate, and free press are the foundations of its democracy. Elementary and secondary education are free, and elementary attendance is required. Ride a public bus at evening rush hour and you'll see everyone reading newspapers.

Ticos, as the Costa Ricans call themselves, are very clean and well-dressed. Their families, usually large, are all-important in their lives. For many, the extended family is the source of all their social life. Children are loved extravagantly and with endless patience. You rarely see a crying child. They grow up to be cheerful, considerate people who will do anything to help you—as long you're polite. They aren't subservient. Cheerful self-respect you'll see everywhere, among the Spanish in the Meseta Central, the Indians and mestizos of Guanacaste, and the blacks of the Caribbean coast.

Costa Rica is not immune to the human problems of the 20th century or of the developing nations. The average salary is less than $200 per month, and many people with responsible jobs are paid only about $300. Earnings haven't kept up with the cost of rent, utilities, and basic foods for the usually large families. Unemployment is high in some areas. Costa Rica is a nation of hard-working people who from early colonial times have struggled to make as good a life as possible for themselves and their families. Compared with the TV generation in other places, their resourcefulness in having fun with little money is impressive. With their families at home or on outings, they find fun or make it.

Population growth and the conversion of field agriculture to cattle range and bananas to palm nuts which take less labor have forced many into cities and towns looking for work. Everywhere there is a serious shortage of low-cost housing, though the government has built many thousands of units near San Jose.

In the outlying areas, and particularly among the people of the Caribbean coast, there is a distrust of what the government and population majority in the Meseta Central may do that affects their life and land. Many women, especially the younger ones, feel caught between the traditional Spanish stereotype of the submissive role and the opportunities that are (or they feel should be) open to them. More women are studying for the professions, especially law. San Jose area is more liberal than the conservative countryside in the choices open to women. You will find many in offices, occasionally even as "la directora."

As I noted earlier, Costa Rica is dedicated to solving these problems and has done much to make its citizens' lives better. Some solutions may wait until the growth of population and the bureaucracy is slowed.

Coffee, shaded by bananas, grows on terraced slopes.

Agriculture

Early agriculture in the tropics was the slash and burn type, with small areas of forest cut and planted for a few years before the soil was depleted and the farmer cleared another plot. Most soil nutrients are actually stored in the trees and plants growing on tropical land. Heavy rains and the rapid breakdown of compost at these temperatures limit fertility of cleared land unless fertilizers are added or crops rotated, or a volcano periodically adds mineral-rich ash to the upper layer. In prehistoric times, people moved on, allowing the soil and vegetation to restore themselves. Very steep hillsides were hard to work and didn't produce well, so were farmed only if easier ground wasn't available.

Modern farms stay in the same place and most crops leave bare ground exposed to the heavy tropical rains. On slopes, tons of soil are lost every year, even from steep pastures. Pressed by population and a growing international debt, Costa Rica has cut half her forests in the past 40 years. Before the year 2000 she will have used all forests not in parks and reserves. Where the soil is gone, forest cannot regrow. The government and even the Peace Corps are doing reforestation, but usually in quick-growing species like pine and eucalyptus which make firewood but do not make food for wildlife or restore the hundreds of species that grow in a tropical rainforest. Lately a few of the tropical hardwoods, including pochote, have been planted. The Costa Rican government recognizes the problem and is working on it. If you are concerned, you'll find suggestions in our "So You'd Like to Help" chapter.

Coffee and bananas were the first two major exports of Costa Rica. Coffee still is the country's most valuable crop though it's concentrated on a small part of the land and subject to wild price fluctuations on the world market. Throughout the Meseta Central, you'll see the glossy green bushes, often shaded by scattered trees, sometimes on incredibly steep slopes. In season, the white blossoms or red berries add to the beauty.

Bananas were first grown on the east coast along the railroad during construction, partly to help pay for completion of the project. That was the start of the United Fruit Company. Later, the Panama disease damaged many plantations and new planting was done on the southwest coast. Some western plantations are now being converted to oil palm, for oil used in margarine and soap. You may want to try varieties of bananas you can find in markets here which have much more flavor than the bombproof ones bred for shipping overseas. They make good snacks to take on buses and trains.

Beef cattle graze beside the road while forest burns on the hill for new pasture.

Recently beef has become the third largest export, grown mostly in the west. Cattle are Brahma purebred or cross, bred to take heat and insects.

Dairy cattle are raised mostly in the highlands, usually above the Meseta Central or at Monteverde. Almost all the beef is grass-fed and relatively lean, exported mainly for fast-food hamburgers and TV dinners. Costa Rica desperately needs foreign exchange, but she is paying a high price for it. Cutting and burning forest from hills so steep a friend noticed "cows falling out of their pastures" on the road to Monteverde, cattle growers are responsible for much deforestation. Fires are started to burn off the coarse grass and brush each year, and many fires burn into adjacent forest. Some cattle fincas in Guanacaste use introduced African grasses and modern methods to increase production on flatter ground.

Sugar has long been a major crop for home use and export. You'll see it along the road in the eastern Meseta Central. There it grows between coffee fields until it becomes the major crop as you drop down past Turrialba and into banana country. Other export crops are pineapples, copra and dried coconuts, cacao, cotton. Rice is a major crop in the west, all of it used in the country as it's a staple in the local diet. Also grown for local consumption are beans, corn, honey, vegetables, mangoes, papayas and many other tropical fruits, pork, chickens, and potatoes,the latter mostly on the slopes of Irazú.

Did your office plants come from this farm near Río Frio?

House plants and cut flowers, grown under acres of plastic screening for shade and rain protection, are a new export crop in the Meseta Central. The plants in your office or home may have been grown in Costa Rica. It's fun to visit these places and see the plants you keep in little pots at home growing by the acre! Cut flowers, particularly carnations and chrysanthemums, grow under screens even on high ridges along the

Interamerican Highway. Such crops are require little land but much labor in a frost-free climate.

Lately, there have been several developments promoting new export crops—oranges for juice concentrate, jojoba for oil, and macadamia nuts, to name several, If you stay in deluxe San Jose hotels, you'll be offered information about investments in these.

Industry

Costa Rica is one of the world's largest per capita producers of hydro-electric power with big installations at Lakes Arenal and Cachí. For years it exported electricity to Nicaragua and El Salvador, but domestic use increased so that much is still generated with expensive, imported oil. Recently Daylight Saving was tried in order to save power usage, but was abandoned due to public pressure and concern for children walking to school on narrow roads in the dark. Though there has been some oil exploration and talk of a trans-Costa Rican pipeline to transport Alaskan and Venezuelan oil, presently no oil is produced in the country, which has made balancing the economy difficult.

Costa Rica offers tax incentives to labor-intensive industries producing items for export. Many plants import textiles and other raw materials, hire Costa Ricans to assemble them, and export finished products such as underwear. My uniform shirts on the Alaska ferry were labeled "assembled in Costa Rica". One successful operator imports used typewriters from North America, reconditions them in a modern plant, and exports them wholesale all over Latin America. There's plenty of room for imagination here! Costa Rica would rather produce many products internally than buy with foreign exchange, but with a well-scattered population only as big as a large city, there isn't the market to make it pay.

Costa Rica's major non-agricultural industry, aside from government, is tourism. Ecotourists can find more species of birds, wildlife, and plants growing naturally here than in any other similar area. With planning, tourism can make preserved tropical forests and beaches more profitable than any other use of the same land—and keep it so forever. Recently Costa Rica has attracted travelers from all over the world and their numbers have grown rapidly. Hotels near San Jose and at the beaches and tours and lodges for nature lovers are increasing though sometimes still are less than the demand. Costa Rica has so much to offer the tourist, and does it so well, that it is rapidly being discovered by thousands who ride jets instead of tossing Spanish galleons.

Launching a dugout from the beach at Puerto Viejo.

PLANNING YOUR TRIP

Do you hope to see as much as possible in the time you have for this trip, or would you rather "sit and watch the coconuts fall," as a relaxed friend in sleepy Puerto Viejo put it?

When I first went to Costa Rica, I hadn't had a vacation in 8 years and really needed to get away from lists of things I had to do. I chose Costa Rica because it was an interesting place I hadn't been, with lots of birds and wildlife where no one shot at you. If the tropical heat proved too much after years of living in Alaska, I could go up to the cloud forests and look for quetzales. Planning for everything from snorkeling to high altitudes of course made packing harder.

San Jose, nearly in the center of the country, is a well-located base for touring. With 23 days to spend, I flew into San Jose and spent several days there learning my way around and getting bus, train, and boat schedules. Most hotel managers in San Jose will store extra baggage while you travel if they know you're coming back to stay there. Leaving dressy and warmer clothes there, I traveled a lop-sided figure 8 with a loop on each coast, and returned to San Jose for a few days in the middle and at the end of of my trip. From San Jose, I rode public buses up Irazú and Poás, toured Cartago and Alajuela, and went to the bird zoo. In San Jose, I toured museums, the national zoo, and attended performances of the National Symphony and a Venezuelan modern dance troupe in the

53

National Theater.

I rode the train to Puerto Limón, spent a night there, and rode the bus to the village of Cahuita. It was so peaceful that I spent four days, staying in a primitive but clean cabina, snorkeling and birdwatching in the national park. Back by bus to Limón for another night because there wasn't any boat north that day. Then up the canales for two days at Barra Colorado before riding boat and bus back to San Jose.

The electric train west to Puntarenas didn't go when I wanted to, so I rode the bus and spent two nights there. I enjoyed the Calypso tour in the Gulf of Nicoya and caught the early morning ferry the next day to the Nicoya Peninsula. There are more direct routes to Liberia and Santa Rosa National Park, but I wanted to see the country. The bus dropped me at the park entrance, and I hiked into the campground and spent three days hiking, swimming, and wildlife watching before returning by bus to San Jose.

I've never seen or learned so much in 23 days! However, my stopovers for several days helped keep the trip from being a race. With all that travel and just two nights camping out, the trip would now cost about $30 per day for everything but souvenirs. You can spend a great deal more, or perhaps less if you stay more in one place.

What are your interests? What kind of trip do you want? What is your energy level in tropical weather?

An experienced traveling friend past 70 said "We found we traveled differently in our 50's than we did in our 40's, differently in our 60's than we did in our 50's, and still differently now". Sleeping in a noisy, basic hotel with a thin mattress on boards may have been tolerable in college days, but now would keep you from getting enough rest to enjoy the next day of your trip. Or maybe you are still at an age when you can't bear to let comfort stand in the way of adventure and you stretch your dollars for experiences to remember.

Exchange

Please note: you need to know the current exchange rate (the number of colones you'll get for each dollar you change) to plan and budget your trip. For the past several years the Costa Rican government has de-valued the colon in small steps every two weeks. It partly compensated for inflation. However, in 1991 the rates for devaluation and inflation are about 25% annually, and edging higher. You can get the current rate from the nearest Costa Rican consulate or embassy, or by calling the Costa Rican Tourist Board office in Miami (the ICT office in the U.S.), 1-

800-327-7033 in the U.S.; (305) 358-2150 from Florida and elsewhere. Address: 1101 Brickell Ave., BIV Tower, Suite 801, Miami, FL 33131.

You can legally exchange money only at banks or at hotels where you are staying. Penalties for exchanging money otherwise are severe and not worth the risk. The banks will charge a commission to exchange travelers' checks, but not cash. You may want to carry some cash, carefully, in U.S. dollars especially for airport taxes, baggage charges, etc., when you may have used up your colones before leaving or for arrivals on holidays or after bank closing hours. Paying in colones rather than dollars avoids exchange ripoffs. If you will arrive during the latter part of Easter Week or between Christmas and New Years when the whole national banking system is closed, you should try to exchange some money at your airport of departure for Costa Rica.

Travelers' checks and currency in U.S. dollars can be exchanged in any good-sized town. Other currencies may have to be exchanged at a particular bank, usually only in San Jose. Banco Nacional in San Jose will cash German marks for colones, but on holidays the marks would be nearly impossible to exchange. Canadians should bring U.S. dollars in U.S. travelers' checks since Canadian banks don't have correspondence arrangements with Costa Rican banks. The American Express office is at T.A.M., Calle 1, Ave. ctl./1. Phone 23-5111. They also get exit visas.

You will be able to exchange only $50 worth of colones back when you leave, so you should have some travelers' checks in small denominations to come out fairly even. If you will be staying in villages, you should carry some colones in small bills, as even a 500 colones note can be a problem to break. Major U.S. credit cards can be used for car rentals, excess baggage charges, and most moderate to expensive hotels. Credit cards are often the simplest way to get funds from home if you run short.

On Costa Rican holidays the bank office at the airport is closed and no one there will change colones back to dollars as you leave. You can buy gifts at the airport shops and pay your departure fee, about $6, in colones.

Safety

What are you to think when the American press refers to the political and military problems of Guatemala, El Salvador and Nicaragua as "Central America"? At least it's better than the former practice of calling everything between Mexico and Peru "banana republics". Even with the regional problems, Costa Rica remains peaceful. Its democracy and neutrality together with lack of an army are its greatest sources of national pride. While residents are concerned about problems in other countries, only the economic instability has spread. One California paper headlined its article "What's a Nice Little Country Like Costa Rica Doing in a Place Like This?"—and then told what a delightful, relaxing place Costa Rica is. During your vacation the only evidence you're likely to see of regional problems is a maid from El Salvador or Nicaragua cleaning your hotel room (as you well might in Los Angeles).

There is far less violence in the entire country in a month than there is in any major U. S. city in a night. The murder rate is half that of the U. S. You are personally as least as safe here as you would be any place on earth, including at home.

Note: drugs are in Costa Rica as elsewhere though most are in transit to North America. Breaking Costa Rica's drug laws is definitely not worth it, as penalties are severe and bail is not always set even for possession of small amounts. Foreign embassies, including the United States embassy, cannot help citizens who break the laws of the country they are in.

Theft has always been here and has increased with the economic crisis and the admission of thousands of refugees who have not been able to find work. The bars across ground floor windows of most houses and other buildings will probably startle you on your first drive into San José from the airport. The majority of the people you see are the most honest people in the world, but here, as elsewhere, there are some of the others— and they are very quick and expert. I take the precautions listed below.

1. When traveling, always look as neat and clean as humanly possible— but don't look affluent. Lots of jewelry and matched sets of leather luggage may make you feel more important when you arrive at a hotel, but unless you have Princess Diana's security forces, they aren't worth it. At best, you are a mark for every cab driver and merchant who can raise his price. At worst, you are an easy target for major theft. In particular, gold neck chains with pendants and pierced earrings of any value may be taken off you in the street (with possible damage to neck or ears). I never wear an expensive-looking watch, and I keep cameras out of sight unless I'm using them.

2. Try to avoid taking more luggage than you can carry at one time. Besides making travel easier, this saves leaving anything behind when moving through airline and bus terminals. Backpacks are handy, but avoiding a hippie look can save trouble with customs and unpopularity with villagers. Don't leave luggage unattended in public places, buses, taxis or parked rental cars.

3. When you are out for day or evening, avoid carrying anything you don't need at the time. Hotels can keep your extra money, cameras, passport, and other valuables in their safes. In villages, I've left my

tourist card and all extra money with the honest owner of the cabina I was using. A photocopy of the first several pages of your passport including its number, your photo, and your entry visa stamped at the airport is sufficient and should always be carried. That saved me when my wallet was stolen from an outside pack pocket I should never have put it in. Of course, passport and credit card numbers should be recorded and kept separately so you have them when reporting a theft. The police can stop travelers on the street and demand to see passports, but the photocopy seems to be acceptable as long as it includes your photo and visa. You do need passport and driver's license if you're driving a rental car.

4. Take local advice, especially in San Jose, Puerto Limón, and Puntarenas, and don't walk in parks and questionable neighborhoods at night. Walk with someone if you can. I take a taxi if I must carry valuables or am out at night in cities. Looking alert and aware of anyone who comes close is a deterrent to theft.

5. Avoid crowds at bus stops and be careful if you're jostled. Don't accept candy or food from people you meet on buses.

Costa Ricans carry nothing of value in pockets, even a cheap pen in a shirt pocket. Men should never carry anything in back pockets. For men or women once in the country, a traveler's pouch worn inside clothes is a relatively safe place to carry money. Some have a loop that fits over a belt, allowing the pouch, big enough for flat bills, to hang down inside trousers or skirt. For women, it's best to avoid nylon zipped bags which seem to be targets, and instead use a purse with secure handles and a short shoulder strap that allows the purse to be carried under your upper arm. I have never had a problem carrying a briefcase which has inner pockets and zips securely outside, but I have had a cloth camera bag unzipped on the street. Utility leather handbags, about $20 in Costa Rica, zip securely and are big enough to hold billfold, shopping bag, and even a camera. Friends who carry these have had no problems.

If you do have a theft, call the ICT at 23-1733 or visit their office under the Cultural Plaza and file a complaint. The police can't hold the thief if they catch him without a complaint. The ICT people speak English and will represent you as needed later so it doesn't interfere with your vacation or leaving the country.

In summary, don't bring anything you don't really need, try not to carry anything you don't need that day, and watch or have someone else watch anything you put down. Try to look and act like a knowledgeable foreign resident of Costa Rica rather than a tourist just off the plane.

These precautions apply as well anywhere you travel and are not unique to Costa Rica.

Tide Rips

Tide rips occur whenever waves approach a shore over a wide area but can only retreat in restricted places, forming a strong current out to sea. Even strong swimmers cannot swim against these currents directly toward shore but must swim parallel to shore until they get out of the current before heading for the beach. Waders who find their legs being pulled strongly by a current should walk parallel to shore or stand still and then move toward only when an incoming wave gives them a boost.

A strong tide rip makes this break in the surf line at Playa Hermosa, south of Jacó.

Any long open beach such as Jacó, Esterillos, or First Beach at Manuel frequently has these currents, often visible as a muddy area where incoming waves are much lower than elsewhere. These currents may stay in one place or may move along the shore. Their strength and location change with tide and weather. The gentle waves you played in yesterday may be treacherous today even though they only look a little higher.

Many people drown every year on these beaches, wearing themselves out trying to swim back to shore against the current. Unless you are very experienced in ocean surfing and are a strong swimmer who can swim for an hour or more, don't swim or wade more than ankle deep at these beaches. A friend wading waist deep in front of the cabinas on First Beach was knocked down and couldn't move at all toward the beach until two strong young Costa Ricans came in and dragged her out. There are very few lifeguards at beaches in Costa Rica (I've never seen one) so it's up to you to swim safely. Find a sheltered beach or cove such as

Third Beach at Manuel Antonio, and don't swim alone.

Atide rip at Manuel Antonio's First Beach makes this low spot in the breaking surf.

For a safe thrill, look down from a plane at a long exposed beach such as Playa Savegre which extends for miles south of Manuel Antonio Park (on your way to or from the Osa Peninsula or Golfito). Every quarter mile you will see a muddy break in the white surf line with a mushroom-shaped plume of muddy water extending out several hun-dred yards from shore. You can see a dozen of these at one time! A person caught in one would be carried out as much as a half mile before being released to try to find a safe way back!

Enjoying Nature Safely

Common sense and the ability to admit you're in unfamiliar conditions and take advice from the locals will help anywhere in the world. I've discussed sunburn, snakes, and Africanized bees (with the appropriate cautions for each) in the Health section of this chapter. Getting lost while hiking alone in the rainforest or insisting on climbing volcanoes that erupt periodically has cost some their lives and spoiled vacations for others. Be careful, take advice, use a guide when you should, and you'll enjoy the untamed world safely.

Traveling With Children

Costa Rica is a fine place to bring children. Costa Ricans love them and welcome visitors with them. The cleanliness of food and water leaves you few worries. There's lots for them to see and do. They'll pick up Spanish quickly if they play with local children. Readers who have trav-eled with infants note that disposable diapers are expensive and not always available outside San Jose. They advise bringing all you'll need but say that will leave you lots of room in your baggage going home for souvenirs and gifts. Restaurants often have high chairs and booster seats, but car seats are not generally available. Milk which has been radiated so it doesn't have to be refrigerated until it's opened is available in any large town.

Children play on Manuel Antonio's sheltered Third Beach.

Children, even infants, need passports. If they are under 18 and stay in Costa Rica more than 30 days, they require permission from the Patronato Office (Calle 19, Ave. 6) to leave the country. Both parents must go to get it, or a single parent traveling alone must have the permission of the other parent notarized by a Costa Rican consul in the parent's home country. A travel agent may be able to get the permission from Patronato if you give him the child's passport and two extra passport photos.

Some parents find it simplest to make their trips with minor children for 30 days or less.

Cultural Sensitivity

Nowhere in the world are people more helpful, hospitable, and friendly than in Costa Rica. Most have had enough contact with North Americans (many have lived for years in the United States or else-where abroad) to be understanding and to forgive us our gringo differences. When I asked a young Costa Rican how he spoke such accent-free English, he said "Oh, I lived in Los Angeles for 15 years." He made some of the comments and suggestions given here.

Dress—San Jose is more cosmopolitan than elsewhere in the country, and slacks on women are acceptable here. You will see young ticas in blue jeans. Do dress up for performances at the National Theater and other occasions important to the Costa Ricans. Wearing jeans there doesn't show respect to the people or their culture. For men or women, shorts are for sports and the beach *only*. Shorts worn on the streets of San Jose label one a tourist from a block away. In villages which may be less liberal, I wear skirts unless I'm going hiking or riding horses.

All Latin Americans consider themselves as American as citizens of the United States of America. Travelers from the United States can show consideration, and it will be appreciated, if they refer to themselves as "norteamericanos" or North Americans.

Machismo still exists in Latin American, but much less in Costa Rica than elsewhere and is less a problem for foreign women than in most other places. The most obvious sign I have seen in all my rambling is polite surprise from men and women alike at the weird things gringo women do—travel alone, hike, ride, swim and live alone, fly planes, operate their own boats and businesses, and make all the important decisions in their own lives. When I was camping by myself in Santa Rosa National Park, the mother of a large family swarming around the campground asked, "Are you a writer?" Apparently writers are forgiven for being even crazier than other tourists and wanting solitude. I have never had an incident involving a Costa Rican despite my often being the only woman present.

A Costa Rican advises, "Don't be blatant in manners, dress, or voice. Blend in. The locals catch on quickly if you stand out. Explain clearly (not loudly) what you need and want. Check things said to you for truth. People sometimes want to please you enough to say 'si', yes, to anything you ask. Single North American girls have a bad reputation, so many men think they're an easy catch. Show that you respect yourself."

Nude bathing is at best completely offensive to Costa Ricans. At worst, it's downright dangerous to bathers in some areas and has led to serious incidents. The white sand beach at Cahuita may look like a deserted island to you, but it's these people's front yard and the path behind it through coconut palms is the walkway to their homes. In some coastal villages where there's little affordable entertainment, local girls are never taught to swim, though they miss safety and enjoyment because their parents don't want them exposed to nudity on the beach. What a shame!

Men traveling to Costa Rica planning to find an accommodating Tica should know that real romance takes time and much adjustment on both sides to cultural differences. Prostitution is legal, and registered prostitutes are tested periodically for disease, but many are not registered, and AIDS is here too. Take care.

Costa Ricans are polite and possibly more considerate than you are used to. One can be a lady or gentleman anywhere. Here you'll find that an interest in the people and their concerns makes your trip really enjoyable and enlightening.

Cruise ship *Regent Sea* passes Portete heading for the dock at Moín.

How To Get There

The easiest way to get to Costa Rica is by airline to San Jose with the exception of stopping through on a cruise ship for a day. Most flights from points in the U.S. other than Miami have at least one stop enroute, often in Mexico City and at the capital city of any Central American airline you ride. Check with your travel agent to find the best flight and schedule for you. Many stops may be tiring, but they do give you a glimpse of the other countries enroute. If you will be stopping in Mexico but not staying over, ask your travel agent for an *in transito* pass so the Mexican authorities can't request a charge for customs clearance ($10 each way).

Do you want just a quick look at Costa Rica now, and maybe plan to come back later for a longer visit? Each year more cruise ships, usually running between Mexico and the Panama Canal, stop for a day at the Pacific port of Caldera. Their passengers ride the electric train on part of its scenic route, have lunch in San Jose with tours of the National Theater and National Museum, do a bit of shopping, and visit Sarchí's oxcart factory before returning to their ship. It's a full day and a fine introduction to Costa Rica. Other ships stop on the East Coast at Moín, just north of Puerto Limón. Cruise lines stopping in Costa Rica include Regency

Cruises, Royal Viking Lines, Bermuda Star Line, (
Ocean Cruises, and Special Expeditions.

For the lowest air fares, especially if you're g
have your travel agent search carefully for excur
package plans which may involve some night?
often take a discount off the regular fare.

Students with an International Student Card (from any
agency) can get 40% discounts on PanAm flights.

Recently during the high season from December into April, **Fiesta Holidays** in Toronto, (416) 498-5566, **Go Travel** in Montreal, (514) 735-4526, and **Fiesta West** in Vancouver, (604) 688-1102, have offered remarkably cheap charters from Canada to Costa Rica, flying weekly so you can select the length of your trip, with or without the hotel part of their packages.

There are many well-informed travel agents willing to make the effort. Space will not allow us to list them all, but we include four who are especially capable in organizing Costa Rican trips for any budget.

Travel agents can get the best fares available to fit your schedule at no additional cost to you. Some also run tours to Costa Rica. All can design an individual itinerary for which they will make a reasonable charge. Phone calls to Costa Rica are expensive and the travel agents usually must post deposits to assure your reservations. You will be happiest if you allow the travel agent plenty of time to make reservations before hotels are full where you want to go, if you don't change your mind any more than necessary at the last minute, and if you make the required deposits when the agent requests them.

America's Tours & Travel
Javier Pinel
1402 Third Ave, #1019
Seattle, WA 98101-2110
1-800-553-2513
(206) 623-8850 in WA

Worldwide Holidays
Dolores Batchelor
7800 Red Rd., Suite 112
So. Miami, FL 33143
1-800-327-9854
(305) 665-0841 in FL

Preferred Adventures Ltd.
Karen Johnson
One West Water St., Suite 300
St. Paul, MN 55107
(612) 222-8131
Fax: (612) 222-4221

Southern Horizons
Laudencio Castro
6100 Simpson Ave.
No. Hollywood, CA 91606
1-800-333-9361
(818) 980-7011 in CA

International Flights

llowing airlines fly to Costa Rica from the United States:

San Francisco: Continental, Pan American, American, Mexicana.

om Los Angeles: LACSA, Mexicana, Continental, American, Pan American.

From Dallas: American (some nonstop), Continental, Pan American.

From Houston: Continental, Aviateca, TACA, SAHSA.

From New Orleans: SAHSA, LACSA, American, Pan American.

From New York: LACSA, American, TACA, Pan American.

From Chicago: Mexicana.

From Miami: LACSA, American, Pan American, SAHSA, Aeronica, Aviateca, TACA, .

Reservation phones, at least within the United States: **American,** 1-800-421-0900. **Continental** (int'l desk) 1-800-231-0856. **Pan American,** 1-800-211-1111. **Aeronica** (Nicaragua), 1-800-323-6422. **Aviateca** (Guatemala), 1-800-327-9832. **LACSA** (Costa Rica), 1-800-225-2272, in Canada 1-800-663-2344. **Mexicana,** 1-800-531-7921. **SAHSA** (Honduras), 1-800-327-1225. **TACA** (El Salvador), 1-800-535-8780.

From Europe, **KLM,** 1-800-556-7777, flies from the Netherlands and **Iberia,** 1-800-221-9741, flies from Spain, and **Pan American** connects its European and Latin American routes in New York. Direct charter flights from Germany starting in November 1991 will be offered by **Medico-Reisen,** a German tour agency. Note that, except for direct flights from Miami to Costa Rica, almost all flights have at least one stop enroute. The number of flights daily, which days of the week the flights operate, and schedules vary widely. Your travel agent can find the schedule most convenient for you.

For their local addresses near you, see your travel agent or phone book. Their San Jose addresses are given here because you need to confirm your return flight at least 72 hours before the flight. A travel agent suggests you ask the airline's representative at the San Jose airport when you arrive for their rules on reconfirmation (in person or by phone, etc.).

American
Edificio Centro Cars
La Sabana
Tel. 22-5655

LACSA
Calle 1, Ave. 5
Tel. 31-0033
Airport tel. 41-6244

Pan American
Ave. 7, Calle 5/7
Tel. 21-8955

Iberia
Calle 1 Ave. 2/4
Tel 41-4125
Airport tel. 41-2591

SAHSA
Calle 1/3 Ave. 5
Tel. 21-5774, 21-5561

KLM
Calle 1 Ave ctl/1
Tel. 21-0922

Mexicana
Calle 1 Ave. 2/4
Tel. 22-1711

TACA
Calle 1, Ave. 3
Tel. 22-1790, 22-1744

Continental
Juan Santamaria Airport
Tel. 33-7146

Aeronica
Ave. 1, Calles 1/3
33-0226

Aviateca
Ave. 3, Calle ctl.
Tel. 55-4949

LACSA flight loads at Juan Santamaria Airport.

Domestic Flights

SANSA   To/From: Quepos, Barra Colorado, Río Frió, Coto 47, and Golfito daily. Liberia, Tamarindo several days a week. Calle 24, Ave. Ctl/1. Tel. 21-9414, 33-0307.

Baggage

Most international airlines allow 66 lbs. of baggage. Some include your carry-on bag. You'll be happier if you don't have to carry or look after more than that anyway. Excess baggage charges can be more than $1 per pound. There's motivation for packing light! Experienced travelers advise you to check your baggage only to your point of departure from your home country and make the transfer to the international airline yourself if you're changing airlines. It's easier to cope with lost luggage in Miami than to wonder where it went after you arrive in San Jose. However, one U.S. airline persuaded me to check baggage through by telling me if it was lost, they rather than the foreign airline would have to make good. Your bags should be secure, locked, and hard to slit with a knife.

SANSA flight to Barra Colorado is met by outboard skiffs from nearby fishing lodges.

Luggage should be well marked and have your address inside as well. I use laundry marking pen on the luggage itself as well as luggage tags. Your carry-on bag must fit under the seat in front of you. It should contain medicine and any really indispensables—or irreplaceables. Mine has my address books, cameras, binoculars, film, glasses, bathing suit, and one set of clothes including shoes. Anything else I can replace in San Jose if I have to. Prescription drugs should be in their original containers. You are allowed to take into Costa Rica $100 value in gifts.

You may bring two cameras and any reasonable amount of film. This is the rule, but I've carried three cameras and over 100 rolls of film many times and never been questioned. If you are doing serious or professional photography and will need more than that, you are advised to take a list of your equipment and serial numbers to the nearest Costa Rican consulate before you leave home. Costa Rica simply wants to be sure you will bring them back with you instead of selling them en route. If your equipment, including watch and binoculars, wasn't made in your home country, you may save some delay on your return by taking the same list and equipment to your own country's nearest customs office for recording.

This list is then good for as long as you own the equipment and doesn't have to be redone each trip.

Driving To Costa Rica

Until recently, driving to Costa Rica from the United States was risky if not foolhardy. Now more people are enjoying the trip and sightseeing along the way through Mexico, Guatemala, Honduras and Nicaragua, avoiding El Salvador.

From the United States you can enter Mexico at over a dozen points, the shortest route being from Brownsville, Texas, about 2300 miles to San Jose. Allowing time for some sightseeing to Mayan ruins and other points of interest, for slow, often unpaved roads, and for driving in the daylight hours only as well as making border crossings during business hours, you need about three weeks each way, at least on your first trip.

You need a passport, driver's license and vehicle registration. Getting a tourist card from the consulate of each country you will enter can speed the process of border crossing. Vehicle liability insurance is required for each country. The simplest way to get this in advance may be from the representative of Sanborn's, the Mexican insurance agency, Charles Nelson, P.O. Box 310, McAllen, TX 78502. (512) 686-0711. He takes credit card phone orders.

Your vehicle should be in the best possible condition but doesn't need to be 4-wheel drive. Anyone bringing an RV will regret *every inch* the vehicle exceeds the width or length of a VW microbus! Costa Rican roads, except for the Inter-American Highway and a few freeways near San Jose, aren't nearly wide enough to be comfortable for standard motorhomes or even large pickup campers. While you'll meet local trucks and buses on secondary roads and at one-way bridges, you'll want the narrowest possible vehicle when you do.

You do need: Road maps for each country, good tires and spare, a tool kit, emergency triangles, flashlights and extra batteries, rain gear, and possibly a cooler chest for drinks, snacks, and your film. Avoid leaving your vehicle unattended with anything in it, but make it as secure as possible and keep your baggage out of sight. Being able to speak some Spanish will make the trip more enjoyable and save frustration when you need directions. Unleaded gas is available in Costa Rica but not at all places en route. You don't need camping gear for the drive down as there are towns with hotels where you'll probably want a comfortable night after a day of tropical driving.

RV parks in Costa Rica haven't thrived during all the years of military action to the north. However, just west of San Jose, 3 km from the airport, is the very attractive, shaded lawn of **Belén Trailer Park**, in San Antonio de Belén. 21 spaces, concrete pads, showers, hot water. All spaces have water, most have electricity and sewer. Dump station and laundry room. Ice and groceries nearby. Propane refills available in Pavas and Alajuela as well as in stores though some don't have com-patible fittings to refill your tank. The helpful North American park owners can advise. From the stoplight on the autopista near the Herradura Hotel the park is 2 km. south. Rates less than $8 day. Belén Trailer Park, Apdo. 143, Belén, Heredia. Phone 39-0421.

Minivans from the United States stay in Belén Trailer Park near San Jose.

At **Punta Leona Beach Hotel** between Puntarenas and Jacó there are RV spaces within the resort. Phone 63-9249, Fax 32-0791. The resort's other facilities are described in the Southwest Region section. More RV parks and spaces are planned—we'll add them in the Flash section as they develop.

Entry & Departure Requirements

While documentation and procedures vary somewhat depending on your citizenship, the requirements for U.S. citizens given here are fairly typical.

For all visits you now do need a passport, even for infants, but you don't need a visa. U.S. Passport Service offices in major cities can get you a passport in less than three working days if you go to them with your airline ticket (showing you really are leaving soon) as well as passport photos and embossed copy of your birth certificate. Obviously you can be more relaxed if you apply for the passport at least six weeks ahead. You must have a round trip or onward ticket showing you will leave Costa Rica. You may be required to show proof of adequate funds to live in the country for the length of your trip.

U.S., Canadian and most European citizens are allowed 90 days in Costa Rica with the entry date stamped in their passports. Citizens of most other countries can extend the original 30 or 60 day entry to 90 days upon application. No extensions are given beyond 90 days, except for the automatic 30 days that comes with an exit visa. At the end of that time you must leave Costa Rica for at least 72 hours.

Using a Costa Rican travel agent to get extensions and exit visas: find one who does this and furnish your passport, 3 photos, your departure ticket, and evidence that you have $400 per month for the additional time you want to stay in the country. Make a copy of the first pages of your passport showing its number, your photo and the entry visa stamp, and carry these pages while the agent uses your passport to get the exit permit. That exit permit, which includes a stamp from the court that you don't owe child support, then gives you an automatic 30 days beyond your original 90 days. The exit visa costs $12 if you're leaving by air, $40 if by land. The travel agent will charge a small fee for all of this. The time and hassle saved are worth it—two trips to Immigration and at least half a day's time standing in line. The travel agent or his staff speak English. Many people behind Immigration's windows don't, or don't admit it. T.A.M. and Tikal agencies are among those who will get exit visas.

Extensions and exit visas on your own: If you decide to get an exit visa or extension to 90 days on your own, here's the procedure. The Im-migration offices at Puntarenas and Puerto Limón are reported to have shorter lines than San Jose has, especially before holidays. Be sure to bring all the material mentioned above and enough travelers' checks to show that you have at least $400 for each month you plan to stay. Avoid the young fellows in the courtyard who will offer to help (for a price). One took me to the wrong department and cost me a day.

Immigration is now in new offices in La Uruca, a suburb northwest of San Jose, near the Irazú and San Jose Palacio hotels (on the Bernardo Soto highway, 8 blocks west of LACSA headquarters). It's open from 8 to 4, Monday through Friday. Get there by 7:15 a.m. early in the week. Go to the window with the sign "Prorrogas de Turismo". Some people in that office do speak English. They'll look at your passport and other documents, have you copy a form in Spanish and tell you which line to stand in next. Be sure to ask them how much value in revenue stamps you'll need when you get to the head of that line. If you go stand in the stamps line now, you can avoid waiting twice in the other line! You will have to surrender your passport for which you'll get a receipt to carry for the several days before they will give back the passport. If you get your own exit visa, you'll also have to go across San Jose to the Court Building (Tribunales) and stand in line at the window where they take your passport and check the child support records. The system works, but it's quite a test of patience.

Entering Costa Rica: Costa Rica has made entry at the airport as simple and convenient as I've seen it anywhere. You line up before Immigration's windows just inside the terminal and they check your passport and look in the big book of computer records to see if you've been in trouble here before. If you haven't, you're quickly allowed on past the bank office for exchanging money or cashing travelers' checks into colones, open M–F 6:30 a.m.–6 p.m, Saturday and holidays 7–1. The ICT airport office can call hotels downtown to find a room for you, open 8 a.m.–9 p.m. daily except Jan. 1, Easter Thursday and Friday, and Dec. 25. (Note that changing money from colones back to dollars when you leave is impossible at the airport if the bank is closed.) If you use either of these services, your baggage will already be waiting for you in the claim area when you get there. Customs check of your baggage is quick and efficient (perhaps more detailed if you come from cocaine growing countries to the south), and 20 minutes from the time you entered the terminal, you may be climbing the stairs to the street outside! Welcome to Costa Rica!

Outside you'll find cabs, minibuses, car rentals and the bus stop for the San Jose-Alajuela bus just across the driveway. The latter is only a few cents all the way to San Jose, but won't take any more than carry-on luggage. It's worth remembering if you ever turn in a rental car at the airport. With tourist luggage, the cheapest way to town is the minibus owned by the airport taxi company which will stop at hotels. Airport cabs cost about twice as much per mile as all other cabs in the country and they won't bargain. It's about $10 to town by cab. Enjoy the ride to San Jose on the modern *autopista*, (turnpike) past coffee plantations, several industrial plants, Hospital Mexico, several deluxe hotels, and the Cariari Country Club. You pass Sabana Park as you enter San Jose.

What to Bring

You'll undoubtedly have some items you'd add to this list, but keep it light and leave room for what you may want to bring back. If you select a base color and make sure everything else goes with it, you'll have a variety of costumes with a limited wardrobe. Cotton is cooler than synthetics, but everything should be wash and wear. I never travel with light-colored slacks, shorts, or skirts as they look grubby after I've sat down twice. I bring a navy lightweight suit with skirt and slacks, a navy or khaki skirt, field pants and hiking shorts. All blouses are in light colors that go with the skirts and pants. Birkenstock sandals soften the miles of San Jose's stone sidewalks and go with a cotton blend skirt for days at a time in buses and jeeps in the countryside. A skirt is far cooler on the coasts than slacks, and should be full enough for climbing into bus or boat.

Field pants for hiking, riding, or going to forests and parks with insects should be cotton/poly blend rather than all cotton or denim jeans, so they will dry overnight in humid conditions (jeans take forever to dry in a rainforest lodge). Note that khaki or light blue is much cooler than navy in pants or skirts.

Men should bring a lightweight suit and one or two ties (for travel and evening in San Jose), plus slacks. As soon as possible, you'll want a *guayabera* shirt, the white or cream shirt Latin American men wear open at the neck, not tucked in. It's cool but dressy enough for almost any occasion and saves wearing ties, etc. to dinner. You don't need coat and tie outside of San Jose. Flowered Hawaiian-style shirts will mark you a tourist and are suitable only at the beach.

Women:
1 suit w/skirt & slacks
2 skirts (1 plain, 1 print,)
3 blouses (capped or short
  sleeves)
1 dressy dress
1 pair slacks or field pants
1 pair walking shorts
1 bathing suit
Sweater or light jacket
3 sets underwear
3 pairs socks, 2 pairs
  pantyhose
1 pair street shoes (walking)
2 pairs sandals (1 pair each,
  dressy, walking)
Manicure set

Men:
1 suit
2 dress shirts
3 sport shirts
2 pairs slacks
1 pair cotton/poly field pants
1 pair walking shorts
1 pair swimming trunks
Sweater or sport jacket
3 sets underwear
4 pairs socks
1 pair street shoes
1 pair sandals
Shaving gear

Both Men and Women:
1 pair running or tennis shoes
Towel (hotels won't let theirs

Ear plugs (if you can sleep
  wearing them)

go to the beach)
Washcloth
Universal flat drain cover for
   wash basin
Sun hat
Sun glasses
Toilet paper (small amount)
Sunscreen (SPF # 6 and #15+)
Cup (unbreakable)
Insect repellent
Anti-itch ointment
Bandaids
Q-tips
Moleskin
Aspirin
Kaopectate
Pepto Bismol
Toothbrush , paste, cup
Hairbrush & comb
Vitamin pills (optional)
Umbrella, folding. Cheap in
   San Jose. *Essential.*

Sewing kit
Alarm clock
Flashlight (important)
Plastic bags, clothespins & line
According to your special interests:
Fins, mask snorkel
Day pack
Cotton bandanna
Sleeping or bivouac bag
Canteen & water drops
Pocket knife
Spoon, bowl
Powdered sulfur and "Chiggarid"
Binoculars
Photographic gear & film
Battery-powered fan
Hiking boots
Goretex parka, pants or poncho
Pile jacket
Stocking cap
Malaria pills
Gaiters, optional for hiking in mud

Note that electricity in Costa Rica is 110 volt A.C. 60 cycle throughout the country. However a few rustic nature lodges depending on their own generators may have D.C. Ask. If you plan to spend many nights in the discos of San Jose, or you're a field biologist or in the Peace Corps, your interests will affect your choices of essential baggage.

Time

Costa Rica is on Central Standard Time, 6 hours behind Greenwich Mean Time. Since it's as far east as Miami, in the Eastern Time Zone, the sun comes up around 6 a.m. all year and sets in early evening. The whole country seems to start the day early. Costa Rica tried daylight savings time and rejected it three times, most recently in 1991. Near the equator daylight hours vary only slightly throughout the year.

Telephones

You can dial direct between Costa Rica and most other countries. It's more expensive to dial from Costa Rica to the U.S. than in the other direction, especially if you use the low cost times of day. The access numbers for Costa Rica from abroad are 011-506 plus the number. From Costa Rica to the U.S. or Canada dial 001 plus the number. To call collect or use a telephone credit card, dial 116 to get the international operator who speaks English. To get AT&T direct from Costa Rica, dial 114. In San Jose, the Radiográfica, at Calle 1, Ave. 5 is open from 7 a.m. to 10 p.m. From it you can wire or telephone another country, with English-speaking assistance if you need it. They will send Faxes and receive them for you at their number (506) 23-1609. If your correspondent lists the number of your hotel, Radiográfica will call you or you can check with them at 87-0513. Unfortunately the phone on the busy corner outside is the only one to use for calls within Costa Rica.

Costa Rica has some villages with just one phone number with or without an exchange and extension, e.g. Cahuita. Many hotels on the coasts do have a San Jose number. This can be the easiest way to make reservations for lower-priced hotels which don't have foreign representatives. Usually if you want to call hotels that cost less than $16/night, you'll need to speak Spanish.

Pay phones in San Jose all seem to be on busy corners with loud diesel trucks shifting gears. Costa Rican coins come in old, new, and newer denominations, and the phone you're facing usually takes coins you don't have. You need the new 2, 5, and 10 colones coins so it's worth saving these. As soon as the party you're calling answers, give him your pay phone's number so he can call back if you get cut off. Passersby will help if they can. Use their help or find a phone inside somewhere. There's a pay phone outside the ICT office under the Cultural Plaza, a quiet spot.

Many foreigners who've moved into Costa Rica haven't been able to get phones in their own names so the phones are listed in someone else's, effectively making them unlisted. Be sure you have your friends' numbers as you won't be able to look them up.

Many private phones in Costa Rica can't take or make international calls. Their monthly charges are less, and it saves landlords the risk of being left with big phone bills. However, if you're renting, you should ask as it means no one from your home country can call you!

Addresses

Most Costa Rican mailing addresses are "Apartados", abbreviated "Apdo.", meaning post office box. Street numbers don't exist or aren't used. Neither are street names outside of San Jose. All directions are given in meters or varas (33 inches) from something else which may not still be there. The tree was cut down or the Coca Cola bottling plant is long gone, but everyone knows where it was! I lived in a very nice house in a good suburb of San Jose, but the address was (in Spanish, of course) "225 meters south and 100 meters west of the church, near the brown garbage container." Don't try this in the dark the first time, especially from a bus and bus stop you don't know. A taxi driver might be able to find it. A friend who had to pick me up was smart enough to ask whether those directions were from the front or back of the big church. You may want a compass as well as some patience.

Note: Many towns, especially those named for saints, have the same names in different parts of the country. It's important to use the province name in the address. e.g. Santa Barbara de Heredia, not just Santa Barbara. Puerto Viejo de Limón is on the east coast south of Puerto Limón. Puerto Viejo de Sarapiquí is on the Sarapiquí River in north central Costa Rica. The two Puerto Viejos ("old port") are mentioned often in this book and other tourist literature.

Mail

Air mail takes about five days each way between Costa Rica and the U.S. or Canada, the same to Europe. Surface mail takes weeks. If you're sending mail from Costa Rica, mail it at your hotel desk or a main post office, for reliability, and don't put anything but a letter in it. The main post office in San Jose is on Calle 2, Ave. 1/3. Open 7 a.m. to 6 p.m. weekdays, 7 a.m. to noon on Saturdays. Mail to you should be sent in care of your hotel or to you at "Lista De Correos", general delivery. Zip or postal codes are put before the name of the town, e.g. 1000 San Jose, or with a hyphen, after the apartado number, e.g. Apdo. 51-1000, San Jose. Do underline both Costa Rica and Central America on the envelope, in hopes the U.S. postal clerks won't send it to Puerto Rico!

Stamps can be bought at post offices or in San Jose at Banco Credito, around the corner from the main post office, where you can get a collection of beautiful ones for mailing and souvenirs at a 10% discount.

Try not to have anyone send you anything but letters. A few personal photographs in a standard letter envelope do seem to go directly through the mail. Other items go to customs warehouses, often in another town, and the duty can be very high, with no relation to the value of the item. Getting there at the right time to pick it up can be a big nuisance. Even cassette tapes with messages on them aren't worth it. The same applies to presents you want to send Costa Rican friends after you get home. Don't do it. They might have to pay $15 in duty and make several trips to pick up a $5 present. Maybe you'll have a friend visiting Costa Rica who won't mind taking something small in the $100 in gifts a traveler can bring.

Getting Around

Public transportation within the country is subsidized and is very reasonable.

Air **SANSA** is the airline within Costa Rica with daily prop plane flights between San Jose and Liberia, Quepos, Golfito, and Coto 47 near the Panamanian border. SANSA flies to Tamarindo and Barra Colo-rado several days a week. Most fares are under $20 and the flights are about half an hour. *Note:* SANSA requires full payment in advance at their of-fice to hold reservations. Tour agents can to this for you (be sure they do), but you'll have to do it yourself if you're traveling independently. You can plan fine excursions from two days to many using SANSA to and from the coast, leaving you more time to enjoy beaches, canales and parks. Riding a bus one way and flying the other is economical and lets you see the country well. The airline now has several tours that include nights at hotels.

Trains We've discussed the train between Turrialba and Siquirres and the electric train to Puntarenas, both recommended scenic rides at mini-mal cost. Check with the ICT for schedules. In San Jose, the station for the Pacific train is on the south side of town at Ave. 20, Calle 2. The Pacific train leaves daily about noon. In December it changes schedule to accommodate shoppers in San Jose, leaving later than usual from San Jose for Puntarenas. Question any schedule you're given then.

Buses Costa Ricans ride buses to go anywhere. If there's a road, there's probably a bus, though it may not be daily. Buses on main highways to Golfito, Puerto Limón, Puntarenas, and Liberia are very comfortable. Fares are low—$4 will take you a long distance. The following comfort-able bus rides are among the world's most scenic. The only drawback to riding on a bus is not being able to stop for pictures.

The bus from San Jose to Golfito takes about seven hours including a lunch stop, and follows the Inter-American Highway from Cartago south over the summit of Cerro de la Muerte, over 11,000 ft. On a clear day, you have glimpses of both the Atlantic and Pacific Oceans as the road winds along the backbone of the Talamanca Range through nearly treeless high altitude brush country. It drops down to the Valle de General across a slope where landslides during the rainy season sometimes do block it, and reaches Golfito in mid-afternoon, for about US$6! This makes a nice round trip if you use SANSA one-way.

Buses to Puerto Limón and the Sixaola express bus which stops at Cahuita and Puerto Viejo de Limón offer a beautiful ride through Braulio Carrillo National Park and its cloud forest. The views are more apt to be clear in the morning than in the afternoon when the cloud and rainforest lives up to its name.

Buses in San Jose cost only a few colones, usually less than a dime.

Often 15 or 20 cents in colones is the fare for a half hour ride in from the suburbs. It's a good use for the small change you accumulate. Most buses to suburbs start at or near the "Coca Cola", site of the long-gone Coca Cola bottling plant at Ave. 1 and Calle 16. It's a rough neighborhood, best avoided at night and a place to be careful by day. From here you can get buses to Ciudad Colón, Santa Ana, Escazú, Sarchí,and Naranjo, as well as Quepos and Orotina. Nearby are stops for most areas west of San Jose, including Guanacaste. Other bus stops in San Jose are:

Alajuela: Ave. 2, Calle 12/14

Cahuita: Ave. 11, Calle ctl/1 (Sixaola bus, twice daily)

Cañas: Calle 16, Ave. 1/3

Cartago, Turrialba: Calle 13, Ave. Ctl./2

Golfito: Ave. 18, Calle 4 (near Pacific RR)

Guápiles: Calle 12, Ave. 7/9

Liberia: Calle 14, Ave. 1/3 (near Coca Cola)

Limón: Ave. 3, Calle 19/21 (Hourly)

Monteverde: Calle 12, Ave. 5/7

Nicoya: Calle 12, Ave. 5 (near Coca Cola)

Puerto Viejo de Sarapiquí (La Selva area): Calle 12, Ave. 7/9

Puerto Viejo de Limón: Ave. 11, Calle ctl/1 (Sixaola bus, twice daily)

Puntarenas: Calle 12, Ave. 7/9 (near Coca Cola)

San Isidro de El General: Calle 16, Ave. 1/3

Santa Cruz: Calle 16, Ave. 1/3 (near Coca Cola)

Tilarán: Calle 12, Ave. 9/ll.

Turrialba: Calle 13, Ave. ctl/2, hourly.

Zarcero: Calle 16, Ave. 3 (near Coca Cola)

Zona Sur: Ave. 11, Calle 4.

Even for suburban buses, your best chance of having a seat is to catch the bus at its terminal instead of at one of its later stops. For buses going farther, you should get your ticket the day before (especially for weekends or holidays) and get there an hour early. Buses run from early morning until 10 or 11 at night, so you often have no choice but taxis after theater or dinner with friends. Taxis at such hours don't bargain easily, but sometimes you can share. In other areas, such as Quepos and Manuel Antonio, the buses stop running much earlier and you are left with taxis.

To get to some areas not well served by buses, such as parks, the cheapest way often is to take a bus to the nearest large town and take a taxi, possibly 4-wheel drive, from there.

Nicaragua: Tica Bus leaves from Calle 9, Ave. 4 on Mon., Wed., Fri. at 7 a.m. , 10 hour trip. SIRCA bus to Managua, 12 hours, starting at 5:00 a.m. Wed., Fri., Sun. from Calle 11, Ave. 2. Both charge around $10. There's also a local bus to the border at Peñas Blancas, but you have to walk four kilometers to catch the bus on the other side. A visa is not required for US citizens (I'd call 33-8747 and check on this for latest info), but you are required to change at least $60 in US dollars at the official rate at the border. You must have at least $200 in travelers' checks or cash with you.

Panama: Passport and visa required, plus a return or onward ticket. TICA Bus, Calle 9, Ave. 4, Mon., Wed., Fri., Sun.,runs to Panama City. TRACOPA bus, Ave. 18, Calle 4, runs daily, to David, Panama, and you take another bus to Panama City. Fare about $20.

Airlines also fly direct from San Jose to both capitals. Another choice is to take SANSA's morning flight to Coto 47, catch a taxi to the Panamanian border to catch a bus on the other side.

If you're going to ride buses often, some Spanish is essential for at least one member of your party. You have to be able to ask and receive directions and schedules. Around tourist hotels, someone always speaks English. In and around public buses they don't necessarily. You don't need very much, however, if you're polite and prepared for some confusion. Be careful of your possessions, especially around the San Jose stations, and don't show much money when buying tickets. Carry as little luggage as possible. Some buses have storage below, but local buses don't, and backpacks or large suitcases don't fit on the overhead racks inside.

Taxis

Taxis are quite inexpensive, except for the airport cabs, which charge double. San Jose cabs have meters, called "marias", but many drivers refuse to turn them on. They'll tell you "it's broken". Lately the government has been cracking down on drivers who don't use the meter. You can take the driver's number and make a complaint to the MOPT office in Plaza Viquez.

If the driver doesn't use the meter, fares are a matter of bargaining— the more Spanish you have, the better. You should agree on the fare *before* getting into the cab. Fares can vary according to the time of day, the driver's attitude, yours, how affluent you look (don't expect to bargain about 30 colones with a Nikon hanging around your neck!), and whether you're going or coming from an expensive hotel. My mail was held at a friend's office in the Corobicí Hotel. I soon learned to save 40 colones every trip by naming the nearest street intersection instead of the hotel when agreeing on the fare, though I could later direct the cab to the door.

You can ask several drivers to reach a consensus. Some hotel desks are good sources of advice, while those at deluxe hotels may add a bit. The ICT office under the Cultural Plaza may tell you the going rate is about 60 colones for the first kilometer and 25 for each additional in San Jose. For example, from the center of downtown to the east end of Sabana Park near the Museum of Art should be about 100 colones. Our San Jose street map shows kilometers so you can calculate what the fare should be. The meters only read to 15 kilometers, so if you're going farther, you'll have to bargain. Drivers are allowed to charge more at night.

In San Jose taxis are easiest to catch at the Limón bus station, the Coca Cola bus station, and at Parque Central in front of the Metropolitan Cathedral. The *taxistas* on Avenida 2 in front of the Gran Hotel and National Theater are the least cooperative in town. They'll tell you they're waiting for a fare from the hotel if you look like one who would bargain.

In outlying areas some cabs are 4-wheel drive. Particularly if there are several in your party, it may be practical to hire a cab and driver for the day for some trips, e.g. from Puerto Limón to Cahuita or Puerto Viejo and back. They'll add some for the state of the road, but it may save you hours of waiting for a bus to come back. Taxi drivers are not tipped.

Tours

Tours are increasing rapidly throughout Costa Rica, although most are still based in San Jose. New tours and tour agencies appear almost weekly. There are multi-day tours to the more remote national parks, Barra Colorado, Tortuguero, Monteverde, and the Nicoya Peninsula. There are many half day and all day tours in and around San Jose, mostly in new minivans. Operators listed on page 279 have been giving good tours for years. They pick you up and drop you off at your hotel and may visit several sites in one day, e.g. Irazú and the Orosi Valley or Poás Volcano and Sarchí's oxcart factories. The driver speaks English and any other languages required. He'll tell you about what you're passing en route to the main object. You spend your time sightseeing instead of waiting in bus stations or perhaps riding crowded buses, and the vans are clean and comfortable. You pay for the extra service and you meet few Costa Ricans except for your driver. Tour drivers are tipped.

The tours I have been on have been excellent, even to places I have also reached by public bus such as Irazú and Poás. There are also nature and other special interest tours described in our next section, and bicycling diving, and kayak tours listed with their sports in our first chapter. One day adventure tours are offered by **Calypso Tours** with boat tours in the Gulf of Nicoya (and now advertising multi-day tours to Cocos Island 500 km. west) , **Costa Rica Expeditions** with rafting on the Reventazón River, and **Rios**

Tropicales with rafting on several rivers including wildlife viewing from rafts on the Corobicí River. **Swiss Travel** was a pioneer in Costa Rican tours. **Interviajes** offers very reasonably priced tours on a weekly schedule to nearby and multi-day destinations. All of these are well done and fun.

Some "one day" tours are now being stretched to a distance that may be beyond your limit if you're not up to sitting five or six hours a day in a bus. Ask about the itinerary before you sign up. If the trip calls for more than two hours each way (they're often optimistic) plus seeing or doing whatever the object of the trip is, I think you'll enjoy it more if you take at least an overnight.

Examples are tours from San José to Arenal Volcano or to the Sarapiquí River and back in one day. There are good places to stay over-night at each destination. At Arenal, staying overnight gives you a better chance of seeing the volcano erupt. On nature tours, staying longer allows you to see more birds and animals in the evening and early morning when they're most active.

Museums are usually open Sundays but not Mondays. You may want to schedule a city tour (or even a walking tour of San José) for any day but Monday when it will be mostly a shopping tour.

Tours on the train use refurbished cars with comfortable seats. The tour operators who contributed to that cost have priority in reserving space which may or may not be available to independent travelers. More tours and operators are being added to the list you'll find at the back of this book.

Senior Tours
Elderhostel runs informative, reasonably-priced tours to Costa Rica for people 60 and over (spouses can be younger). 80 Boyleston Street, Suite 400, Boston, MA 02116. **Lifestyle Explorations** has tours several times a year to Costa Rica led by Jane and Joseph Parker, for people thinking of retiring here. Besides beaches and natural areas, they look at communities and meet with authorities on the pensionado law. Lifestyle Explorations, Inc., World Trade Center, Suite 400, Boston, MA 02210. Phone (508) 371-4814 and Fax (508) 369-9192.

Special Interest Tours to Costa Rica
Many churches, volunteer groups, universities, and even cities have tours to Costa Rica, at least occasionally. These offer a way to meet Costa Ricans you otherwise never would.

Camcorder enthusiasts, willing to rough it a bit taking their own films and learning how to make these better may be interested in rainforest tours for camcorders by Adams & Co. Travel Services, 24 BAFP Dr., Watsonville, CA 95076. (408) 761-5551.

Nature Tours and Lodges

Ecotourism is growing fast in Costa Rica with all its natural attractions. Day tours are offered by the operators listed under Nature Tours on page 280, adding new ones constantly. **Jungle Trails** (Apdo. 2413, San Jose, phone 55-3486, fax 55-2782) offers a one day tour to Carara Biological Preserve, stopping at a forestry nursery where you can plant a tree in a reforestation project, helping Costa Rica! **Geoturs** offers excellent day trips to Carara and Braulio Carrillo. **Costa Rica Expeditions** has one-day trips to Tapantí and other good birding spots. **Guanacaste Tours**, described with Liberia, offers tours from Liberia to Guanacaste parks, reserves, rivers, and beaches.

Oxen and baggage cart meet air taxi with guests at Tiskita.

Lodges and operators listed here not only preserve tracts of varying acreage but offer competent guides to help you identify and understand what you see. More are opening. These are listed together, by the same regions used for hotels in the second half of this book, to help you choose where to spend time on your trip according to what you most want to see. For a short trip you might select one. With more time you might select two, offering different habitats, plants, and wildlife.

"Come get muddy and learn how the rainforest works" is Rara Avis's slogan. Wilderness lodges offer varying degrees of comfort, usually more rustic than an urban hotel in the same price range. Their costs include bringing supplies in by plane or boat, keeping staff all year for varying occupancy, and maintaining boats, horses, and trails, as well as water and electric systems. Prices include meals and are often in package tours

80

including transportation. Access by small plane or boat is usually cheaper for 4 people than for 1 or 2, but often they can coordinate. English is spoken. All of these are recommended.

You will select according to your interests, and can encourage preservation of habitat by patronizing those who protect it with low impact use. You should inquire about the availability of guides who know the local wildlife. Use whatever transportation the lodge offers for getting there—they know the conditions and have arranged the best possible. Bring raingear, walking shoes or boots (they may have rubber boots), bug repellent, and a flashlight with spare batteries. Keep the weight of your gear down if you will be flying. With flexibility and a sporting attitude, you'll have experiences you'll never forget!

Central: Rancho Naturalista—Two-story lodge on hilltop in 125 acre American-owned ranch, 15 km from Turrialba. Ten rooms, all different, with shared or pvt. bath, hot water. In transition zone, they've counted 300 bird species within 2 miles. Extensive trails. Guests staying a week have a free day tour to another habitat. Excellent food, great view. Range A+ includes transportation from San Jose, meals, guide, horses, laundry. Single supplement. Apdo. 364-1002, San Jose. Phone 39-7138.

Eastern: All the lodges and cabinas in Tortuguero and Barra Colorado are discussed in their villages, though several are primarily for nature tourists. In Puerto Viejo on the southeast coast, Cabinas Chimuri owned by Mauricio Salazar is a nature lodge with an opportunity to learn about the Bribri Indians as well (listed in Puerto Viejo).

Southwest: Tiskita is on Costa Rica's mainland coast south of Golfito. All others are on the Osa Peninsula and offer trips into Corcovado Park. Drake Bay, La Paloma, and Marenco also offer trips to Caño Island for snorkeling on its reef and hiking to prehistoric burial grounds in the rainforest. They offer hiking in nearby rainforest, swimming in ocean and in streams, and birding even at the lodge. Access is by boat or air taxi. Some of these lodges are closed during September and October, the rainiest months in this region.

Tiskita—Lodge is on a clifftop overlooking the ocean on 400 acres, most in natural forest with trails and waterfalls, and many bird species that come only this far north. Owner, Peter Aspinall, planted hundreds of tropical fruit trees from around the world near the lodge to learn what would grow well here. They attract birds and monkeys besides furnishing guests with *super* fresh refrescos! Ten cabinas have double beds, deck for relaxing, birdwatching even from the pvt showers—it's an idyllic spot. You can fish, explore tidepools below the lodge, snorkel with gear provided, and surf at Pavones a few miles north. Bird list and tidepool list provided with the trail map. Access is by air taxi from Golfito or San Jose, or 2 1/2 hours by jeep taxi from Golfito. If you ride a jeep one way through miles of deforested cow pasture and the Rio Claro, you'll appreciate what Peter has saved with this preserve. Range A+. Costa Rica Sun Tours, Apdo. 1195-1250, Escazú. Phones 55-3418, 55-3518, fax 55-4410.

View from a room at Tiskita on clifftop.

Corcovado Lodge Tent Camp—Rustic tent lodge owned by Costa Rica Expeditions on 390 acres of forest preserve near Carate, south edge of Corcovado Park. Road or small plane reaches 20 minute walk to lodge. Wall tents with 2 bunks, screened dining area, shared bath. Heat and insects are here, but so are jaguars, ocelots, tapirs, monkeys, peccaries, and over 100 species of birds. Range A+ including meals and transportation. Lower rate for 4 people, additional nights. Apdo. 6941-1000 San Jose. Phone 57-0766, fax 57-1665.

Drake Bay Wilderness Lodge—Attractive, well-run lodge facing Drake Bay at mouth of Río Agujitas. Screened cabinas with pvt. or shared bath, on shaded grounds with many birds (we counted a dozen species at noon near the dining room). Excellent food. Camping in your tent or wall tent they rent. Snorkeling gear loaned. Bird and monkey watching, canoeing, swimming in river or bay. Optional fishing and tours via horse (overnight camping) or boat to Corcovado, Caño. Range low A+ including meals and transportation is one of lowest here. Phone and fax, 71-2436.

Nature trail crosses quiet river near Drake Bay.

La Paloma—Thatched cabinas with pvt bath and porch on hilltop overlooking the Pacific near Drake Bay. Not inspected. Range A+. In Costa Rica, phone 39-0954, fax 77-0171. U.S., (305) 785-2269, fax (305) 785-2372.

Marenco Biological Station—Lodge on hill overlooking the Pacific with 1240 acres of forest and beaches, adjacent to north end of Corcovado, with hundreds of bird, animal and butterfly species. Cabinas have 4 bunks, balcony, shared bath. Good food. Swimming, snorkeling, and hiking on trails and to waterfall. Tours, guides, horses available. Research biologists often present. Range A+ includes transportation from San Jose and meals.

Northwest: Monteverde's accommodations, listed with the village, are all occupied by nature tourists. Some lodges as well as local naturalists offer guided walks. Several cattle haciendas farther north now offer nature tourists guided horseback riding on their natural areas as well as on adjacent national parks:

Owner Alvaro Wiessel with keel-billed toucan at Rincon de La Vieja Mountain Lodge.

Rincon de La Vieja Mountain Lodge—Rustic lodge in ranch house on 660 acres adjoining Rincon de La Vieja Nat'l. Park, near hot springs. West slope of mountain range, northeast of Liberia, is less rainy than east but has lots of wildlife including monkeys, peccaries, hundreds of bird species. Nine rooms, some with pvt. bath. Excellent food and hospitality. Horseback tours in park and to volcano summit. Range A+ includes meals, horses, guide. Hostel discount in rustic cabin with shared bath. Deluxe hotel under construction on hacienda. Apdo. 114, Liberia, Guanacaste. Phone 66-0473.

Volcán Orosí dominates the view from Los Inocentes.

Hacienda Los Inocentes—Lodge is Spanish style ranch house with high ceilings, tile, hardwood, and surrounding porch and chairs, overlooking stone corrals and Volcán Orosí. Big rooms, one with pvt. bath, others each have key to unshared bath in nearby room, for up to 35 guests. Great food. Hacienda has 14,000 acres, partly in forest, adjoins Guanacaste Nat'l. Park, and offers tours to Santa Rosa Park. Altitude 900 ft., accessible by paved road. Tractor-drawn wagon available for ranch tours by non-riders. Some rooms wheelchair accessible. Here's nature in comfort with Costa Rican traditional style. Range A+ includes guide and horses. Apdo. 1370-3000, Heredia. Phone and fax, 39-5484.

North Central: Lago Cote Ecoadventure Camp—Lodge for comfort with nature, on Lake Cote near Arenal. Offers hiking, volcano tours, mountain biking, riding, windsurfing, all equipment provided. Shared bath. Range A. Tikal Tours, phone 23-2811, fax 23-1916.

Arenal Observatory—Rustic lodge on a cool, breezy ridge part-way up Volcán Arenal, it sometimes is a volcano research base for scientists from the Smithsonian and universities. Simple rooms with bunk beds and cabinas have pvt. baths. Good, tipico food. A roofed lookout shelters guests, telescope, and cameras. Guests eject from bunks when the mountain booms at night to watch red-hot lava and boulders shower down the slopes across the canyon. Owned by John Aspinall (brother of Peter at Tiskita), it's on a macadamia farm with 300 acres of forest. Howler monkeys wake you at daylight. Besides the very active volcano, there's hiking, birding, nearby Lake Arenal and the hot springs at Tabacón. If you're driving in rainy season, ask if you need 4-wheel drive to cross two rivers. Low Range A+ includes meals. Costa Rica Sun Tours, phones 55-3418, 55-3518, fax 55-4410.

Lookout at Arenal Observatory gives sheltered view of the volcano.

Selva Verde Lodge—Lodge on main road at Chilimate near Puerto Viejo, owned by Holbrook Travel in Florida on 500 acres of private forest with signed and maintained trails. Biologists give workshops and tours. All rooms and dining room screened. Most have pvt. bath. River lodge is deluxe with fans, reading lamps, desk. Second floor looks into canopy. Range A+ includes meals in river lodge, rate lower in creek lodge. Phone 20-2121 for reservations, 71-6459 at lodge.

La Selva Biological Reserve, 3500 acres, near Puerto Viejo, is joined by a corridor recently purchased with Braulio Carrillo National Park, providing a continuous strip of natural habitat from the lowland to the top of Barva Volcano. Over 400 species of birds have been identified here plus equally impressive numbers of tree, mammal, reptile, amphibian, and insect species. La Selva is operated by the Organization for Tropical Studies. The priority is rainforest research, but it has miles of trails you can walk and rustic quarters at the reserve where you can stay. Reservations absolutely required even for day walks. Only 65 people are allowed in the reserve including researchers, so reservations can be hard for individuals to get during high season when tours are booked 3 months ahead. Relatively high charges for tourists help support research in the reserve— about $15 for lunch and use of trails per day, or $76/person for room, board and trails. Rules are strict about staying out of research plots, meal and quiet hours, etc. OTS runs a bus from San Jose to La Selva several times a week, $10. Phone 40-6696, fax 40-6783.

Huge ceiba tree at Oro Verde Camp behind Mariamalia, second from left, and guests.

El Gavilán Lodge and Oro Verde Station—both on the Sarapiquí River. Owners are Wolf and Mariamalia Bissinger. He's German and she's Costa Rican. English, Spanish, German, and French spoken. El Gavilán, on 440 acres near Puerto Viejo by good road, is a gateway to the lower river. It has 11 attractive rooms, 8 with pvt bath, on landscaped grounds, with outdoor jacuzzi, horses and trails. A two hour scenic boat ride down the river brings you to Oro Verde Camp on the river bank in a 1200 acre forest reserve. Thatched, screened shelters here, built almost entirely of local materials, provide simple but comfortable quarters for up to 40 people. Both lodges serve good tipico food. Here are miles of nature trails and the Sarapiquí River which joins the Río San Juan two miles downstream. By dugout you can visit nearby lagoons and a pristine riverbank forest along the San Juan to watch birds, monkeys, sloths, otters, frogs, and butterflies. Fishing is excellent for tarpon and snook.

While a one-day tour from San Jose comes as far as El Gavilán and includes a boat trip and lunch, it's a long day. At least two nights, one at Oro Verde, would be more enjoyable. Range A+ for tours including meals, and transportation from San Jose. Depending on tour package, some boat and horse charges additional. El Gavilán Lodge, Apdo. 445-2010, Zapote, San Jose. Phones 23-7479 and 53-6540, fax 53-6556.

Waterfall Lodge—each room and balcony has 2-way view into the forest.

Rara Avis: Amos Bien, former administrator of La Selva, is demonstrating on 3200 acres of forest adjoining Braulio Carrillo Nat'l. Park that rainforest is more profitable than denuded pasture. The adjacent park and its altitude in the transition zone combine to provide a maximum number of species including rare birds—over 300 species of birds have been counted so far! Getting there, up the last 10 miles of rivers, mud, and wooden corduroy road by tractor-assisted jeep, or wagon or horseback, is a strenuous part of your adventure. Waterfall Lodge has 8 rooms with private bath (including tubs they hauled all that way!) each on a corner of the building with two-way view into the canopy so you can birdwatch from dry chair or hammock when you tire of rain (13–18 *feet* a year), trails, and mud. Nearby is a 180 foot double waterfall, swimming hole, and an aerial tram used by forest canopy researchers sometimes available to ride if you sign a release and pay $25. Two miles lower is rustic El Plástico Lodge, a comfortable renovated former penal colony building with shared baths in a clearing at the edge of the forest with a view over the lowlands. The corduroy road between the lodges has great birding. Range A+ includes meals (excellent), lodging, and guide. El Plástico is about $30 a day per person less than Waterfall Lodge, and also has youth hostel discounts. Transportation cost depends on the number of people. San Jose pickup can be arranged. Rara Avis, Apdo. 8105-1000, San Jose. Phone 53-0844, fax 32-6513.

Jungle River Safari—offers rainforest with comfort for 8-10 guests, cabinas with pvt. bath, meals, open bar. Guided walks, river swimming, above Guápiles. Not inspected. Range A+. 4-day minimum stay. Box 1484, Key Largo, FL 33037. 1-800-TRAILS-5.

South Central: These rustic lodges are in the cool, damp Talamanca Mountains south of San Jose at 7500 and 6300 ft. altitude respectively. For quiet, no-frills birding, away from tour buses and crowds, they are good places to look for quetzales, collared trogons, hummingbirds, and hundreds of others. Both are near the Interamerican Highway and the owners can meet your bus (the San Isidro bus from San Jose) there by arrangement. Mornings on the highway are usually clear, but afternoons are often a whiteout in fog.

Genesis II—Rustic lodge with shared bath, hot water (solar), 12 volt lighting, excellent food, on 90 acre rainforest 4 km east of Interamerican Hwy. Canadians Steve and Paula Friedman built the lodge and offer trails with birdwatching lookouts through the forest, adjacent to large reserve. Low Range A+ includes all meals, naturalist guide and laundry for 3 days or week. Discount for 3 or more guests, days without guide, or add'l days. Can arrange pickup at San Jose Hotel or airport. Message phone 25-0271, fax 23-3873. Friedman, c/o Embajada de Canada, Apdo. 10303, 1000 San Jose.

Finca Chacon—Don Efraín Chacon and his family have rustic cabinas with pvt. bath, hot water and good meals on their farm beside the Río Savegre. Farm has dairy, homemade cheese, grows apples, peaches. Trout fishing in the river, hiking, and birdwatching are featured, with quetzales most easily seen in April and May. Nine km down steep, narrow road toward San Gerardo de Dota from Km 80 on the highway. Range B includes meals. $12 round trip for pickup at highway. Phone 71-1732.

Driving in Costa Rica

Car rental This isn't something to jump into as lightly as you might at home. Costa Rica has one of the world's highest per capita accident rates. Passing on the narrow two-lane (or less) roads is a macho competitive sport. For a real hair-raiser, try Sunday afternoon on the grade above Esparza with the crowd returning from a weekend at the beaches competing with buses and loaded cattle trucks heading for Monday market in San Jose! On the winding, steep road, buses and trucks pass in both directions.

San Jose streets are one-way and narrow with almost no parking except lots and garages. There are freeways for some miles near San Jose, but most other roads are one or two lanes. I can think of few things that would persuade me to drive in San Jose at all.

West-bound on the Guápiles Hwy., entering Braulio Carrillo Nat'l. Park.

Prices for rentals are like those in the United States. For a sub-compact I paid about $300 a week plus fuel for unlimited mileage. International rental chains will take major credit cards for the deposit. Some have 800 numbers that allow you to reserve the cars before you leave home, sometimes for a lower rate than you'll get if you reserve in Costa Rica.

Your valid driver's license is good for three months in Costa Rica. After that you need to get one there. You can get a Costa Rican license good for 4 years by presenting your valid license from home and a brief physical by any Costa Rican doctor for eyes and blood pressure, though physical requirements are being stiffened at presstime. To rent a car you must be at least 25 and carry your passport. Insurance is a state monopoly and is required. You can get it through the car rental agency. Ask the amount of the deductible which may be more important than a slight difference in price between agencies. Rental agencies in the San Jose area are listed below. Note that most are on the west side of downtown San Jose or at the airport. Most whose downtown offices we have listed also have branch offices at the airport.

For a higher rate, some have 4-wheel drive vehicles. Be sure you need one before spending the extra money for a vehicle that's less comfortable for any number of people over two. Most popular beaches can be reached by ordinary cars. Ask about road conditions. Cars can be rented with air conditioning, but you should check to be sure it really cools the air rather than just blowing it. Cars in Costa Rica don't have heaters or defrosters, though the controls may be there. You don't need a heater, but do need the defroster in fog and rain (bring a rag to wipe inside the windshield).

Always rent a car in broad daylight when you can thoroughly inspect for dents, scratches, and nicks even underneath. Be sure each is marked on the diagram of previous damage you'll be asked to sign. Check the tires including the spare for wear or damage.

Some roads require 4-wheel drive—ask.

If you're spending a week at a resort, it may not make sense to have a rental car parked and costing money when there's often some cheaper, less worrisome way to get there. However, if there's a group of you with limited time, it can be a good solution. Cars shouldn't be left overnight except in a fenced area. All baggage should be stowed out of sight in the trunk, but try not to leave *any* baggage in an unattended vehicle.

Driving in Costa Rica requires more concentration than it takes at home, even on the freeways near San Jose. On back roads, you are advised to "drive like a bullfighter," as one friend said, demonstrating how he swerved around holes in the road. Save wear and tear on vehicle and passengers by slowing and shifting as necessary for bumps. Unlit livestock, potholes, and pedestrians make driving at night *dangerous!* Recently bicycles have multiplied everywhere. Few have reflectors, none has lights, most have more than one passenger, and all seem to be black! If you find fresh branches in the road, it means someone has car trouble just ahead.

On rural dirt roads, if you see fresh tracks turning aside before a bridge to go through the stream instead, follow the tracks or ask someone. The bridge may be broken or rotting—another reason for not driving at night.

I'll always remember the reader who rented a car and tried to see all of Costa Rica in nine days. He sent back a marked up copy of this book with "potholes" written on almost every page!

Service stations are far apart, and many villages, especially on the coast, have none. You should fill up in main towns like Liberia, Santa Cruz, or Nicoya before heading to beach resorts. These also may be the only towns in Guanacaste where you can get tire or other repairs. Unleaded gas is now available, called "Super".

Car Rental Agencies

Hertz Rent A Car
Calle 38, Paseo Colón
Phone 23-5959
(800) 654-3131

ADA Rent A Car
Airport and Plaza Viquez
Phone 33-7733

Avis Rent A Car
Calle 42, Ave. Las Americas
Phone 22-6066
(800) 331-1212

Budget Rent A Car
Calle 30, Paseo Colón
Phone 23-3284
(800) 472-3325

Dollar Rent A Car
Calle ctl., Ave. 7/9
Phone 33-3339
(800) 421-6868

El Indio Rent A Car
Calle 40/42, Ave. ctl.
Phone 23-4955

Adobe Rent A Car
Calle 7, Ave. 8/10
Phone 21-5425
Fax 21-9286

Elegante Rent A Car
Calle 10, Ave. 13/15
or Calle 24, Ave. 5/7
Phone 21-0136

Santos Rent A Car
Calle 40, Ave. 3/5
Phone 57-0035

National Car Rental
Paseo Colón, Calle 24/26
Phone 33-4406
(800) 227-7368

Tico Rent A Car, S.A.
Calle 10, Ave. 13/15
Phone 21-0284

Toyota Rent A Car
Paseo Colón, Calle 30/32
Phone 23-2250

Global Rent A Car
Ave. 7, Calle 7/9
Phone 23-4056

U-Haul Rent A Car
Paseo Colón, 75 m west of Toyota
Phone 22-1110, 23-2630
Fax 22-1242

There are more agencies and a total of over 1000 rental cars including jeeps in Costa Rica. During high tourist season, from late November into April, you should reserve as far in advance as possible. Allow at least a month if you want a car over Christmas or Easter holidays. If you reserve a car before you arrive in Costa Rica, get a fax of the reservation and carry it with you. Rental car agencies are now in Liberia, Limón, Golfito, Alajuela, Heredia and Tamarindo. **Aventura Rent A Car** in Liberia in the Bramadero Hotel rents cars and jeeps. Phone, 66-2349 and Fax, 66-2885. Their other offices in San Jose at the Hotels Corobicí and Cariari, in Puntarenas at the Hotel Fiesta, and at the Hotel Tamarindo Diria at Tamarindo, offer returns where you rent or at their other offices. You can also fly SANSA or ride a bus to these resorts and just rent a car or jeep for the days you need it. Phones, 39-4821, 39-4104. Fax, 66-2885, 39-0217.

What do I do now? Sign warns of rockfalls on the Interamerican Highway.

Traffic Police

If you do have an accident, don't move the vehicles until the police arrive and make out a report. Note the traffic police numbers below:

San Jose	22-4305, 23-8045, 22-1005
Alajuela	41-6208
Cartago	51-9064
Heredia	37-0438
Liberia	66-0409
Limón	58-1148
Puntarenas	61-0340

Those same helpful men who write up accident reports and send you on your way are often stationed beside the highway to control speeding drivers. The "TUR" (for tourist) on your rented car's license is a flag some can't resist. Usually when they pull you over, they just ask to see your license, passport, and the rental contract. Some will look for infractions such as speeding or not having seatbelts buckled up and threaten to write you a ticket unless you pay them several thousand colones. *Don't pay.* This practice will only get worse if encouraged.

Tickets are usually only about $10 and are paid in San Jose. One car rental agency tells all its customers to bring the tickets to them. The police cannot legally require payment on the spot. If a policeman is insistent, ask for and write down his identification number and the date, time and place. Often that's enough to end talk of a bribe. If he won't show his identification number and name, let him write the ticket while you note date, time, and place and his car license. Turn these in to your car rental agency. You may still have to pay the fine, but it won't require spending your vacation time in court.

One reader toured Costa Rica with surfing friends in a rental car with the surfboards stacked on top. They were flagged down by traffic police seven times between Puerto Limón and Puntarenas!

Hitchhiking On back roads, you'll meet people trying to get a ride to town because there isn't a bus until tomorrow or the next day. I'm not sure how successful they are on roads with little traffic, but you may not be able to count on getting a ride. With bus fare so cheap, that's the way to go if there's a bus. Otherwise, ask and try to find someone going there.

Maps Maps to help you get around are inexpensive. The ICT and your hotel can furnish maps of downtown San Jose and simple resort maps of the country. Car rental agencies have simple road maps which don't show the smaller roads, and of course none tells you which streams have bridges. The International Travel Map of Costa Rica, published in Canada at a scale of 1:500,000 with text in English, shows back roads and the smallest villages. It even shows which towns have service stations! For driving off main highways where there are few directional signs at intersections, it's essential— at travel bookstores in the U.S. and Canada and by mail from **Windham Bay Press**, publisher of this book. (See order section near back of book.) Possibly you can find this map in Costa Rica. San Jose bookstores, **Libreria Lehmann**, Ave. ctl, Calle 1/3, **Libreria Universal**, Ave. ctl, Calle ctl/1, and **The Bookshop**, Ave. 1, Calle 1/3, have good map sections. Lehmann's sells the aeronautical chart of Costa Rica. At 1:500,000, it shows the mountains in shaded relief so you can see the shape of the country. It's about 2 1/2 by 3 1/2 feet. The Ministry of Transport, Ave. 18, Calle 9, has topographic maps for hiking and street maps of towns.

Hotels in Costa Rica

Tourism in Costa Rica has grown incredibly in the past several years. While you can avoid crowds even in high season in this small country, doing so now requires planning and usually reservations some months ahead. One day in March when I looked at six hotels in central San Jose, they had a total of three rooms available for that night! New hotels are being planned and built, several thousand rooms in the next three years. New tours are offered daily. Roads are being improved so buses now reach places that required 4-wheel drive until recently.

Reservations: High tourist season coincides with the dry season, December through April, plus the two weeks in July when there's usually a break in the afternoon rains. Christmas and Easter Week are peak times when Costa Ricans as well as tourists head for the beaches. If you can, make reservations five months ahead for holiday weeks and three months ahead for high season in San Jose, Monteverde, and at the beaches. Rental cars should also be reserved well ahead.

Most beach hotels and some in San Jose have low season rates 25-40% lower than their high season rates. Reservations are easier to get then for hotels, tours, and rental cars. While your choice of timing depends on when you can come as well as what fishing or birding you may want, I recommend **November**. The country is green and bright after the rainy season, hotels aren't crowded, and low season rates generally apply.

Fax: Costa Rica has adopted fax machines recently. Most hotels with more than 15 rooms have them, and for the first time, this book lists their numbers. I recommend you ask for a confirmation of your reservation by fax and carry it with you when you check in. Some hotels have overbooked, and this is your best defense.

Some hotels, especially at the beaches during high season, won't make reservations for only 1 or 2 nights. Others do. This can limit your flexibility to travel around even mid-week. Do make reservations and call ahead.

If you make reservations, you should make every effort to keep them or to cancel well ahead. A hotel with very few rooms may have turned away business to hold your reservation, put on extra staff, or laid in more food. This is especially important for groups, but should be done by individuals as well.

Accommodations in each town are described as I found them so you can know what to expect in each place. Some travelers want any clean, inexpensive room so they can make their dollars stretch for a longer trip. Some want luxury and can afford to pay for it. I inspect for cleanliness, noise level (very important in a Latin country where locals equate noise with having fun), and hospitality. A recommended hotel is not only clean and attractive, but has a *very hospitable* staff and represents an exceptional value in its price range. It may not be the most luxurious hotel in the area. If you want more facilities or service, it may not be the one you would choose. Our tastes vary. I admit preferring the hospitable 6-40 room hotels Costa Ricans build and operate so well, with natural areas nearby. Big, impersonally staffed hotels that depend on concrete shade after they've removed all natural growth aren't my favorites, though more are being built.

Bougainvillea Santo Domingo, on attractive landscaped grounds near San Jose.

Costa Rica has all types of hotels, some luxurious and some basic where farm workers stay when they come to town on weekends. In between are many inexpensive to moderate hotels with very considerate staffs. You can decide not only what you're willing to pay, but how much luxury you want. Do you want to stay in a *tipico* hotel, where you feel the character of the country and some of your fellow residents are Costa Ricans, or do you want to relax in the same atmosphere you'd find in Hawaii or Palm Springs? Or would you like some of each for variety?

For this book, I inspected (with a checklist) over 300 hotels all over the country, priced from $4 to $150 per night, double. I looked at almost all the moderate to luxurious hotels. However, when I found clean hotels in good neighborhoods for less than $8 double, I felt I could do more for you than spend days wandering the red light districts of San Jose and Puerto Limón inspecting the cheap ones there. Some of these are listed in

The Mexico and Central America Handbook and *Central America on a Shoe-string* chapters on Costa Rica. Some hotels, inspected at quiet midday, may prove to have a cantina pounding nightly in the block behind.

Costa Rica has many small hotels, often far from major towns. Most hotels in San Jose or the surrounding hills don't have air conditioning as nights are cool at that altitude. On the coasts, most travelers from temperate climates want at least a fan or a building designed to catch every breeze. Many inexpensive places at the beaches don't have hot water, but the tap water is lukewarm. Some have hot water only at the shower head, not in the basin. TV without satellite or cable is usually in Spanish only. Cable TV usually has at least one English language channel.

Electricity is 110 volt 60 cycle A.C. throughout Costa Rica. At rustic lodges usingng generators, you should ask, though it's usually the same.

Hotels rated moderate and higher usually cash traveler's checks, a real help when there's no bank in a resort town. They usually take major credit cards. Some have reservation agents abroad whom your travel agent can call free. For hotels which don't, you may have to make your own reservations. Hotels in higher ranges usually have someone behind the desk who speaks English. Tour representatives in the lobby can book sightseeing tours. Some hotels offer courtesy transportation, which may or may not be free, but may be the easiest way to get there. Several beach hotels run buses from San Jose.

In less expensive hotels, you're likely to be more on your own if your Spanish is limited, though the manager will often go to amazing lengths to help you. On the East Coast practically all the blacks speak English. You should inspect the rooms offered you in budget/basic hotels before checking in to see if they're what you want. Everyone has his own definition of basic.

Wheelchair accessibility is noted for hotels, though not all rooms may be stairless. Bathroom doors tend to be narrow. Tropical architects have always depended on stairs as an obstacle to dirt, insects and other crawlies. Custom changes slowly. San Jose sidewalks have high steps.

Hotels are listed with each town later in this book. Since I inspected, the colon has been devalued several times, but most hotels have ap-plied for rate increases with the ICT that more than match inflation. If you find hotels listed in our tables out of alphabetical range order, it's because of price changes after we set type. Expensive hotels give their prices in dollars which they don't decrease with changes in the exchange rate. Inflation will cause some rates to rise.

For the current exchange rate when you travel, you can call the nearest

Costa Rican embassy or consulate or call the ICT office in Miami toll-free from the continental U.S., 1-800-327-7033. Some coastal hotels include meals with the rate, and most have a high season rate for December through March. The price a hotel licensed by the ICT may charge for a room is posted in the room.

	Price	Range
Luxury	Over $80/day	A+
Deluxe	$60-80	A
Expensive	$45-60	B
Moderate	$30-45	C
Inexpensive	$20-30	D
Budget	$11-20	E
Basic	up to $11	F

This scale refers to price for two people in U.S. dollars *before* the 16.3% sales and tourism tax that will be added to your bill (about 1/6) and does not refer to features of the hotel which may include a swim-ming pool in the budget range. Some hotels have no rate for singles and simply charge a rate for the room. A room or cabin for 4 may be a real bargain for a group or family if not for a single.

Couples should ask for their preference in twin or double beds when making reservations. Hotels often have rooms with either. Many budget hotels have some rooms with bath and some without. Expensive hotels usually have deluxe rooms and suites at higher rates than the range we show for basic rooms. Beach hotels often have some rooms with air conditioning and some with fans. In San Jose and at higher elevations you don't need it, but down on the coasts you probably will need at least a fan. Fan or generator noise can make earplugs welcome.

"Apartotels" and "cabinas" are terms you'll see often. An apartotel has rooms with kitchen facilities, often suites, and usually has weekly and monthly as well as daily rates. There are several in the San Jose area and a few elsewhere. They can be economical for families and very conve-nient if one is following a diet. "Cabina" means cabin but often means a motel-style connected row of rooms, and occasionally even is a room in a multi-story building. A "pension" is an inexpensive to basic hotel which usually does not serve meals even if it formerly did. A "motel" in Costa Rica (none listed here intentionally) is a hotel with discreet entrance and staff used by couples not married to each other.

Bed & Breakfasts

B & B's are a small but rapidly growing sector of tourism in Costa Rica. In most villages you could find someone who will rent a room and provide breakfast or all meals. Many don't advertise. Now some are seriously advertising, particularly in *The Tico Times*., often owned by retired North Americans, but some offering a chance to stay with an English-speaking Costa Rican family. Most are Range C and some have weekly or monthly discounts. You'll find new ones in almost every issue of the paper. There are no associations such as you'll find in other countries, but several do list homes besides their own. Since these change rapidly anywhere, we can't list each one in Costa Rica, but will note two with multiple listings among the following: **Bell's Home Hospitality** has a brochure describing over 20 houses in and near San Jose, which they personally inspected. Price Range A (have single rate, about $40) includes breakfast. Dept. 1432, P.O. Box 025216, Miami, FL 33102-5216. In Costa Rica 25-4752, Fax 24-5884. **Costa Rican Homestays Bed & Breakfast** offers lodging in Costa Rican homes, private bath, breakfast, laundry, airport pickup. Brochure. Apdo. 8186, 1000 San Jose. Phone 40-6829. **La Posada De La Montaña** in the hills 20 minutes northeast of San Jose, is on 5 acres of coffee plants and other trees, has some units with kitchenettes. Accepts credit cards. Reservations: P.O. Box 308, Greenfield MO 65661, USA. Phone or Fax (417) 637-2066. In Costa Rica, Apdo. 1-3017, San Isidro de Heredia. Phone or Fax 39-8096. **Park Place**, in hills overlooking Escazú and Central Valley, is 4 room (two floors) guest house with kitchen across street from owners (real privacy). No young children. Near bus. Range C and up. Glade and Pat Murchison, owners. Apdo. 1010, 1250 Escazú. Phone 28-9200. **Tres Arcos**, owned by Mr. and Mrs. Eric Warrington, 20 year residents of Costa Rica, has 10 units for 1-5 people near the University of Costa Rica in Los Yoses, two kms. east of central San Jose. Can arrange airport pickup and tours. Apdo. 161-1000 San Jose. Phone/Fax 25-0271.

Youth Hostels

Toruma Youth Hostel in San Jose was the first youth hostel in Central America when it opened a few years ago. Now there are others including some which operate as hotels but give lower rates to those with IYH cards (includes national hostel associations). Group trips to outlying hostels are sometimes organized by Costa Rican Youth Hostels in San Jose, phone, 24-4085, which can also make reservations for you at any of the hostels. **Albergue Lago Arenal** overlooks Lake Arenal. **Kiskadee Hostel** is in Puerto Viejo de Limón (not inspected), **Rincon De La Vieja Mountain Lodge** has hostel rates for some rooms, and **Rara Avis** has hostel rates with meals at rustic El Plástico Lodge. **Cabinas San Isidro**, 8 km east of downtown Puntarenas has hostel rates. At Manuel Antonio, **Costa Linda** is on the hill back from the beach. **Albergue La Calzada** is 1/4 mile from Guayabo Nat'l. Monument, Range E.

Camping

Camping at beaches and national parks is practical, especially if you're in a group or can arrange with a local person to watch your camp. Sometimes the nearest hotel is miles away. There are a few commercial camping areas, e.g. at Jacó Beach, and others where camping is OK as long as you're not in someone's yard or field without permission. Surfers at Pavones south of Golfito often bring mountain tents and camp in a group. If you're camping high in the mountains, as on Rincon de La Vieja, you'll need a good sleeping bag and tent, though sometimes there are shelters or huts. For mid-altitude camping here in the tropics, I've found my 18-ounce Goretex bivouac bag plus a foam sleeping pad works, though in real heat it can feel like a sauna. In rain, I'd want a plastic sheet overhead. The bivouac bag zips closed with a bug net panel, and I think I could sleep on an anthill. However, a tent is more comfortable in heat than being zipped into a bag. A hammock is the ideal tropical camp bed for those whose backs will tolerate one. Avoid grassy stock pastures, which often have chiggers and ticks.

Crabs are camp scavengers near the beach, even crawling under loose doors.

I used the grassy, tree-shaded campground at Santa Rosa Park two nights. The first night I was concerned about crawling creatures and tried sleeping on a picnic table. Unfortunately, it had a loose plank on one side and at midnight, it dumped me. Falling off a table while zipped up in a bivvy bag is a very helpless feeling! Peace ended at 4 a.m. when a family of howler monkeys on one side of camp joined a chorus of coyotes in the next field.

Camping is the only way to be nearby for turtle nesting or hatching on west coast beaches, and in such unpopulated places, keeping supplied with food and reliable water is your main concern. In settled areas, camping is beautiful except during holidays. More camping areas being added at beaches like Jacó and at Moín on the Caribbean. Watching your gear or finding someone else to watch it is a problem if you're alone or in a small group and want to leave camp. I've sometimes stayed in a hotel or cabina simply to have a place to leave gear. Often your best bet is to camp with others so someone is always in the area. Putting your name with permanent laundry marker on your gear to destroy its resale value may help.

While some are planning RV parks at presstime, usually as part of a development, there is just one near San Jose at Belén and one as part of the Club Punta Leona, south of Puntarenas.

Food

While I've met travelers who can remember after two weeks in New Guinea which night the meat was tough, I'm not one of them. If food is one of your real interests as a traveler, you'll have have fun exploring the well-advertised restaurants of every nation in San Jose. For inexpensive meals, small places called *sodas* serve good plain food for $1.50-$3 for lunch. The best ice cream in Costa Rica is at the Pops chain. *Refrescos* are delightful drinks made with such tropical fruits as mango or tamarind blended with water or milk. My favorite is *maracuyá*.. *Gallo pinto* is the staple rice and bean dish that Costa Ricans eat for breakfast and at other meals. It can be very plain or have peppers and other goodies added. *Casado* is the meal of the day, the best value at small restaurants, with meat, gallo pinto, and vegetables. Shrimp (not cheap) and fish dishes are excellent. Corvina, sea bass, is cooked many tasty ways. *Langosta* (lobster) is expensive, but more reasonable in beach areas where they're caught the same day. Steak is grass-fed, lean, and inexpensive.

In coastal heat, I especially enjoy fruit salads and*ceviche*, a cool fish cocktail made with corvina pickled in lemon juice and seasoning. The best recipe I've eaten follows, courtesy of Yolanda Kaye and Martha Thomas at Costa Rica Expeditions:

Ceviche Recipe, Serves 6.

Fresh sea bass	l kilo
Coriander (fresh if possible)	l bunch
Sweet red peppers	2 medium
Onion	l large
Garlic	3 cloves
Lemons	6-8 medium
Worcestershire sauce	1/2 t
Salt & pepper to taste	

Cut up sea bass (or any firm-fleshed white fish such as sole, snapper, halibut, shark, but not tough octopus) into 1/2 inch cubes and place in non-metallic container. Finely chop coriander, peppers, onion, and garlic and mix with fish. Peel and wash the lemons. Then cut in half to juice. Peeling is very important as the oil in the skin will cause the ceviche to be bitter. You need enough lemon juice to cover the fish. Add worcestershire sauce, salt and pepper. Cover and refrigerate overnight.

Hotels where I've enjoyed the food will be mentioned with my individual comments. Restaurants noted are excellent, cheap and in places you might not easily find. For the environmentally concerned, a note— tortuga (sea turtle) eggs are served in some bars, and the meat is served in restaurants in Limón. All species are endangered and taking eggs or meat is illegal in most places. Poaching probably will continue as long as people maintain the market by buying them.

Health

Costa Rica is the cleanest, most healthful, tropical country I've visited. The people and government are concerned about health and have spent heavily on water supplies, hospitals, and health programs. You can safely drink the water in San Jose and other major towns, as well as in licensed tourist hotels in outlying areas. In basic places with shallow wells or at roadside pulperías,stay with soda drinks from the bottle, coffee, or beer. In the dry season, December through April, some outlying towns, including Santa Ana and Escazú near San Jose, have water problems and you should not drink or brush teeth in it. I carry and use water purification drops when I'm refilling my canteen from streams or wells on hikes.

Food. Milk is pasteurized, and market stalls in community markets are incredibly clean. Fish stalls in San Jose, over 70 miles from the sea, don't even smell fishy! In choosing restaurants, I don't take any more care than I would traveling in the U.S., and I have rarely been sick despite eating in a wide variety of places all over the country. If you buy fried food from streetside stalls or vendors on buses and trains, or eat salads in doubtful-looking places, you're on your own. Washing your hands and the knife you use to peel fruit before eating is important.

Insects, etc. Any tropical area has more insects than you usually see in temperate climates. A biology professor once told my class that the reptiles had their age, the mammals are having theirs now, but he felt that the next would belong to arthropods (insects and all others with jointed legs). If you travel in the tropics you may feel that the insects have always had the upper hand! In warm damp climates they flourish. If you see ants or an occasional cockroach in an otherwise clean establishment, it is not a sign of filth but only means no one has mopped there in the past few minutes. Relax and enjoy the fantastic array of butterflies, moths,, and caterpillars that brighten garden and forest here (and feed those wonderful birds you came to see).

Africanized bees arrived in Costa Rica several years ago. You should assume that any hive or swarm you see is Africanized and stay away. Their venom is no worse than common honeybees, but they are more aggressive when disturbed so more of them sting. Avoid wearing perfume. Some guides advise not swatting the first one that comes near you, as the smell may incite others. If attacked, you should run away, and if possible, get underwater in a stream or pond. People who are seriously allergic to bee stings at home should carry antivenin kits.

At low altitude, especially near beaches, several types of gnats, sand-fleas, etc. may appear (or you'll find later that they bit without appearing) in the evening. Insect repellent and wearing shoes and socks helps.

Hikers and campers should bring insect repellent. Note that "deet", the active ingredient in many repellents, makes many people more sensitive to sun and dissolves plastic luggage if it leaks. You can use slightly diluted Avon bath oil instead (except in African bee areas)! If you walk across lowland cattle pastures you may encounter chiggers, an almost invisible mite, also found in the southern U.S., whose bite raises welts with a fierce itch that lasts some days. Staying on trails and roads is the best prevention. Being completely covered around the ankles, etc. and changing clothes immediately after hiking helps. You can dust sulfur powder on socks and pants to repel the mites. Clear nail polish applied to the red dots indicating mites is reported to help. A product called "Chigarid" has been recommended by readers. It's worth carrying a soothing anti-itch lotion. Some people take an antihistamine before bedtime to reduce swelling and itching if they've been bitten.

If you camp or stay in primitive quarters, hang up all clothing and shake out your shoes and clothes before putting them on.

Snakes Except for the Arctic, most areas of the world have poisonous snakes. Despite looking carefully anytime I step off a trail or put my hand up to a tree, I have only seen one poisonous snake outside the laboratory in Costa Rica (the non-poisonous boa constrictor in a national park doesn't count). However, I will keep looking for the fer-de-lance (called *terciopelo* or velvet snake here) which is highly poisonous and very aggressive, the coral snake, and bushmaster. Except for the coral snake, most are **very** well-camouflaged. In urban areas they aren't a problem. In rural places or wilderness, watch where you are walking, and avoid stream banks at night. To see them safely, visit the snake lab in Coronado, a northeastern suburb of San José, and watch them milked for venom Friday afternoons at 1:30, from behind a window. The lab is open, free, weekday afternoons from 1 to 4, with live snakes of each kind displayed. The **Serpentarium** in San Jose, Ave. 1, Calle 9, second Floor, is open 7 days a week, 10 a.m.-7 p.m. Admission $1. Excellent displays of live snakes of Costa Rica and elsewhere. Feeding is early Thursday morning when you can come if you've asked earlier for an appointment.

Sunburn. Ten degrees north of the equator, the sun's effect on unprotected skin is serious. A burn from one day in the sun can spoil the next several days of your trip. Long-term exposure can, besides giving you a tan, age your skin drastically. I don't think the leather look has improved the appearance of anyone since Sitting Bull. Fortunately, you can avoid this and still go home with a healthy glow.

Using shade where available, a sunscreen lotion, a sun hat, and discretion with the midday sun and length of exposure are sensible. Here you will tan through a thin shirt or while lying in the shade near a beach. I wear a long-sleeved shirt and long pants anytime I'm riding horses or open boats. Bring effective sunscreens with you. They are labeled now with sun protection factors (SPF), supposed to indicate how much longer an average person can stay out without burning. You will *not* be in average conditions. As a blonde who tans well, I use creams rated SPF 6 for daytime moisturizers even in the Central Valley. On the beach or outdoors, I use gels with SPFs of 15 or higher. These have names like Block Out and Total Eclipse! Bullfrog is a waterproof sunscreen, SPF 18, highly recommended by raft trip leaders, available at REI stores in the western U.S. In the tropics, you will tan through these sunscreens. It's important to put more on after swimming and every 3 to 4 hours in any case.

Immunizations. Officially there are none required or listed as recommended for Costa Rica. If you're staying in major hotels and not camping or snorkeling, that's fine. If you will be hiking, camping, or traveling near Costa Rica's borders which might not be recognized as barriers by germs and mosquitoes, you should take the precautions you would for any tropical area. A gamma globulin shot makes you more resistant to many viruses, including hepatitis, for up to 6 months. Tetanus is a good shot for any outdoor person to keep current. Costa Rica eliminated malaria some years ago, but cases have occurred recently in the eastern lowlands. You can get a weekly pill prescribed by your doctor to be taken for several weeks before, during, and after the trip if you will be near the borders or going to other tropical countries on the same trip. No immunizations are required for reentry to the United States. Carrying a copy of your immunization records and prescriptions (written in their chemical names rather than trade names) is always sensible when traveling.

Medical Care. Costa Rica has excellent doctors and hospitals, with the majority in the San Jose area. All hospitals have English-speaking staff members and many doctors have trained in the U.S. or England. For emergency care, go to the hospitals or clinics. For other care, your consulate can provide a list of private doctors. Check with your health insurance before you leave home to see if you need additional coverage or forms. Usually you will have to pay with cash or credit card and apply later to your insurance for reimbursement. Medicare does not cover medical treatment outside the U.S.

Because costs are much lower and skills are high, many people from abroad come to Costa Rica for plastic surgery (especially face lifts), cataract operations, sessions at health spas, dental work, and even some heart operations. A nursing home specializing in long term care for Alzheimer's patients has opened, taking advantage of Costa Rica's lower labor costs to provide more staff and care at less cost than in other countries.

HOSPITALS

SAN JOSE	Address	Phone
Clinica Biblica	Calle ctl./1, Ave. 14	23-6422
Clinica Catolica	Guadelupe	25-9055
Clinica Santa Rita (Maternity)	Ave. 8, Calle 15/17	21-6433

The hospitals listed above are private and can give any medical care you need. They will take credit cards, but you will have to pay them and bill your own insurance later. The hospitals listed below are under Costa Rica's Social Security system. They will provide free emergency care to anyone.

Calderon Guardia	Ave. 9, Calle 17	22-4133
Children's Hospital	Paseo Colón, Calle 20	22-0122
Hospital Mexico	Autopista General Cañas	32-6122
San Juan de Dios	Paseo Colón, Calle 14	22-0166

Phone # 128 for medical emergencies requiring help or ambulance in the San Jose area. This number will be extended through-out Costa Rica, the medical equivalent of 911 in the U.S.

Red Cross (Ambulance)   21-5818

OTHER CITIES	Telephone	Red Cross (Ambulance)
Alajuela	41-5011	41-2939
Cartago	51-0611	51-0421
Heredia	37-1091	37-1115
Liberia	66-0011	66-0994
Limón	58-2222	58-0125

Puntarenas   63-0033   61-0184

Clinicas are private hospitals, available to foreigners at reasonable rates. Others are social security hospitals which provide emergency services to foreigners. All have laboratories, x-rays, and pharmacies.

Photography

Costa Rica is a great place for photography, whether you're a professional or just carry an Instamatic. The tropical flowers and blossoming trees, wildlife, and constantly changing scenery offer more choices than you'll be able to film in one trip.

Using the Tarcoles River bridge to steady my 400 mm lens to photograph a crocodile.

Those who've traveled with a camera in the tropics know what they want to do. For those who haven't, here are some suggestions:

For any trip, take time to know your camera well before you leave home. If it's new or borrowed, load and shoot some film and get it back to study before you start this trip. Read the manual and practice. Bring all the film you think you'll need for the trip, plus a bit more. Bring extra batteries for your camera and flash. Radio and electronic stores at home receive many stock items packed with silica gel and may be able to give you some to protect gear and film from dampness. You can get lead-foil envelopes made for taking film through airport security—but then carry all your film in your carry-on bag and ask that it be hand-checked instead of x-rayed. Some professional photographers simply put all film in a see-though plastic bag so inspectors can see it in the original containers quickly when they hand-check the bag.

You are allowed to bring two cameras and any reasonable amount of film into Costa Rica, but should get your equipment list with serial numbers reviewed by a Costa Rican consul at home if you want to bring more cameras. Film is very expensive, several times what you pay at home. If you have to buy extra film during the trip, get it from a busy photo store like the IFSA store on Ave. Central across from the Cultural Plaza, where they sell enough so any film they have is fresh.

Color film is very sensitive to heat. I leave any I won't need on a coastal trip back with my baggage in San Jose. Both color and black and white film soften in high humidity. They may jam the film winding mechanism of your camera or their sprocket holes may break so the film won't wind at all. I keep the film in its original cans in a sealed bag with silica gel and dry the gel weekly in an oven. I bring the exposed film back from a trip of three months or less to process at home.

Electronic cameras are delicate creatures in the humid, salty air on the coasts. A small amount of corrosion forming on any contacts can stop them for the trip. Keep your cameras as dry as possible and wipe them off before storing even for the night. After a multi-day field trip, I remove lenses from cameras and put all bodies, lenses, and my binoculars in a plastic bag with silica gel at least overnight. Mildew growing between lens components is impossible to remove.

If possible, bring at least one backup camera, preferably not a super miniature whose parts are tiny and extra fragile. If you should have to get a camera repaired, you will be lucky if parts are available. The IFSA store can send you to the repair shop they use. Note that batteries are considered accessories and your camera may be returned without them if you don't make the person writing the receipt list them.

I use two Pentax ME bodies, one loaded with black and white and the other with color (Kodachrome 64 or Fujichrome 100). The lenses I switch as needed are a Macro-Zoom 70-210 mm, 50 mm, 28 mm, and 400 mm (not worth carrying unless you're trying for wildlife close-ups). The wide angle lens is good for buildings, narrow streets, and tall trees. It shows both the rim and bottom of a volcano crater. Both cameras stopped on one trip, one repairable and the other not. I bought a Pentax K-1000 body when I got back—a larger, heavier model that takes the same lenses and isn't as automated, but is much more rugged with fewer electronics to corrode. I take all three cameras on trips.

I use a flash to fill in shadows or get more light in the forest. A tripod or monopod is useful. Filters protect the lenses as well as correct light— yellow or green for B-W film and skylight or ultraviolet for color. A *greenish-yellow filter* for B-W film makes the hundreds of rainforest species show in different shades of grey without using 3/4 of the available light that a green filter absorbs. If you're using fast film, you'll want a neutral density filter to cut tropical midday sun.

Greenish-yellow filter separated plant species on a trail at Tiskita.

If the sky is overcast, a camera with automatic exposure will pick up so much light from the sky that it underexposes everything else. If you set the meter for double the light, the picture subjects will come out. When the sky is blue and you don't have glare off the sea, the automatic meter is fairly accurate. In the forest, it's wise to use a separate light meter.

I carry my cameras in my camera bag securely zipped rather than around my neck when I'll be using them, and leave the bag at the hotel desk if I don't need them that day. On the streets of San Jose, Puntarenas, or Puerto Limón, I'm careful of my camera bag (or have a companion watch it) while I take pictures or load film.

Arts, Crafts, Souvenirs

Costa Rican craftsmen make beautiful pieces from metal, leather, ceramics and tropical hardwoods. Artists paint designs derived from the Moors who invaded Spain on oxcarts such as those that used to haul coffee to Puntarenas and still work on back roads. Preserving the art today, they paint the designs on trays, wall plaques, and oxcarts ranging from toy size to barbecue stands. You can watch them do it at small factories in Sarchí, near San Jose. Many tours as well as public buses go there. All wooden crafts are generally less expensive there than in San Jose, though you can find any crafts in San Jose gift shops. Plain wooden trays, lamps, candlesticks, etc. show the grain of tropical hardwoods.

Beautiful chairs, tables, beds, and other furniture are made from the same woods. The shop can probably ship something home for you. Do be sure the wood was well-dried before a large or valuable piece was made. Two artists whose furniture is well-designed and built are Barry Biesanz, 28-1811, in Escazú, and Jay Morrison, 28-6697, in Santa Ana, west of San Jose. Call for appointments and directions to their shops.

Note: If you buy valuable pieces, including furniture, you may consider paying the excess baggage charges to carry them back with you rather than shipping—cheaper than air freight and customs brokers. You will be there to discuss with zealous U.S. Customs agents why they shouldn't bore holes in your purchases to check for drugs. My air-freighted hardwood desktop acquired holes and gouges in their search.

Several shops, some of them artists' coops, have a good stock of crafts in San Jose:

Gift shop in Hotel Don Carlos, Calle 9, Ave. 7/9. This shop features samples of all the arts and crafts in Costa Rica, one-stop shopping.

Apple store on Ave. Ctl, near Pizza Hut.

La Galeria, Calle l, Ave. 1.

Artesania CANAPI, Calle 11, Ave. 1

Mercado Nacional de Artesania on Calle 11, Ave 2.

The northeastern San Jose suburb of Moravia, is best known for leather crafts including wallets, purses, briefcases, and belts. Leather is comparatively expensive, though you can find good values in the zippered handbags some Costa Ricans carry, even in San Jose. A bag big enough for anything I'd want to carry around all day, plus a camera, is less than $20. In the weeks before Christmas, vendors have stalls in downtown San Jose that are worth checking. I've seen fine buys in leather wallets and writing folders at the weekend market in front of the National Theater. Hammocks are a good buy at the same place, especially at day's end when the sellers don't want to take them home.

Bandanas featuring Costa Rican animals, bird, or flowers are made by **Go Bandanas** and sold in most gift shops. They're attractive and packable. **Costa Rica Expeditions Travelers' Store**, Ave. 3, Calle ctl, has wildlife posters and comfortable rocking chairs with leather backs and seats packed for shipping or taking with you.

Gift shops have gift packs of Costa Rican coffee and the liquor departments in supermarkets, *supermercados*, have Cafe Rica, a coffee liqueur like kahlua. Bags of roasted coffee beans are cheapest in supermarkets. *Puro* on the label means that no fillers or sugar have been added. Vanilla beans and extract are better quality here than you may find at home.

San Jose has many art galleries with original works and prints by Costa Rican artists. Exploring the galleries is fun and some of the work is very impressive. The gift shop in Parque Bolivar, the national zoo, has wildlife and rainforest posters and T-shirts made from photos of the animals to benefit the park system.

Full-size painted oxcart at Sarchí factory.

A Costa Rican told me one could bargain anywhere, even in department stores. That may work if one looks native and speaks excellent Spanish. You might try it in the central market, and you definitely should bargain with cab drivers. Most stores have fixed prices.

The central markets are an experience, with individual stalls selling anything from cheese to birdcages. The San Jose and Alajuela markets are especially interesting. One useful item you'll find is the shopping bag made from rice sacks that Costa Rican housewives use to carry purchases home. It's large, very strong, and is white or has the rice brand label and design on it. Costing less than $1, it folds to nothing in your purse, but is very handy in Costa Rica and back home for shopping. The markets are the cheapest, most interesting place to buy a cotton canvas campesino's sun hat, cool protection in boats or on hikes, especially if you wet it before wearing. You probably already have that absolute essential, an umbrella, but if you don't, downtown shops and the market stalls have folding ones made in Panama for about $6.

Returning Home—Customs

Most countries will not allow you to bring home birds, animals, or plants without a great deal of extra paperwork or permits. Some are prohibited outright, especially live endangered species or products from them. In Costa Rica, you may see items made from turtles, alligators, or jaguar or margay skins. These will be confiscated by customs at your port of entry if you get that far with them. It's best to buy your orchid plants at home except for the tissue cultured ones in sealed vials you'll find in some gift shops. I think if you've read this book, you probably have sense enough not to carry drugs across borders. Flights coming from Central or South American into any other country are particularly searched. A Labrador retriever worked the baggage carousel diligently in New Orleans when I returned from Costa Rica. Trained dogs work at Costa Rica's Juan Santamaria Airport during both arrivals and departures.

There's lots you can bring, much more than your airline baggage allowance. You'll save time at the airport of entry by putting all your purchases and receipts for any expensive items together in one bag. Canadians absent from Canada for more than 7 days are allowed to bring in duty free $150 per year in value plus 40 ounces of liquor. Canada Customs publishes a useful brochure, "I Declare", worth studying.

United States citizens who've been abroad for 48 hours or more are allowed a value of $400 each, no matter what age. One quart of alcohol may be included if you're of age and the state you enter allows it. Useful pamphlets are "Your Trip Abroad" from the United States Dept. of State, Washington, D. C. 20520 and "GSP and the Traveler", from the Department of the Treasury, U.S. Customs Service, Washington, D.C. 20229. The latter explains the Generalized System of Preferences, a list of 2,500 products from developing countries, including Costa Rica, allowed into the United States duty free.

With a U.S. passport reentering the United States is very easy. Instead of having to prove your identity in a slow-moving line at the airport, you are almost waved through, especially if you look awfully square and don't fit that fascinating stereotype the drug agents are looking for.

LIVING IN COSTA RICA

Costa Rica encourages foreigners with a guaranteed pension income of at least $600 per month to become *pensionados*, living in the country with all the privileges of a citizen except the right to vote and to work for hire. The intent of the law is to bring money into Costa Rica and to bring people with education and skills from whom Costa Ricans can learn. Thousands of people from many nations, including many from North America, presently live in Costa Rica in any of several resident statuses.

Pensionado Margot Frisius with a pizote (coatimundi) she raised. She and her husband breed several specials of macaws and provide refuge for wild animals confiscated from poachers.

Some are having a wonderful time, enjoying the friendly people, climate, low cost of living, and a new chapter in their lives. Others are like the retired aerospace engineer I met at the theater who used his slightly impaired hearing as an excuse not to learn Spanish and who spent his days in his apartotel watching TV. He hadn't thought to go over to the university and volunteer to teach a physics or engineering course in English to keep his brain cells alive. He missed the fun of being part of the country.

Edwin Salas was the inspired, imaginative head of the ICT's Pensionado Department. Officially, it's Departamento de Jubilados, Instituto Constarricense de Turismo, Apdo. 777, San Jose, Costa Rica. Telephone, 23-1733, Ext 264. His advice is the best I've heard: "When you're deciding to retire here, think about your attitude toward foreigners at home and then toward Costa Ricans. You'll find the villagers kind and generous as long as we don't feel rejected. Costa Ricans are very sensitive. An approved pensionado is a Costa Rican. Most U.S. citizens are scared by the language barrier. Don't be scared; it is not a barrier. There are so many fields in Costa Rica that the ground is fertile, but we need the seed."

Costa Rica needs volunteers from babysitters and English tutors to engineers and doctors. The Pensionado Association can offer suggestions or direct you to an area where you could help. It's the best way I've heard to get behind the doors and walls and meet interesting people as well as gain a sense of accomplishment. Volunteers have designed roads and helped train local medical helpers.

I think retiring here, or perhaps anywhere, is like the fenceposts you'll see along the road. If a dead log is set, it soon rots in the tropics. Costa Ricans plant live poro tree trunks with the bark left on. They grow into trees that work as fenceposts for a lifetime. You can keep living and growing, or rot.

If you're thinking of moving here, there are two pieces of advice you'll hear everywhere: come for extended visits including the wet as well as dry season, and don't cut yourself off by handling your assets so you can't return to your native country temporarily or permanently later if you change your mind. Since Costa Rican laws are different from the ones you have lived with, it's wise as soon as you have your residence status to arrange your affairs, including wills, with a Costa Rican lawyer so your personal and property rights are protected. Usually one member of a couple applies for residence, covering dependents. If assets and income can be divided to qualify both, it can save many problems in case of death or divorce. However then each would have to cash the required amount of money into colones annually.

There is a Newcomers' Seminar the second Tuesday of every month at the Irazú Hotel to which all are invited. Newcomers' Seminars are also scheduled other Tuesdays at different hotels in San Jose. Some speakers at these meetings have investment projects to sell, but others do discuss any changes in the pensionado law, insurance for foreigners, and they answer any questions.

The **Asociación de Residentes Pensionados y Rentistas de Costa Rica,** Apdo. 700, 1011 Y Griega, San Jose, Costa Rica (Phone 33-8068) is a good place to inquire for information even before you come to Costa Rica., if you're thinking of retiring here. They have a list of the requirements for pensionado status. Their office is next to the ICT Pensionado Office on the ground floor of the ICT building, Ave. 4, Calle 5. Once you're in Costa Rica, they're good people to see for references to effective lawyers to get your residence status. Having the association do it for you, for which they charge less than most, is probably the quickest, surest, and most convenient way. The association represents the interests of pensionados as a group to the Costa Rican government and deserves the support of any foreign resident in the country.

Lillian DeSha, wife of the association's president and one of its pillars, wrote the following letter to a prospective pensionado with useful advice for anyone thinking of retiring in Costa Rica. I appreciate her permission to use it here:

"We recommend that anyone considering retiring in Costa Rica first come here as a tourist at least once... Enjoy the country and the people and learn first hand that a different culture means different responses to a given situation. The adaptability and personality of the individual governs the degree of happiness and satisfaction with life anywhere. Tourist visas are good for 90 days.

There are two resident status categories available for retirement in Costa Rica. Pensionados and Rentistas. Pensionados must prove a $600 per month pension for life from a qualified source such as Social Security. You would provide a police report and be cleared through Interpol. You would have a medical examination here which includes a test for AIDS [this may have changed since her letter] and other communicable diseases. You would be required to prove exchange of $7200 a year from US dollars into colones at a government owned bank in a process called 'updating your file'. You would be required to live in the country four months out of the year, not necessarily consecutively. Your identification (carnet) must be renewed every two years at a cost of $100. You would carry the carnet at all times. Pensionados can own and operate businesses and make investments but not earn a salary or supplant a Costa Rican in a work situation.

Rentistas must prove interest or dividends in the amount of $1000 a month from a qualified investment or annuity. The government decides the qualification. $1000 a month, or $12,000 a year must be converted into colones. Every five years a rentista must again prove the validity of his source of income. The police, Interpol and medical exams also apply.

Passports [with entries and exits stamped in] supply proof of stay in the country for both categories. The same work requirements apply as those for pensionados.

It would be unwise to retire here expecting to earn a living or supplement one's resources, and extreme caution is advised regarding investments. Foreigners who have businesses here say it is extremely difficult.

Property taxes are lower here than in the U.S. or some other countries. Revenues come from a 10% tax on everything including food in restaurants, services, hotels, entertainment, etc. Gasoline is now about $1.30 per U.S. gallon {when she wrote}. The roads are poorly maintained and driving is like running a slalom course for some holes are axle crackers. The sidewalks in San Jose are not for the infirm.

Prices for homes and property vary according to location. Condominiums are available, again at varying prices. Rentals are available. If one owns one's home and car one can live very well on $1000 per month including help, taxes and utilities. Automobile insurance is slightly less here, but not substantially very different, and it is mandatory.

People who have lived here for years hark back to what it used to be like. Violent crime was rare and there has been an increase said to be perpetrated by refugees. Thievery is a constant problem. The iron grillwork on windows and doors is not just a charming facet of Latin architecture. It is to make robbery more difficult. Ads for homes frequently feature 'secure' which means there is a guard in the area. Bureaucracy and red tape is maddening. Nevertheless, after living here three years, we do not intend to go elsewhere. Those looking for the 'perfect place to retire' may be rewarded in heaven.

Should you decide to further investigate retirement in Costa Rica, this organization can do all the work, including legal services, to obtain your status. We have a Provisional Membership for $50 a year which entitles you to all information and services available to members. This sum can be applied to the cost of achieving pensionado or rentista status. You would receive the publication for our members, the PEN REN NEWS. In it is information of actions of the board of directors and the latest developments in our continuing efforts to understand the law and to take whatever actions are necessary to assure that all Pensionados and Rentistas enjoy the full protection of the constitution of the Republic.

If you have any further questions, please do not hesitate to contact us. Requirements for retiring in Costa Rica are patience, patience, patience, a sense of humor and a love of adventure. As they say in the South—first 'Come see us' ".
                                                            Lillian E. DeSha

The paperwork and procedure for becoming a pensionado are no one's joy. Get the ICT's advice in the Pensionado Office and talk to a lawyer recommended by other pensionados who've weathered the process. Be sure any time you deal with Migración that you have all the documentation of birth, bank and pension records they require, usually notarized by a Costa Rican consul near your former home and frequently translated into Spanish by an approved translator. *Important:* Get the required police report that you have no record *last*, as it is only good for 6 months and could expire before you became a resident. Many people have done the whole procedure by themselves, and it is easier now that representatives from the other government departments are in the Pensionado Office, but most still recommend having a good lawyer.

You will be able to bring in any reasonable amount (including one of any usual household appliance and allowing 1 color TV and 1 black and white) of household goods *once*, and a vehicle every 5 years without paying the usual duties. For a vehicle up to $16,000 value including cost of transportation and insurance, you pay 15% tax on that amount. If the value exceeds $16,000, you pay the much higher Costa Rican duties on the excess. You may also buy the car from a dealer in Costa Rica under the same law. At the end of 5 years you can sell the car and import a new one on the same basis. When you sell the car (you don't have to) you or the buyer must pay 70% duty on it. Pensionados and the association are still fighting the tax, but presently it's there. Do be prepared with patience to earn at least part of that pensionado status by out-lasting the procedure for getting it.

Changes are always possible in the pensionado law and the legislative assembly looks longingly at the tax privileges pensionados enjoy. Almost annually revisions are threatened, and at presstime, President Calderon had proposed changes in the exemptions of duties on vehicles and the amount of income required to be converted into colones. The Pensionado Association is the unified voice of foreign residents dealing with the government and is your best source of current information on the law.

Hired help for house and yard costs much less here than elsewhere, but you must get references from past employers for anyone who will be in the house when you aren't home. A good live-in maid is an excellent deterrent to theft, sometimes the only way you can be free to leave your house when you want to. Recently the cost of labor has risen and fewer people than before are willing to live in, so more homeowners, Costa Rican and foreign, are hiring day help.

Be prepared to explain exactly how you want anything done, if necessary in sign language at first while the maid teaches you Spanish! Many houses come with maid's quarters built in and you provide food. Costa Rican law provides for at least half a day off per week, holiday and vacation pay, and severance pay for anyone who has worked at least a year for you. With vacation and severance, you pay 14 months' pay for a 12 month year. You will also have to make social security contributions.

Your maid can help with marketing and is a real asset when you bargain for produce or simply want to pay tico instead of gringo prices for anything not in major stores. She may be able to recommend seamstresses, haircutters, and neighborhood cab drivers who can be counted on at 5 a.m. when you need to catch an early flight. She can show you how to make tortillas, but you may have to show her how you want eggs fried.

Some neighborhoods contribute a monthly charge to have a night patrolman. In ours he pedalled around on a bicycle blowing a very loud whistle all night! This saved him the trouble of encountering a thief and woke most of us several times nightly so we knew he was on duty.

U.S. Medicare doesn't cover costs outside of the United States. However pensionados and rentistas can, once they have gained that status, pay $50 a year for Costa Rican Social Security health coverage including surgery at government clinics and hospitals. You wait as long as Costa Ricans do for treatment, but it is good when you get it. Treatment, including surgery, is much cheaper even in the private clinics not covered by Social Security than in the United States.

Recently several residential care facilities have opened for long term care. **Villa Confort Geriatric Hotel**, in La Garita is a senior citizens' hotel featuring another aspect of the growing health tourism business in Costa Rica. It offers special diets and 24-hour available medical care, recreation facilities and landscaped grounds, but is not a nursing home. The same owners offer custodial care to Alzheimer's patients at nearby **Golden Valley Hacienda**. Phone 43-8575 and 43-8191. Fax: 24-3821. With Costa Rica's lower labor costs, they feature more staff and lower cost per patient than similar homes in North America.

Costa Rican life runs at a more comfortable pace than in many other places, but you may have to get used to not worrying about whether something gets done this week or next. *Ahorita* means "a little now'" literally, but really means (if you ask when the car will be fixed or when so-and-so will be back in his office) soon, sometime, next week, or maybe never! It's much worse than *mañana*.

Pets

If you want to bring a dog or cat into Costa Rica, you need to write ahead to Jefe del Departamento de Zoonosis, Ministerio de Salud, 1000

San Jose, Costa Rica, C.A. Ask for a form for Importation Permission. There will be a small fee required when you send it back (make a copy first in case it is lost in the mail). Allow time for the validated form to get back to you. You also need a health certificate signed by a local vet and certified by a Costa Rican consul. The health certificate needs to state that the animal is free of internal and external parasites, and in case of a dog, has had shots for distemper, hepatitis, leptosporosis, and parvovirus, and has a rabies shot at least 30 days old but not more than 3 years old. With all of this done in time, the entry is very smooth at the airport.

When I took my German Shepherd to Costa Rica for two months, I went first to her vet at home and got a store of worm pills and flea and tick dip. She caught a mild bout of canine turista probably from drinking ditch water on our morning jogs, but that easily cleared with terramycin. Very short-haired dogs are vulnerable to stinging insects and the screw worm fly which lays its eggs under the skin of livestock, leaving a large abscess with the larva. A medium coat seems to be adequate protection. I wouldn't consider taking any pet on a short trip as it vastly complicates finding housing—remember that $1 a pound in excess baggage!

Returning to the U.S. was simple. A Costa Rican vet filled out another health certificate which I took to the Dept. of Zoonosis in the Ministry of Health building behind San Juan de Dios Hospital, Calle 16, Ave. 6/8. It took just a few minutes and a few colones for the revenue stamp (much easier than getting my exit visa). You also need a Permiso de Exportación from Banco Central, which you can get as early as 15 days before you leave. All the U. S. authorities required was the rabies certificate.

There are good vets and boarding kennels in the San Jose area. If you'll be living outside the Meseta Central, you may want to make up a pet medical kit. If you will be living on the coast, you might think again before bringing a cold weather breed. There are well-bred dogs available in Costa Rica.

If you're living and housekeeping in Costa Rica, you'll want *Living In Costa Rica*, published by the United States Government Women's Association, the embassy women's club. It lists suppliers of any repair or service you could need. The book is in bookstores and gift shops.

Learning Spanish

You say you had two years of Spanish in high school 30 years ago, taught by the football coach because he had to have a few class hours? Costa Ricans appreciate any effort you make to speak their language. It shows that you care about them and their culture, besides making travel easier and allowing you to meet a wider variety of people than if you can only speak to those with English. They will help you and tell you words, unless they're too busy practicing their English on you. They also speak a bit more slowly than some Latin Americans which gives you a chance.

If you can, take a class before you leave home. There are now some excellent taped language courses you can practice at home, from quick travelers' phrases needed in restaurants to the level the State Department employees are supposed to know. In between are some for the business traveler. Most of these now stress Latin American Spanish rather than 18th century Castilian. If you call the Spanish teachers at your nearest community college or adult education program, they may have a class, know where there's a Spanish conversation club, or help you find a good native speaker who'd like to practice English with you in return.

In San Jose, there are excellent Spanish schools which teach short and long courses, some of which are very intensive. The **Costa Rican-North American Cultural Center** in Los Yoses has an excellent library and offers classes and programs at reasonable cost. It's a good place to meet people, both Costa Rican and foreign residents—in Los Yoses, on the main route leaving San Jose to the east. Apdo. 1489, 1000 San Jose. Telephone 25-7344. The *Tico Times* has ads for most schools, and we have a list in our Sources Of Information at the back of this book.

You will be surprised how fast you can pick up some Spanish if you're not shy about trying to use it and make the effort to speak with local people instead of talking mostly to fellow foreigners. Spanish is probably the world's easiest language, and once you learn some, more doors are open in Costa Rica and you're set for travel all over Latin America.

Investing in Costa Rica

We've mentioned agricultural projects for which you'll see investment advertising—for plantations of established and new crops such as macadamia nuts, jojoba oil, oranges, cardamom (spice), vanilla, and cashew nuts. You'll also see ads for real estate developments, either as raw land or condominiums, built or not yet constructed. There are industrial plants and tourist developments seeking investment capital.

You will have to make your own assessment of the projects and of the honesty and business sense of those promoting them. It's definitely "buyer beware." For example, some agricultural projects have been worn out cattle land with seedlings of the latest fad crop planted under climatic conditions that gave no chance of profitable growth. You're wise to live in Costa Rica for awhile, at least on extended visits, and see the project on the ground as well as look at similar projects before investing. You'll want to have someone honest with excellent Spanish, if yours is not, read any documents before you invest or sign. Many projects are promoted by foreigners rather than Costa Ricans.

Note that many agricultural projects make heavy use of pesticides and herbicides exported liberally by U.S. chemical companies to developing countries where their use isn't banned or controlled as it is at home. Sometimes the names of products are changed so you can't recognize them (e.g. read the billboards along the road up Irazú) and the instructions and cautions are written in English so the campesinos using the chemicals may not dilute or apply as directed.

"Reforestation" investment projects are usually row plantings of a single species, often not native to Costa Rica, which in no way replace the multi-species ecosystem of a rainforest needed by the insects and wildlife who lived in the former forest. Some projects use chemicals to control competing growth. If a native forest wasn't cleared simply to qualify for the tax benefits of new tree planting, some projects do provide fast-growing wood for local needs so real rainforest elsewhere can be saved. Well-managed plantings should hold the soil and may affect water run-off and humidity.

Reforestation planting in Guanacaste.

Real estate in the Meseta Central is controlled as are building permits much as they are where you come from (check to see if you'll be able to build on the lot). Outside the area, some developers have simply run bulldozers wherever they could make the most lots, without regard for the land, slope, or erosion. There are also some excellent projects (look during or just after the rainy season). When buying land, you must have a very careful lawyer. A friend attempting to buy acreage found there were two recorded deeds so that the land had two owners, neither of whom knew about the other!

Waterfront land on the coast is controlled by federal laws which prohibit building within 50 meters of the high tide line and give the government considerable control over the next 150 meters, for a total of 200 meters back from the shore! Additional legislation is pending to allow the Costa Rican government more power to preserve critical habitat and keep some natural areas. If you are considering buying coastal land, be sure you will be able to build on it.

With Costa Rica's many climates in such a small area, you have a wide choice of temperature, humidity and rainfall. Explore the country in wet and dry seasons before you buy (you can rent indefinitely before and after you get residence status) to find what suits you. The beaches are still easy to get to if you decide you'd rather live higher and cooler.

Credit is expensive and often not available. Your real estate purchase will probably be on a cash basis—and so will the next buyer's if you later decide to sell. This is worth thinking about when you make the initial investment **and** when you add to its value with improvements. It accounts for many of the bargains you see in newspapers.

In addition to concern for the safety of your investment, it will be up to you and your conscience where you draw the line on chemical use, deforestation, or on real estate developments which raise the price of Costa Rican land beyond the ability of Costa Ricans to buy their own—or send it to the sea more rapidly than nature intended. Some projects are extremely well designed and well managed. The choice is yours.

Cashew fruits and nuts growing. The fruits attract many bird species.

REGIONS

Meseta Central

The Meseta Central, often called the Central Valley, is the heart of Costa Rica. High enough to be comfortable all year just north of the equator, with never a frost, and with little need for either heat or air conditioning, it's an ideal climate for people, most flowers and plants, and for doing whatever you want to almost any day of the year. Here there's a variety of scenery at every turn. Each village has a different character to explore, and the center of it all is bustling San Jose.

San Jose
(pop. 275,400)

Downtown San Jose.

San Jose is by far the largest city in the country, surrounded by a cluster of communities whose residents commute to work in the city daily. All national capitals should be this size—just big enough to be a city with fine restaurants, night clubs, excellent hotels in all price ranges, and cultural activities of all kinds. From discotheques, movie theaters with films in several languages, to big and little theater groups, sports events, art galleries, museums, shopping for anything, it's all here in a city small enough for you to walk around the central part in a day and to leave in a few minutes by bus or car. You can explore the city for a few days and vary your trip with day tours to nearby towns in the Meseta Central or up several volcanoes as well as to each coast. People-watching, night or day, is always entertaining.

When the stone sidewalks get hard, you can sit in one of the many parks to relax even a few feet from the busy streets. Do watch your step on the sidewalks as most are the responsibility for maintenance of the property owners they pass—and the stones and concrete vary accordingly. Some parks are the scene of weekly band concerts or art shows.

Stop by the ICT information desk under the Cultural Plaza at Ave. Central and Calle 5 for information and maps. Pick up the latest issue of the *Tico Times* at the newsstand on the west side of the Plaza, and you'll see what an array of choices you have. San Jose is really very easy to find your way around in, especially on foot when you don't have to worry about one-way streets. Do assume, however, that pedestrians have no rights, especially at corners where cars whip around from behind you. That assumption can save your life!

San Jose's streets run north and south, the *calles*. *Avenidas* run east and west. Near the center of town is Avenida Central. North of it all the avenidas are numbered in odd numbers, to the south in even numbers.

Actually Avenida 2 (Dos or Segunda) is a bigger boulevard downtown than Central. On the west end of downtown, west of San Juan de Dios Hospital, Avenida Central is called Paseo Colón and is a wide, tree-lined street ending at Sabana Park. Calle Central runs north and south near the center of town and the streets to the east are numbered in odd numbers, to the west in even numbers. Numbers are usually on the corner buildings rather than on street signs. But there aren't any building numbers, and directions are in meters or varas from a corner. A block is supposed to be 100 varas long, a bit less than a hundred yards. An address might be given as "Ave. 3, Calle 5/7". That means the building faces Avenida 3 on the block between Calles 5 and 7. It may be on either side of the street. This gets more sporting in the suburbs or out of town when everything is in meters from trees, bridges, or prominent buildings.

The National Theater.

Besides the museums we've already discussed in San Jose, there's **Parque Bolivar**, the small national zoo (entrance on Calle 9, Ave. 11) with examples of Costa Rica's birds and animals. The site and facilities are inadequate, and the zoo is supposed to be moved to a larger site in the western suburb of Santa Ana, but money is needed. If you're lucky, you might see one of the sloths in the trees landscaping the zoo. A small shop sells T-shirts and other souvenirs to help raise money for the zoo and other national parks. You can also get information brochures about some of the other parks and their wildlife. Tues–Fri 8–4. Sat, Sun. 9–5.

Admission $.20.

The **National Liquor Factory**, a government enterprise, is on Calle 11 between Ave. 3/7. You can watch liquor made from Costa Rican fruits and sugar. For guided tours with samples, available after 4 p.m. weekedays, call 23-6244.

San Jose is a city to enjoy, and the gateway to all the other things to see and do in Costa Rica.

Entertainment

At night it's best to walk in groups and avoid going through the parks (especially Parque Central and Park Morazán in front of the Aurola Holiday.Inn), but the Plaza de la Cultura is a busy spot and worth a stroll any night you're downtown. On a balmy evening, several small bands may be playing, teenagers dance to tape recorders, a student orchestra may be playing at the bottom of the stairs outside the ICT information office. Street performers juggle or play marimbas—wander by and see what's happening tonight, but don't carry anything for the pickpockets. You can sometimes get tickets to National Theater performances even at the last minute, but get them earlier if possible. (Closed for performances during 1991 and possibly 1992 for earthquake repairs.)

The "What's Doing" page in the *Tico Times* has enough to keep you busy for a month, and will be out with a new list next Friday! There you'll find plays, dance performances, movies (most in English with Spanish subtitles, but some European and Latin American films as well), art exhibits, lectures, and club meetings including the local chapters of some like the American Legion and the Lions Club you may belong to at home. You're welcome at their activities here.

Teatro Melico Salazar , Ave. 2, Calle Ctl./2, has plays, musicals, and dances. It's especially busy while the National Theater is closed.

Josephine's, Ave. 9, Calles 2/4, phone 57-2269, is a new supper club with the most ambitious floor shows in town. Open 9 p.m.—2 a.m. every night but Sunday. Shows start at 10. Most other night clubs in San Jose are really strip joints.

La Esmeralda, Ave. 2, Calles 5/7, besides being a restaurant, is the headquarters of the mariachis' association and has groups playing most of the long hours it's open.

El Pueblo, north of downtown, has bars and clubs with live music, discotheques, a roller skating rink, and restaurants of many nationalities.

Casinos are now in most large hotels, with roulette and a variety of rummy. Among them are the Aurola Holiday Inn, Balmoral, Gran Hotel

Costa Rica, to name just the ones in San Jose's center.

Sala Garbo, Ave. 2, Calle 28, features excellent foreign films.

Performing dog in the Cultural Plaza.

Restaurants

San Jose has many restaurants to enjoy, from international class places like the **London Club** and **The Lobster** on Paseo Colón to simple tipico spots called *sodas*, where you can get a simple meal or snack very reasonably. Fast food chains are here, including McDonald's, Mr. Pizza, and Pollos Fritos Kentucky. **Pops** has great ice cream including several with tropical fruits like mango and guanabana, a local favorite. It's on the corner of Ave. Central and Calle Central, next to the Cultural Plaza, as well as at several suburban spots.

Hotels particularly noted for their restaurants include the **Bougainvillea, Amstel**, and **L'Ambiance**.

The expensive restaurants advertise so heavily, particularly in tourist guide magazines and newspapers, that you can find them easily. There are inexpensive to moderate ones that serve good food which may be harder to find. Here are some my Costa Rican friends and I like:

La Esmeralda, Ave. 2, Calles 5/7. Tel. 21-05-30. Good food and prices, mariachi groups.

Restaurante Los Antojitos, On Paseo Colón, Calles 26/28. Tel. 22-90-86. Also in Los Yoses in Centro Comercial Cocorí.

Atlas Complex, across from the Park Hotel, Ave 4, Calles 2/4 has several

German restaurants including a biergarten and also has a disco. New.

Candilejas, Ave. 4 near the ICT building. Tel. 22-56-42. Family-owned Tico restaurant with very good food at budget prices. Open 8:30 a.m. to 8 p.m. M-W, to 10 p.m. Th, F, and to 6 p.m. Saturday.

Chips, Calle 5, Ave. Ctl./2, across from the Cultural Plaza. Budget restaurant with Tico dishes, pizza, breakfast. Open daily except Easter Thursday and Friday, 8 a.m.–11 p.m. Tel. 33-3246.

Churreria Manolo, Ave. Ctl., Calles Ctl/2. Tel. 21-20-41.

Dennie's Restaurant, S.A., Ave. Ctl, Calle 19/21.

Restaurant Peppermint, Centro Comercial Cocorí.

Mordisco, Paseo Colón near Calle 22, next to Mercedes Benz and Rios Tropicales. Natural foods, great soups and salads. Tel. 55-2448.

Restaurant Balcón de Europa, (Italian), Ave. Ctl. Calles 7/9.

Floridita, (Cuban), Ave. 1, Calle Ctl/2.

La Macrobiótica, Ave. 1, calle 11/15. Natural foods. Health food store.

Manzana, Calle 11 or 13, Ave. Ctl. Tipico Costa Rican food.

Spoon, Ave. Ctl, Calle 5/7 downtown and in Los Yoses and Pavas near the U.S. embassy. Features great desserts, pastries.

El Pueblo, near the Hotel Bougainvillea north of downtown, is a restaurant and entertainment complex with many restaurants, several discos, nightclubs and a skating rink. **Cocena de Lena** features Costa Rican food.

Where to Stay

San Jose hotels, more than others in Costa Rica, have a wide range of rooms in the same hotel. Most higher priced hotels have junior suites and executive suites. Our price ranges indicate rates for two people using a standard room during high season before tax and service charges, listed alphabetically within ranges, starting with luxurious. Any hotels out of range order are due to price changes after we set type.

Aurola Holiday Inn: Convention facilities, separate exercise rooms for men and women, sauna, pool, casino. Non-smoking floor available. Std. room has two double beds; superior room has king-sized beds. Wheelchair accessible. Live music. Most luxury downtown. Ave. 5, Calle 5.

Cariari: Luxury hotel on grounds of Cariari Country Club. Attractive design, stonework. Presidential and bridal suites. Rate includes breakfast, full use of country club except golf green fees and horse rental, lessons, dressage, jumping. Tennis and international class 18-hole golf course. Convention facilities, discotheque, casino. Autopista, between airport and San Jose.

Corobicí: Near Sabana Park at west end of San Jose, Calle 42, Ave. 3. Fourth floor and up have best view of mountains. Two double beds in room, satellite TV. Wheelchair accessible. Tennis, sauna, gym, jacuzzi, large pool in court with bandstand. Convention facilities. Casino.

Herradura: Luxury hotel adjacent to Cariari. Satellite TV from U.S. Church with mass in Spanish & English. Japanese restaurant. Health spa. Has golf package at 9-hole course, Los Reyes Country Club. Conference rooms for 10-200 people. Autopista between airport and San Jose.

L'Ambiance: Seven room luxury hotel in quiet neighborhood. Each room different, furnished with antiques around courtyard with fountain. Cable TV. Travelers checks, no credit cards. Staff speaks German. Excellent restaurant with larger room for banquets. Recommended. Calle 13, Ave. 9.

San Jose Palacio: New luxury hotel on clifftop between airport and San Jose. Tennis, spa, sauna, jacuzzi, beauty salon, restaurants, casino. TV by satellite. Suites with offices for business travelers. Conference rooms for up to 800.

Gran Hotel Costa Rica: Overlooks Plaza de la Cultura and plaza in front of National Theater. Inner court and garden with glass elevator. Casino. Dining room top floor. Open air coffee shop is good place for sightseeing break. Ask for room far from casino for quiet. Ave. 2, Calle 3.

Irazú: Biggest hotel in Costa Rica, west end of town beside autopista. All rooms have balcony, tub & shower, TV, phone. Lighted tennis courts, beauty shop, sauna, casino, suites. Rates less without air conditioning. Convention facilities. Shuttle bus to town, 30 colones. Taxis extortional.

Torremolinos: Cable TV, sitting area even in smallest rooms. Sauna, landscaped courtyard, quiet neighborhood west of downtown. Courtesy transportation downtown. Conference room. Calle 40, Ave. 5.

Ambassador: Outer rooms have mountain view over street, inner rooms face landscaped well. Sixth floor all suites. Big rooms, two dbl beds. Cable TV, phone. Safety boxes for valuables. Paseo Colón, Calles 26/28.

Balmoral: Conversational lounges each floor. Interior rooms face center well. Street-facing rooms have dbl glass., back rooms quieter. Rooms big. TV, phone. Convention facilities, casino, beauty shop, suites. Ave. Ctl., Calles 7/9.

Bougainvillea: Modern, very attractive hotel several blocks north of town center. Phone and wall safe in room. Beds 2-twin or queen. Wheel-chair accessible. Tub and shower. Children's pool. Excellent food. More restaurants and nightlife in El Pueblo center nearby. Recommended. From traffic circle at north end of Calle 3, go 100 m east. If full, try their Bougainvillea Santo Domingo a few miles north of town by free shuttle.

Price Range for 2 people in high season, before taxes—A+ Over $80/day, A $60–80, B $45–60, C $30–45, D $20–30, $E $11–20, F up to $ 11, U.S. $

Hotel	Range	Single Rate	Cleanliness	Noise Level	English Spoken	Pool	Wheelchair Acc	TV	Elevator	Cooking Facil	Bar	Restaurant	Air Cond or Fan	Parking	Recomm Access	Courtesy Transp	On Waterfront	In Town	Hot Water	Pvt Bath	No. of Rms	Telephone (Fax)	Address
Aurola-Holiday Inn	A+	•	Exc	Exc	•	•	•	•	•	•	•	•	•	•	Taxi / Car				•	All	200	33-7233 US 1-800 HOLIDAY (55-1036)	Apdo. 7802-1000 San Jose
Cariari	A+		Exc	Exc	•	•	•		?	•	•	•	•	•	Taxi / Car					All	181	39-0022 (39-2803)	Apdo.737 Centro Colón San Jose
Corobici	A+	•	Exc	Exc	•	•	•	•	•	•	•	•	•	•	Taxi		•		•	All	150	32-8122 1-800-CARIARI exc Florida (31-5834)	Apdo. 2443-1000 San Jose
Herradura	A+	•	Exc	Exc	•	•	•	•	?	•	•	•	•	•	Taxi / Car		•		•	All	145	39-00-33 (39-2292)	Apdo. 7-1880-1000 San Jose
L'Ambiance	A+	•	Exc	Exc	•	•	•	•			•	•	•	•	Taxi / Car				•	All	7	22-6702	Apdo. 1040 San Jose
San Jose Palacio	A+	•	Exc	Exc	•	•	•	•	?	•	•	•	•	•	Taxi / Car		•		•	All	254	20-2034 (20-2036)	Apdo. 458-1150 San Jose
Gran Hotel Costa Rica	A	•	Exc	Exc	•		•		•	•	•	•	•	•	Taxi / Bus		•		•	All	107	21-4000 (21-3501)	Apdo 527-1000 San Jose
Irazú	A	•	Exc	Exc	•					•	•	•	•	•	Taxi / Car		•		•	All	350	32-4811 (32-4549)	Apdo. 962-1000 San Jose
Torremolinos	A	•	Exc	Exc	•	•	•	•			•	•	•	•	Taxi / Bus		•		•	All	73	22-5266 (55-3167)	Apdo 2029-1000 San Jose

Costa Rica Tennis Club: On south side Sabana Park (with jogging paths). Rooms pleasant, on two floors. TV & phone. Eight kitchenettes. Sauna, 14 tennis courts, bowling, basketball, huge pool often occupied by swimming classes. Good value.

Europa: Only moderately-priced downtown hotel with large pool. Has rooms with balcony overlooking pool in inner court without street noise and fumes. Cheaper rooms face street. Large rooms, suites. Phone, TV. Some rooms wheelchair accessible. Excellent food. Good value. Calle Ctl, Ave 3/5.

Presidente: Inside rooms have windows to skylighted wells, so are airy & quiet. Rooms large, double or twin beds. Bathroom has step up. Phone, TV. Conference room. Restaurant, bar, disco, casino. Ave. Ctl, Calle 7.

Royal Dutch Suites: Family owned and operated. Big rooms with tubs and showers. Calle 4, Ave. Ctl./2.

Santo Tomas: Restored former coffee planter's house built when the surrounding neighborhood was a coffee finca. On busy street in a good neighborhood. North American owned. Continental breakfast included. Big rooms, 12 foot ceilings, antiques, original tiled hall. Queen-sized beds. Small quiet patios. Ave. 7, Calles 3/5.

Artist painted tile mural of nearby old buildings in Hotel Don Carlos.

Don Carlos: Delightful, quiet, small hotel in historic building with small courts, prehistoric sculptures, original paintings. Marimba players some afternoons. Truly feels Costa Rican. Hospitable staff. Rate includes con-

Price Range for 2 people in high season, before taxes—A+ Over $80/day, A $60–80, B $45–60, C $30–45, D $20–30, $E $11–20, F up to $ 11, U.S. $

Hotel	Range	Single Rate	Cleanliness	Noise Level	English Spoken	Pool	Wheelchair Acc	TV	Elevator	Cooking Facil	Bar	Restaurant	Air Cond or Fan	Parking	Recomm Access	Courtesy Transp	On Waterfront	In Town	Hot Water	Pvt Bath	No. of Rms	Telephone (Fax)	Address
Ambassador	B		•	Exc	Exc	•		•		•		•	•	•	Taxi / Car				•	Al	78	21-8155 21-8311 (55-3396)	Apdo. 10186-1000 San Jose
Balmoral	A		•	Exc	Exc	•		•		•		•	•	•	Bus / Taxi	•			•	Al	121	22-5022 21-1919 (21-7826)	Apdo. 3344-1000 San Jose
Bougainvillea	B		•	Exc	Exc	•		•		•		•	•	•	Taxi / Car				•	Al	80	33-6622 (22-5211)	Apdo. 69-2120 San Jose
Costa Rica Tennis Club	B		•	V gd	Exc	•	•	•	•	•		•	•	•	Taxi / Car				•	Al	27	32-1822 32-1266 (32-3868)	Apdo. 4964-1000 San Jose
Europa	B		•	Exc	Exc	•	•	•		•		•	•	•	Taxi / Car				•	Al	72	22-1222 (21-3976)	Apdo. 72-1000 San Jose
Presidente	B		•	Exc	Exc	•	•	•		•		•	•	•	Taxi / Bus				•	Al	51	1-800-532-1052 22-3022 (21-1205)	Apdo. 2922-1000 San Jose
Royal Dutch Suites	B		•	Exc	Gd	•		•		•			•	•	Taxi / Bus				•	Al	30	22-1414 22-1066	Apdo. 4258-1000 San Jose
Santo Tomas	A+		•	Exc	Exc	•							•		Taxi				•	Al	20	22-3946 55-0488 (22-3950)	Av. 7, c. 3/5 San Jose
Don Carlos	C		•	Exc	Exc	•						•	•	•	Taxi / Car				•	Al	25	21-6707 (55-0828)	Apdo. 1593-1000 San Jose

tinental breakfast. Restaurant serves light Costa Rican entrees. Gift shop has well-chosen variety of crafts at good prices. Highly recommended. Reservations essential. Calle 9, Ave. 7/9.

Dunn Inn: Friendly North American-owned simple hotel in good neighborhood. Cable TV in common area. Partially glassed over courtyard. Price includes continental breakfast, good value for two people. Fax available to guests. Corner Ave. 11, Calle 5.

Garden Court Hotel: New five story budget hotel in rough neighborhood. Phone, TV, sauna, gym, pool, elevator, cafeteria. shuttle bus from Irazú Hotel to downtown stops here or take taxi. Rate includes breakfast. Very good value, but don't walk alone outside at night. Ave. 7, Calle 6.

Plaza: Small lounge each floor. Faces central banking square downtown. Manager helpful. Phone, TV in room. Rooms small, adequate. Have increased permitted rate but may only charge Range C. Ask. Ave. Ctl., Calles 2/4.

Royal Garden: Dining room well known for Chinese food, including breakfast. Pleasant rooms, well furnished, phone and TV, sitting areas. Suites. Quieter in back rooms. Casino. Good value. Calle Ctl., Ave. Ctl.

Alameda: Rooms at back quieter. Light and airy. Cheerful dining room. Family style—no liquor or cigarettes sold, and no street friends allowed. Phone in room (TV with charge). Up to 5 beds for family in some rooms. King-sized beds slightly higher. Neighborhood looks rough after dark. Good value. Ave. Ctl., Calles 12/14.

Amstel: Well-run with super food. Rooms with air conditioning slightly higher. Rooms facing Calle 7 quietest. Central, good neighborhood. Cable TV. Phone in room small charge. Can arrange babysitting. Get fax of reservation and any cancellation. Good value. Calle 7, Ave. 1.

Capital Hotel: Newly redone, central location. King-sized beds. Cable TV (charge). English, German spoken. Good value. Calle 4, Ave. 3/5.

D'Galah: Very pleasant, across from north side of the University of Costa Rica gardens. Rooms, suites, kitchenettes. Courtyard with plants. Two pianos in lobby. Feels like Costa Rica. Very good value. Recommended.

Diplomat: Pleasant, cheerful rooms, quieter at back. Good restaurant on second floor. Good neighborhood.and value. Calle 6, Ave. Ctl./2.

Fortuna: Family hotel. Phone, TV in room. Safety box. Many Canadian and European guests. Chinese restaurant with garden on ground floor. Neighborhood good. Good value. Weekly rates. Ave. 6, Calles 2/4.

Price Range for 2 people in high season, before taxes—A+ Over $80/day, A $60–80, B $45–60, C $30–45, D $20–30, $E $11–20, F up to $ 11, U.S. $

Hotel	Address	Telephone (Fax)	No. of Rms	Pvt Bath	Hot Water	In Town	On Waterfront	Courtesy Transp	Recomm Access	Parking	Air Cond or Fan	Restaurant	Bar	Cooking Facil	Elevator	Wheelchair Acc	TV	Pool	English Spoken	Noise Level	Cleanliness	Single Rate	Price Range
Dunn Inn	Apdo. 1584-1000 San Jose	22-3232 22-3426 (21-4596)	11	Al	•	•			Taxi	•	•	•	•				•		•	Exc	Exc	•	C
Garden Court Hotel	Apdo. 962-1000 San Jose	32-5627 32-5359 (32-3159)	70	Al	•	•	•		Bus Taxi Car	•	•	•	•		•		•	•	•	V gd	Exc	•	C
Plaza	Apdo. 2019-1000 San Jose	22-5533 (22-2641)	40	Al	•	•			Taxi Bus	•	•	•	•		•		•		•	V gd	Exc	•	A
Royal Garden	Apdo. 3493-1000 San Jose	57-0022 57-0023 (57-1517)	52	Al	•	•	•		Taxi Bus	•	•	•	•		•		•		•	Exc	Exc	•	C
Alameda	Apdo. 680-1000 San Jose	21-3045 23-6333 (22-9673)	52	Al	•	•			Taxi Bus	•	•	•			•		•		•	V gd	Exc	•	D
Amstel	Apdo. 4192-1000 San Jose	22-4622 (33-3329)	54	Al	•	•			Taxi Bus	•		•	•		•		•		•	Gd	Exc	•	C
Capital Hotel	Apdo. 6091-1000 San Jose	21-8497 (Fax same)	15	Al	•	•			Taxi	•	•				•		•		•	V gd	Exc	•	D
D' Galah	Apdo. 208-2350 San Jose	34-1743 53-7539	14	Al	•	•			Taxi Bus	•	Caf eter ia						•		•	Exc	Exc	•	D
Diplomat	Apdo. 6606-1000 San Jose	21-8133 21-8744	30	Al	•	•			Taxi Bus		•	•	•	•	•		•		•	V gd	Exc	•	D

Price Range for 2 people in high season, before taxes—A+ Over $80/day, A $60–80, B $45–60, C $30–45, D $20–30, $E $11–20, F up to $ 11, U.S. $

Hotel	Address	Telephone (Fax)	No. of Rms	Pvt Bath	Hot Water	In Town	On Waterfront	Courtesy Transp	Recomm Access	Parking	Air Cond or Fan	Restaurant	Bar	Cooking Facil	Elevator	Wheelchair Acc	TV	Pool	English Spoken	Noise Level	Single Rate	Range
Fortuna	Apdo. 71570 San Jose	23-5344 (23-2743)	26	All	•	•		Taxi, Bus			•	•	•	?				•		V gd	•	D
Galilea	C. 13, av. ctl. San Jose	33-6925 (21-1505)	26	All	•	•		Taxi, Bus									•	•	Gd	V gd	•	D
La Gran Via	Apdo. 1433-1000 San Jose	22-7737 (22-7205)	32	All	•	•		Taxi, Bus			•	•		•			•	•	Exc	Exc	•	C
Park	Apdo. 4604-1000 San Jose	21-6944	16	All	•	•		Taxi, Bus			•	•						•	V gd	Gd	•	D
Talamanca	Apdo. 449-1002 San Jose	33-5033	54	All	•	•		Taxi, Bus	•		•	•	•	•			•	•	V gd	V gd	•	D
Troy's	Av. 2, c. 19/21 San Jose	22-6756	5	3	•	•		Taxi, Bus	•	•							•	•	V gd	V gd	•	D
Bella Vista	Apdo. 3151 San Jose	23-0095 / 33-5477	17	All	•	•		Taxi, Bus		•	•						•	•	Gd	V gd		E
Cacts	Apdo. 379-1005 San Jose	21-2928 (21-8616)	13	8	•	•	•	Taxi, Bus		•	•							•	Exc	Exc	•	E
Centro-americano	Apdo. 3072-1000 San Jose	21-3362 / 21-3955	45	All	•	•		Taxi, Bus		•	•				•			•	V gd	V gd	•	D

Galilea: Pleasant, friendly. Rooms quieter at back. Phone. Student discounts, some also available for outlying hotels when arranged through Galilea. 1/2 block from Cartago bus station. Ave. Ctl., Calle 13.

La Gran Via: Rooms at back very quiet. Front rooms have balcony overlooking street. Top floor rooms have great view and breeze. Two double beds all rooms. Cafeteria, coffee shop. Good value. Ave. Ctl., Calle 1/2.

Park: Rooms open onto inner court. Some rooms have cable TV. Weekly, monthly rates. Laundry service, mail. Most residents North American men with escorts. Ave. 4, Calles 2/4.

Talamanca: Light, pleasant rooms with phone, good beds. Rooms at back quieter, upper floors with view. Disco, casino. Takes credit cards. Ave. 2, Calles 8/10.

Troy's: Small friendly place with North American manager just east of central city. Sandwiches, American breakfast. Room service. Lobby with cable TV in English. Allows street friends. Ave. 2, Calles 19/21.

Bella Vista: Some rooms have windows open to center, planted well—quiet. Not all rooms have windows. Fans and TV on request. Readers report OK, alternative when youth hostel full. Ave. Ctl., Calles 19/21,

Cacts: Friendly, helpful budget hotel in converted house. Two floors with stairs. Includes continental breakfast. Mail service, safety boxes, self-service laundry. Good neighborhood. Offers reasonably priced tours to canales, other areas. Recommended. Ave. 3, Calle 28.

Centroamericano: Most room windows open to hall with plants, simple, slightly dark rooms with phone. No street noise. Small lobby with TV. Hotel busy with foreign and tico residents. Friendly place, permissive with street friends. Ave. 2, Calle 6/8.

Costa Rica Inn: Helpful. Tipico hotel in good neighborhood. Good place for budget traveler with limited Spanish to start in Costa Rica. (I did.) Many guests North Americans who live in country. Ask for room with windows, quieter at back. Weekly and monthly rates. Recommended. U.S. address: P.O. Box 59, Arcadia, LA 71001. Calle 9, Ave. 1/3.

Johnson: Sitting area each floor. Hotel begins on second floor of building and has elevator from there. Phones. Rooms not facing street quieter. Restaurant serves breakfast only. Some Peace Corps guests. Good value. Calle 8, Ave. Ctl./2.

Morazán: Dark rooms on ground floor. Lighter rooms with shared bath on upper floor, across from park, near Limón bus station. Basic, fairly quiet, double beds.Ave. 3, Calle 11/13.

Price Range for 2 people in high season, before taxes—A+ Over $80/day, A $60–80, B $45–60, C $30–45, D $20–30, $E $11–20, F up to $ 11, U.S. $

Hotel	Address	Telephone (Fax)	No. of Rms	Pvt Bath	Hot Water	In Town	Recomm Transp	Cooking Facil	Bar	Restaurant	Air Cond or Fan	English Spoken	Noise Level	Cleanliness	Single Rate	Range
Costa Rica Inn	Apdo. 10282-1000, San Jose (See text)	22-5203 (23-8385) US: (800) 637-0899	35	All	•	•	Bus / Taxi					•	Exc	Exc	•	E
Johnson	Apdo. 6638-1000 San Jose	23-7633 23-7827	57	All	•	•	Taxi / Bus	•		•	•		Exc	V gd	•	D
Morazan	Apdo. 550-1000 San Jose	21-9083	8	3	?	•	Taxi / Bus						Gd	V gd	•	E
Musoc	Apdo. 1049-1000 San Jose	22-9437 (39-1657)	45	2	•	•	Bus / Taxi					•	Vgd	Vgd	•	D
Petit	Apdo. 7694-1000 San Jose	33-0766	14	7	•	•	Car / Taxi						Exc	Exc	•	E
Ritz	C. ctl., av. 8/10 San Jose	22-4103 (22-8849)	15	9	•	•	Taxi / Bus		•			•	V gd	Gd	•	E
Asia	Apdo. 7427 San Jose	23-3893	20	7	•	•	Taxi / Bus				Cafeteria	•	V gd	High		F
Astoria	Av. 7, c. 7/9 San Jose	21-2174	18	2	?	•	Taxi / Bus						Exc	V gd	•	F
Boston	Apdo. 3202-1000 San Jose	21-0563	23		?	•	Taxi / Bus						Gd	Gd	•	F

Musoc: Clean, friendly, basic. Rooms light and airy. Hot water in shower only. Rough neighborhood overlooking Coca Cola bus terminal. Calle 16, Ave. 1/3.

Petit: Very pleasant with good beds. Manager helpful. Many returnees. Some rooms have sitting areas. Cheerful, good neighborhood. Light cooking possible. Inside back rooms quieter away from service station next door. Bi-weekly, monthly rates. Good value. Recommended. Calle 24, 50 m. s of Paseo Colón. (In budget hotels many choose between this and Cacts, which is quieter.)

Ritz: Swiss-owned. Guests are foreign students, businessmen. Friendly place. Breakfast served. Rooms at back quieter, all somewhat dark. Lobby with TV, plants. Calle Ctl., Ave. 8/10.

Asia: Helpful Chinese manager. Rooms quieter at back. Small lounge. Basic, but safe and clean. Good value. Calle 11, Ave. Ctl./1.

Astoria: Basic, older Spanish style building with religious paintings, tiled hall. Rooms simple. Hot water and washing machine. Most rooms don't have windows. Garden courtyard, TV in lobby. Ave. 7, Calles 7/9.

Boston: Rooms larger than most similar hotels. Back rooms quieter, open to stairwell. Hot water. OK neighborhood. Ave. 8, Calle Ctl./2.

Cocorí: Clean, back rooms quieter. Nice rooms, no lobby. Clean soda downstairs. Rough neighborhood, but Cocorí is best in it, next to bus to Liberia. Calle 16, Ave. 3.

Generaleño: Clean, basic. Rooms at front and back have windows, ones in between don't. Each floor has hall balcony overlooking Ave. 2. Some shared baths. Street friends allowed. Doors have hasps on which one could provide own lock. Ave. 2, Calle 8/10.

Pension Americana: Very clean though beds worn. Friendly, basic hotel in good neighborhood, doesn't allow guests in rooms. Dormitory and single rooms. Ask for room with windows. Lobby with TV. Family place used by ticos and foreigners. Calle 2, Ave. Ctl.

Pension Centro Continental: Basic, clean hotel downstairs from Ritz. 4 rooms have windows, rest don't. Light lobby. Friendly. European and North American guests. Calle Ctl., Ave. 8/10.

Pension Otoyo: Pleasant family with limited English has had hotel for 30 years. Light and airy with tile hallways, plants, TV in lobby. Pvt. and shared baths. Tipico basic hotel in good neighborhood. Good value. Calle Ctl., Ave. 5/7.

Poás: Very basic, but clean hotel with hot water in good neighborhood.

Price Range for 2 people in high season, before taxes—A+ Over $80/day, A $60–80, B $45–60, C $30–45, D $20–30, $E $11–20, F up to $ 11, U.S. $

Hotel	Address	Telephone (Fax)	No. of Rms	Pvt Bath	Hot Water	In Town	Recomm Access	Parking	Air Cond or Fan	Pool	English Spoken	Noise Level	Cleanliness	Range
Cocori	C. 16, av. 3 San Jose	33-0081	26	All	•	•	Taxi Bus	•		•	Gd	V gd	•	F
Generaleño	Av. 2, c. 8/10 San Jose		47	8	?	•	Taxi Bus				V gd	V gd	•	F
Pension Americana	Apdo. 4853-1000 San Jose	21-4171	32	0	?	•	Taxi Bus				V gd	V gd	•	F
Pension Centro Continental	Apdo. 5554-1000 San Jose	33-1731 (22-8840)	11		•	•	Taxi Bus				V gd	V gd	•	F
Pension Otoya	Apdo. 6226-1000 San Jose	21-3925	13	1	•	•	Taxi Bus				V gd	V gd	•	F
Poás	Av. 7, C. 3/5 San Jose	21-7802	18			•	Taxi Bus		•		V gd	High	•	F
Toruma Youth Hostel	Apdo. 323-1002 San Jose	24-4085	10	8		•	Taxi Bus			•	V gd	High		F

All rooms share bath. Clean, inexpensive soda at front. Street level. Ave. 7, Calles 3/5.

Here are some additional basic to budget hotels in San Jose. You may want to look at them. I'd start with the ones that have both calles and avenidas in odd numbers, for a better neighborhood.

American, Ave 7, Calle 2/Ctl. **Bienvenido,** Calle 10, Ave. 1/3, pvt. bath, hot water, new. Range E. Apdo. 389-2200, San Jose. Phone 21-1872. **Boruca,** Calle 14, Ave. 1/3, near Coca Cola bus station, clean. 23-0016. Range F. **Central,** Ave. 3, Calle 4/6. Clean, Range F. **Lido,** Ave 3, near Calle 14. **Lincoln,** Calle 6, Ave. 10/12. **Principe,** Ave. 6, Calle Ctl./2. Phone 22-7983 Apdo. 4450, 1000 San Jose. 48 rooms, pvt. baths. Range F. **Rialto,** Ave. 5, Calle 2. **Sheraton,** Ave. Ctl., Calle 12/14. **Tala Inn,** Calle 11 Ave 7/9.

Scene from Don Quixote in tile on historic brick wall on Calle9 across from the Jade Musem.

Youth Hostels

Toruma Youth Hostel: Central America's first youth hostel is on Ave. Ctl., Calle 31 in Los Yoses, San Jose's eastern suburb, across from Kentucky Fried Chicken. To a taxi or bus driver you ask for "Albergue Juvenil

Toruma cerca de Pollos Fritos Kentucky". Friendly atmosphere in an older building with high ceilings and a cool breeze. Dormitories for 6-20 people. Hot water. It's open 24 hours a day, and guests can stay as many days as they wish. Soda restaurant serves 3 meals a day, but there are no facilities for doing own cooking. Often has live bands and cultural events, mostly musical. $4 with International Youth Hostel Federation card available at hostel. Card gets holder youth hostel rates at affiliated hostels in Costa Rica if reservations are made through Toruma. Fax 24-4085.

Casa Ridgway: Quaker hostel near Peace Center. Rooms and dormitory bunks. Light cooking. Range E. Apdo. 1507, San Jose. Phone 33-6168. Ave. 6, Calle 15.

Gran Hotel Costa Rica faces plaza where vendors sell everything from whistles to hammocks.

San Jose Area Apartotels

Apartotels are apartments catering to weekly or monthly tenants who want cooking facilities, room for families, and possibly the swimming pools and other amenities that most apartments here do not have. They are completely furnished, including linen and dishes, so you don't have to set up housekeeping. Most, like hotels, have some suites or larger units. Generally they are less expensive than hotels with the same facilities, but more expensive than apartments catering to long-term tenants. We have listed them in ranges based on their daily rates though weekly

Price Range for 2 people in high season, before taxes—A+ Over $80/day, A $60–80, B $45–60, C $30–45, D $20–30, $E $11–20, F up to $ 11, U.S. $

	Los Yoses	Castilla	Don Carlos	Lamm	La Perla	Napoleon	Rango	San Jose	El Conquistador
Range	B	C	C	B/C	C	C	C	C	D
Single Rate	•	•	•	•	•	•	•	•	•
Cleanliness	Exc	Exc	Exc	Exc	Exc	Exc	Exc	Exc	Exc
Noise Level	Gd	Exc	Exc	V gd	Exc	V gd	Exc	Gd	Exc
English Spoken		•	•	•	•	•	•	•	•
Pool	•					•			
Wheelchair Acc									
TV	•		•		•	•	•	•	•
Elevator									
Cooking Facil	•	•	•	•	•	•	•		•
Bar									
Restaurant						•			•
Air Cond or Fan	•								
Parking	•	•		•		•	•	•	•
Recomm Access	Car, Bus	Car, Taxi	Car, Taxi	Car, Bus	Taxi, Car	Car, Taxi	Taxi, Car	Car, Bus	Taxi, Car, Bus
Courtesy Transp									
On Waterfront									
In Town	•	•	•	•	•	•	•	•	•
Hot Water	•	•	•	•	•	•	•	•	•
Pvt Bath	All	All	All	All	All	All	All	All	All
No. of Rms	23	15	9	20	14	26	16	12	29
Telephone (Fax)	25-0033 (25-5595)	22-2113 21-2080	21-6707 (55-0828)	21-4920	32-6153 20-1547 (20-0103)	23-3252 23-3282	32-3823 (22-0694)	22-0455 (21-2443)	25-3022
Address	Apdo. 1597-1000 San Jose	Apdo. 944-1007 San Jose	Apdo. 1593-1000 San Jose	Apdo. 2729-1000 San Jose	Apdo. 2148-1000 San Jose	Apdo. 8-6340 San Jose	Apdo. 1441-1000 San Jose	Apdo. 5834-1000 San Jose	Apdo. 303, San Pedro Montes de Oca, San Jose

and monthly discounts and sometimes low season rates can reduce their cost. Apartotels are often used by embassy personnel and business families newly moved to Costa Rica while they look for permanent housing.

Los Yoses: Some without kitchen facilities. Floor plans vary. Some have BR curtained (not walled) from living room. 3-burner stove, TV. Safety boxes. Medium-sized pool. Ave. Ctl. in Los Yoses and Calle 45.

Castilla: Excellent quiet neighborhood off Paseo Colón. 1 and 2 BR apartments with living and dining room, parquet floors, kitchen and laundry room, 4-burner stove. 20% monthly disc. (low season). One BR apartments open to well, quiet. Two BR apartments have balcony facing quiet street. Recommended. Calle 24, Ave. 2/4.

Don Carlos: On side street 25 m south of Kentucky Fried Chicken on Ave. Ctl. in Los Yoses. Pvt. phone, cable TV, sundeck. Roomy, quiet, secure, well equipped for entertaining. Mountain views. Same owner as Hotel Don Carlos. Language schools within few blocks. Recommended.

Lamm: Near legislative assembly. Very helpful owner speaks fluent English. Separate bedroom, kitchen, living room. Some suites with maid's quarters. Daily linen change. Laundry and dry cleaning on premises. 24 hour porter and switchboard service. Can order refrigerator stocked before arrival. Weekly disc. No pets. Recommended.

La Perla: Near Irazú Hotel and Hospital Mexico west of downtown. three floors, one and two BR apartments. No elevator. Kitchen, phone, cable TV. Guarded parking on street.

Napoleon: Coffee shop. Residential neighborhood several blocks from Sabana Park. Balcony, TV, phone. Some floors carpet, some tile. Cheaper rooms without kitchen. Kitchen units have 2-burner stove, very small cooking area. Pool large. Pets allowed. Calle 40 near Ave. 5.

Ramgo: On quiet street across from south side Sabana Park. Supermarket one block. Has lawn with courtyard. All apartments have 2 BR, roomy kitchen, laundry room, 4-burner stove, phone, cable TV. Small pet OK. Weekly and monthly rates. Embassy personnel use.

San Jose: 1 BR apartments have no table, only dining counter. 2 BR apts. have table. Parquet floors. Living room has day bed. Apts. smaller than some. Weekly, monthly rates. Ave. 2, Calles 17/19.

El Conquistador:: In Los Yoses, 200 m north of Almacen Electra and bus stop for San Pedro bus. Large pool with jacuzzi jets, wading pool, walled garden. Most second floor rooms have mountain view. Cheapest are studio apartments, others have separate living room, all are roomy. Tiled floor, 3 or 4-burner stove. Pets allowed, $4/day. Recommended.

Villas Cariari: Luxury apartments with balcony, overlooking Cariari golf course. Golf, tennis, swimming and wading pools, phone, gym, sauna, whirlpool. Restaurants nearby. Range A+ all year, low season rates 20-30% lower. Off highway between airport and San Jose. Apdo. 471-1000 San Jose. Phone 39-2706, fax 39-1153. (Not in our hotel table.)

Outlying hotels in the Meseta Central vary from basic hotels you'll find in any Costa Rican town to small super-deluxe quiet places on hills overlooking the valley. These include some of the nicest hotels in Costa Rica.

More General Information

Earthquakes—note that in this volcanic belt every hotel in San Jose has withstood an earthquake of 7.1 on the Richter scale. Emergency lights in stairwells and corridors come on in the event of a power outage. During an earthquake guests are advised to brace themselves in an interior doorway or get under substantial furniture, but not to head for the street until the quake is over. Major earthquakes are rare. They happen as often in coastal California

Religion—Since the Roman Catholic church is the principal denomination in any Latin country, the Metropolitan Cathedral (Calle Ctl, Ave. 2) and other churches are beautiful expressions of faith, and saints' days are important events. Parades you'll see in San Jose consist mainly of school students, appropriately for this peaceful country. Because San Jose is so cosmopolitan, you will find churches or assemblies of most other denominations in or near the city. If you don't find information on services for yours in the *Tico Times*, call their office 29-8952, 22-0040, or ask the ICT information center under the Cultural Plaza.

Banking is a government monopoly with regulations for safety *and* to control the flow of foreign exchange in a country which badly needs it to pay foreign debt. The branch bank across from the Amstel Hotel on Ave. 1 Calle 7, is open Saturday mornings, but only changes travelers' checks before 3 p.m. on weekdays. While foreign banks can't offer a full range of banking services here, one way for North Americans to have money sent to you in Costa Rica is to have it wired to the Costa Rican bank yours corresponds with. Learn which one before you leave home. Most major credit cards will allow you to charge them for cash in a foreign country. You should check with yours before leaving home to learn which banks you can use. The American Express office is at T.A.M. Travel, Calle 1, Ave. ctl./1. Villages and beach resorts don't usually have banks, though tourist hotels will exchange dollars for guests.

OTEC, the student organization, runs budget tours for students and teachers within and outside Costa Rica. Students and teachers from abroad should bring identification as to their status (a letter from school administration on letterhead will do, or you can bring an international student card). OTEC's office is at Ave. 3, Calle 3/5. Mail: Apdo. 323, 1002 San Jose. Tel. 22-0866. There is no age limit for full-time teachers or college staff. For students, the maximum age is 25.

Laundry—Any hotel can do laundry or have it done—charges vary. Apartotels and some inexpensive hotels have a laundry sink and hang up area you can use. In villages or rural areas there's someone who will wash and sun dry clothes cheaply. *Lavanderías* aren't self-service, but do offer same-day laundry. In San Jose there is one on Paseo Colón near Restaurante Bastille (west of downtown). Lavantia Doña Ana, open Monday through Saturday, is on the Autopista to Zapote, 125 m. east of Plaza Gonzales, near the Ministry of Public Transport in the southeastern part of town. There's another in the Centro Commercial on the north side of the road to San Pedro, a suburban district east of Los Yoses. New self-service laundromats will wash and dry a load for about $3.50—**Betamatic** (near Burger King), 34-0993, and **Lava Más** next to Spoon restaurant in Los Yoses, 25-1645.

Dance Instruction—If you'd like to learn the *salsa, meringue, cumbi*a, or *socca,* to have more fun in the discos here and to take home with you, **Bailes Latinos** offers small group lessons in English especially to visiting foreigners. Phone, 21-1624.

The Museum of Modern Art is in the former airport terminal in Sabana Park.

Clubs

Costa Ricans and foreign residents have organized clubs for almost any activity, often chapters of groups you may belong to at home. Here's a way to meet people who live here. This list is biased toward groups where English is spoken.

Asociación Nacional de Bridge welcomes players and beginners. Meets Mon. 1:30 p.m. and Wed 8 p.m. Phone 32-9154.

Orchid Association of Costa Rica Meets 3rd Monday, monthly, 8 p.m. Has lectures, tours to nurseries, growing tips. Apdo. 6351-1000 San Jose.

Coffee Picking Square Dancers, Mondays 6:30–9 at Centro Cultural. Visitors invited. Grace Woodman, 25-9433.

Little Theater Group meets monthly, does two productions a year. Lee Warrington, 21-6847.

Canoeing, Kayaking group has weekend trips on Costa Rica's milder rivers. Beginners welcome. Having a boat helpful. Jay Morrison, 82-6697.

Masonic Lodge meets first & third Tuesdays, 8 p.m. , open to Masons in good standing. Ave. Ctl., Calle 19. Ralph Phillips, 28-9764.

Monarch Lion's Club, English-speaking club, meets at the Hotel Herradura, on third Saturday, 10 a.m. Stefan Baumgartner, 32-6565.

Hash House Harriers, for fun run every Monday, 5 p.m. Men and women, 17-71. William Barbee, 28-0769.

American Legion has several posts in Costa Rica. Post 10 in Escazú is open 1:30–7:30 daily, meets last Saturday of month. Phone, 28-1740.

Tsuli Tsuli, the Audubon club of Costa Rica, Apdo. 4910-1000 San Jose. Phones, 56-6431, ext. 237, and 40-8775. Fax, 56-1533.

There are groups for almost any interest. Check the *Tico Times* "What's Doing" page for ideas and information.

Buses

Unless you ride taxis all the time, you'll soon learn the local bus routes you need though the others may remain a mystery. Downtown the Sabana Cementerio bus runs an elliptical route from Sabana South to town on Ave. Central and 2 and back out on Ave. 3. If you're coming into town from western suburbs, you can catch it at any of several stops near Sabana Park for the ride downtown. Going back out, you can get off near the Coca Cola station area and walk the block or two to that stop to catch your bus home. Try to avoid doing this at rush hour or in the dark, especially the first time. From Los Yoses or San Pedro, the San Pedro bus can drop you a block from the Atlantic Railway station where there are lots of cabs or it's an easy walk downtown. The Alajuela buses leave from the Coca Cola area every 10 minutes or so and stop at the airport. Some are minibuses for a slightly higher rate. The ICT information office under the Cultural Plaza has a current list of bus stations and other transportation and can answer questions.

Note the list of San Jose bus stations in the Planning Your Trip section. For buses to Puntarenas, Limón, or Guanacaste, get your ticket the day before, and get there at least 45 minutes early to be sure of a seat. Returning to San Jose, you should do the same. If you get on these at the terminal, you have a much better chance of having a seat than if you get on at one of the stops.

Tara Resort Hotel.

Escazú

Tara Resort: Deluxe classic pre-Civil War style mansion on hill above Escazú with grand view over San Jose. Hardwood-floored rooms upstairs in hotel, wheelchair-accessible bungalows planned. Includes airport pickup and breakfast. Meeting rooms.

Apartotel Maria Alexandra: Deluxe apartments & townhouses on quiet street in Escazú. Sauna, pvt. phone, cable TV, laundry room and washing machine, barbecue area. Excellent restaurant. Reserve at least 6 months ahead in dry season. Recommended.

Mirador Pico Blanco: Tropical landscaping with fine view of San Jose 1000 ft below. Dining room has volcanic rock wall with cascading water. Attractive rooms, some with balcony, all with Costa Rican flavor. English owned. Up Calle 1 and follow signs. Recommended. Same owner (& phone) has new rustic **Volcan Barva Lodge,** good for birders, hikers.

Posada Pegasus: Front deck with great view of mountains and San Jose. Rooms large, most with view. Serves breakfast, light suppers. Just uphill from Pico Blanco. Jacuzzi. German and French spoken. Living room TV, hi fi and library of mystical books. The Cross of Alajuelita on top of the mountain is a scenic hike above. Children and trained pets welcome.

Alajuela
(pop. 145,600)

Alajuela is a delightful town about 20 km. northwest of San Jose, easily reached by bus, and only a few miles south of the airport. Its cathedral is beautiful with hardwoods inside and dark red shining corrugated metal covering its dome. In front is the central park with a bandstand and spreading mango trees. Another park honors Costa Rica's hero, Juan Santamaria, killed in the battle of Rivas. There's also a museum honoring him which often has current art exhibits. The central market is interesting and open even on Sundays when you might be in Alajuela to catch the special bus that departs from the south side of the church on an excursion up Poás Volcano at 8 a.m.

Nearby attractions include **Campestre del Sol** a former country club now open to the public, with swimming pools, gym and dance hall, open Tuesday through Sunday, 8-4. Tel. 42-0077. There are soccer games in the stadium almost every Sunday. Across the road is the Butterfly Farm.

The Butterfly Farm, opened in 1990, is a "don't miss". Breeding thousands of butterflies in many of Costa Rica's 900 species for export, they have a *big* walk-in enclosure where you can see and photograph butterflies you'd be lucky to glimpse in the forest. You can also see the stages of growth larvae go through, and, if you arrive early in the morning, may see butterflies emerging from their chrysalides. Guides explain and identify butterflies. Open every day, 7-4. Admission 700 colones for adults, less for students with I.D. and children under 12. It's at La Guácima de Alajuela, 450 m. south and 100 m. east of the main entrance to Los Reyes Country Club, about 35 minutes from San Jose. The La Guácima bus route from San Jose ends only 300 m. from the farm. Tel. 48-0115. If you're driving, get a brochure from ICT with map and watch for butterfly signs as you get near. Tours booked through Costa Rica Sun Tours.

Between Alajuela and Atenas, a private bird zoo, **Zoo Ave,** has over 450

146

birds of many tropical species. Opening a new facility nearby in late 1991 with walk-in aviary. The bus from Alajuela to Atenas or La Garita can drop you off there. The driver won't speak English, so you'll have to ask for Dulce Nombre and watch for the sign on the right side of the road several miles out from Alajuela, across from a tropical plant farm, "vivero." Open 9–5, Tuesday-Sunday. Admission 100 colones.

Bosque Encantado (Enchanted Woods) is an amusement park in La Garita, with animal sculptures, pool and lake. La Garita also has a hydro-electric dam and many nurseries with house plants. It's fun to walk through such places and take photos if you're traveling and can't take plants home. If you buy property in Costa Rica, you'll enjoy low-cost, beautiful plants, including orchids. At La Guácima, there are car and motorcycle races on the track every weekend.

North from Alajuela on the old road, or you can go back out on the autopista to another turnoff, are Grecia, Sarchí, and Zarcero. Grecia is the center of pineapple growing and has an interesting church entirely covered in dark red painted metal. Sarchí, as I've discussed, has factories making painted oxcarts in traditional designs and painting the designs on other souvenirs. The furniture alone is worth the trip to see. Farther along, Zarcero is famous for boxwood hedges shaped into animals, dancers, and even a plane and a helicopter! There are tours to these towns or you could see them all in a day with a car. Buses go regularly from San Jose to Zarcero and Sarchí via Alajuela. Some Poás tours stop in Sarchí.

South of the airport, is the spring **Ojo de Agua** (Eye of Water), where over 6,000 gallons of water a minute rush out, supplying water to the city of Puntarenas, several other towns, and several big, clean swimming pools and an amusement area. It's such a popular outing spot, that I'd recommend going on weekdays unless your purpose is people watching. In that case, go on Sunday and watch Costa Rican families having fun at one of their favorite places. You can get there by bus or car from San Jose (ask ICT for the bus stop and schedule).

Where To Stay

Chatelle Country Resort: garden chalets, phone, 3 with kitchen. Near La Garita, 12 km. from airport. Includes continental breakfast. Shuttle to town, airport. Weekly, monthly and low season rates.

Alajuela Hotel: Exceptional value in tipico hotel 25 m south of central park. Several apartments with living room, kitchen, and 4-burner stove often reserved by tourists who can afford to rent them even while touring the country. Clean, quiet, not plush, with phone, outdoor laundry area, pleasant lobby, courtyard. If you're on a budget and don't have to

Price Range for 2 people in high season, before taxes—A+ Over $80/day, A $60–80, B $45–60, C $30–45, D $20–30, $E $11–20, F up to $11, U.S. $. * = Meals included.

Hotel	Address	Telephone (Fax)	No. of Rms	Pvt Bath	Hot Water	In Town	On Waterfront	Courtesy Transp	Recomm Access	Parking	Air Cond or Fan	Restaurant	Bar	Cooking Facil	Elevator	Wheelchair Acc	TV	Pool	English Spoken	Noise Level	Cleanliness	Single Rate	Range
ESCAZÚ:																							
Tara Resort	Apdo. 1459-1250 Escazú	28-6992 (28-9651)	5	Al	•			•	Taxi / Car	•	•	•	•				•	•	•	Exc	Exc		A+
Apartotel Maria Alexandra	Apdo. 3756-1000 San Jose	28-1507 (28-5192)	5	Al	•	•			Taxi / Car	•	•	•	•	•			•	•	•	Exc	Exc	•	B
Pico Blanco	Apdo. 900-1250 Escazú	28-1908 28-5189 (28-4812)	11	Al	•				Taxi / Car	•	•	•	•						•	Exc	Exc	•	C
Posada Pegasus	Apdo. 370-1250 Escazú	28-4196	5	4	•				Taxi / Car	•		•						•	•	Exc	Exc	•	D
ALAJUELA:																							
Chatelle Country Resort	Apdo. 755 Centro Colón San Jose	31-7328 48-7095	6	Al	•			•	Car	•				•				•	•	Exc	Exc		A-B
Alajuela	Apdo. 110-4050 Alajuela	41-1241 (41-7912)	50	47	•	•			Taxi / Bus										•	Exc	V gd	•	E

148

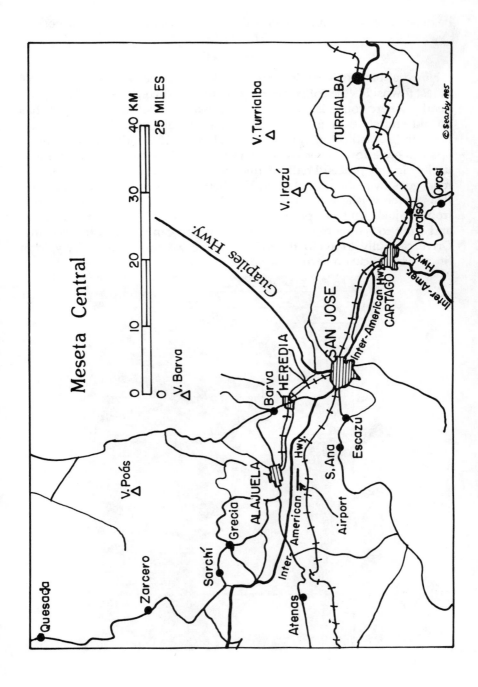

Meseta Central

be in San Jose, this is recommended. It's a quick bus ride to the airport.

Heredia

(pop. 62,300)

Heredia, like Alajuela, is a provincial capital and one of Costa Rica's oldest towns. It's the coffee growing center and there are several *beneficios* nearby where coffee is dried and hulls removed before shipping. It has an old church, now a historic shrine, with bells brought from Cuzco, Peru, in Spanish colonial times. Several very old buildings, including a Spanish-style fort tower (with its gun slits wider from the *outside* and useless in this peaceful nation), line the central plaza. From Heredia, the road goes over the mountain saddle between the volcanoes, Barva and Poás, to the northern plain. A side road winds to a meeting with the road from Alajuela up Poás, providing an alternate way if you're driving a car and want to see more country. In season you can watch coffee picking. Drive carefully to avoid the loaded coffee wagons going slowly from finca to beneficio on narrow, winding roads.

Nicaraguan coffee picker working on hillside near Heredia.

El Castillo Country Club above Heredia has a miniature train to ride, a gym, pool, and Costa Rica's only ice skating rink! Closed Mondays.

Where To Stay (near Heredia and in hills above)

Finca Rosa Blanca: Secluded comfort on coffee finca 8 km. from airport, near attractive village, Santa Barbara de Heredia (good restaurants). Original art and hardwood throughout house. Honeymoon suite in tower has view in all directions and bathroom with waterfall into tub. Separate 3 BR house for families. Breakfast included. Recommended.

El Pórtico: 8 km. above Heredia on slopes of Barva. Rebuilt after fire, it has polished burnt brick original dining room floor (beautiful), heavy beams and hardwoods. Large rooms, sauna, jacuzzi. Helpful management. "We have lots of tranquility." They have smashing views and lovely nearby walks on slopes of Barva Volcano. Guests are often other Central Americans on weekends when reservations are a must. Cater to seminars during week. Recommended.

Apartotel Vargas: 5 double, 3 single apartments, kitchens, TV, laundry. 8 km from airport, transportation. Not inspected. Monthly rates.

Bougainvillea Santo Domingo: Attractive, well-run hotel on quiet, landscaped grounds surrounded by coffee fincas, near Guápiles Highway. Large rooms with two double beds, phone, TV, balcony with view over grounds or south over San José. Tennis, pool, good food. Hourly shuttle to their Bougainvillea Hotel on north side of San José. Recommended.

Chalet Tirol: Alpine style chalets and hotel rooms. Adjacent to Braulio Carrillo Nat'l. Park, river. 16 km from airport, cool climate. Meeting rooms, playground, tennis, several miles of hiking trails on grounds, into park, to river with waterfalls, birding, horses available. Near Castillo Country Club. French restaurant. Weekly, monthly rates. Recommended.

Cabañas de Montaña Cypresal: Two styles of rooms here. Newer rooms have brick fireplaces, a double bed and settee, and sound insulation. The older ones are in wood cabinas with sitting room and patio but walls that carry sound. Phones, sauna, barbecue, volleyball, meeting room. From the road to Poás, turn right at sign.

Volcan Barva Lodge: New cabinas for 2-4 people, under same ownership as Pico Blanco in Escazú. No cooking facilities but restaurant nearby. Near Sacramento above Heredia.

Price Range for 2 people in high season, before taxes—A+ Over $80/day, A $60–80, B $45–60, C $30–45, D $20–30, $E $11–20, F up to $11, U.S. $. * = Meals included.

NEAR HEREDIA:

Hotel	Range	Single Rate	Cleanliness	Noise Level	English Spoken	Pool	TV	Wheelchair Acc	Elevator	Cooking Facil	Bar	Restaurant	Air Cond or Fan	Parking	Recomm Access	Recomm Transp	Courtesy Transp	On Waterfront	In Town	Hot Water	Pvt Bath	No. of Rms	Telephone (Fax)	Address
Finca Rosa Blanca	A+	●	Exc	Exc	●								●		●	Taxi				●	All	6	39-9392 (39-9555)	Apdo. 4-3009 Santa Barbara de Heredia
El Portico	A	●	Exc	Exc	●								●		●	Taxi				●	All	13	37-6022 (38-2930)	(Apdo. 289-3000 Heredia
Apartotel Vargas	B	●	Exc	Exc	●	●	●				●				●	Car Taxi	●			●	All	8	37-8526 (23-9878)	Apdo. 87-1300 Heredia
Bougainvillea Santo Domingo	B	●	Exc	Exc	●	●	●					●	●		●	Taxi Shuttle	●			●	All	44	40-8822 (40-8484)	Apdo. 69-2120 San Jose
Chalet Tirol	B		Exc	Exc	●		●			●		●	●	●	●	Taxi				●	All	10	39-7070 (39-7050)	Apdo. 7812-1000 San Jose
Cabañas de Montaña Cypresal	C	●	Exc	Exc	●							●	●		●	Taxi				●	All	24	23-1717 (21-6244)	Apdo. 7891-1000 San Jose
Volcan Barva Lodge	C		Exc	Exc	●		●				●				●	Car Taxi	●			●	1	1	28-1908 28-5189 (28-4812)	Apdo. 900 Escazú

The Basilica of Nuestra Señora de Los Angeles.

Cartago
(pop. 100,120)

Cartago, 14 miles east of San Jose, was the capital of Costa Rica during colonial times and later until 1823. At the base of Irazú, it has been shaken by earthquakes during every eruption so there are few old buildings. Several roads and the railroad meet here, making it the marketing and social center for a large area. Buses run between San Jose and Cartago every 20 minutes. Public buses run from Cartago up Irazú with stops at villages along the road twice a day. From here you can also take buses to Orósi and Paraiso.

The parish church in central Cartago, **La Parroquia,** was damaged by several earthquakes and not rebuilt after one in 1910. Instead the ruins have been converted into a delightful walled park with ponds, shrubs and benches. The street in front was restored in early style cobblestones.

The **Basilica of Nuestra Señora de Los Angeles** (the Patroness Saint of Costa Rica) is a magnificent Byzantine church on the east side of Cartago. Inside is the tiny image of the Black Virgin, and the walls are lined with cases of the gold and silver gifts by pilgrims in thanks for healing miracles attributed to her. Many are in the shape of body parts healed—hands, arms, legs, etc. The church is built over the spring where the image of the Black Virgin was found. Behind it is a shrine where water from the spring flows and where people bring bottles and other containers to take some of the holy water. The saint's day is August 2, Cartago's biggest annual celebration.

Southeast of Cartago, on the road to Paraiso, are the **Lankester Gardens**, started by Dr. Charles Lankester as an orchid farm. On its 649 acres you can see 800 species of orchids as well as bromeliads, ferns, and many other tropical species. The farm is now run by the University of Costa Rica biology department, open to the public for about $1 which helps pay maintenance, 9- 3:30. daily. Guided walks on the half hour, or they'll assign someone to go with you. The Paraiso bus from Cartago can let you off about 1 km from there, or you can take a bus tour from San Jose. Orchids are in bloom all year, but at their peak in March.

Just before Paraiso the **Auto-vivero Del Río** has a small private zoo of native animals including agoutis, pizotes, and birds, and a greenhouse. Donations. Open Tues–Sun, 9–6.

While Cartago has basic hotels, there are so many better ones in San Jose that with buses every 20 minutes, you'll be more comfortable there.

Orósi Valley

The Orósi Valley is a beautiful area and a fine day trip from San Jose. There are two scenic overlooks built by ICT with grand views of the valley, picnic facilities, play areas for children, and, at the Ujarrás overlook, a restaurant. The Reventazón River winds down the valley, dammed at the lower end by Cachí Dam making a lake that generates electricity for the Central Valley.

The village of Orósi is nestled at the valley's head and has the oldest active church in Costa Rica, built in 1743. Its simplicity says much about the struggling colonial farmers almost forgotten by Spain but keeping their religion. Adjacent to the church is a small museum of Costa Rican religious history. Open daily except Wed. and Sun., 9–5. Tel. 73-3051. Orósi has hot springs and several "balnearios", public baths. The road circles the valley and crosses Cachí Dam. You can visit the power house.

Below the power house is the river gorge rafted first by some river guides working in Costa Rica. They scouted it several days before their trip, but arrived to find the water much lower. By phone they located the manager who asked "How much water do you want?" and then released enough for their trip.

On the north side of the lake is **Charrara Recreation Park** with picnic ground, camping area, playing fields, swimming pool, restaurant, and boat launching ramp for fishing on the lake.

The ruins of Ujarrás church, built in 1693 and abandoned in 1833 when the village was flooded and moved to higher ground, are now a historic shrine. Watch plants now growing between the stones on the walls and try to imagine what this place meant to people so far from Spain.

Tapantí National Wildlife Refuge is about 6 miles from Orósi, by good gravel road. Bring rain gear *any* season—it's always wet, often cool. Trails through forest canyon and beside river offer great birdwatching. Jaguars and many other animals are here, mostly nocturnal or hidden in thick forest. Does their fur *ever* get dry? Picnic grounds, ranger station at entrance with interpretive center. Open 6-4. Admission fee about $1.

Motel Río: Hotel, pool and restaurant beside river at lower end of Orósi Valley. Many day tours from San Jose stop here for lunch.

Turrialba
(pop. 28,250)

Turrialba is a good excursion or tour from San Jose (40 miles each way). You pass increasing areas of sugar cane and bananas after you leave Cartago. From ridgetops you look south to rainforest protected in Chirripó National Park and Tapantí National Wildlife Refuge to see how this country looked as wilderness. The early Spanish settlers in the Central Valley above really were isolated until first the train, and later the roads, were built. Dropping down into Turrialba on the road, you're passing the lower edge of Costa Rican coffee growing. The town is in a scenic basin at the bottom of Turrialba Volcano. It's a bustling market town serving a wide rural area. Until the new highway opened recently from San Jose to Puerto Limón, it was everyone's rest stop on the route. From here you can ride rail cars on the most spectacular part of the former "jungle train" route along the Reventazón River to Siquirres.

If you're determined to get up the volcano, from Turrialba or Cartago you can go by bus to the village of Pacayas, from which horses or 4-wheel drive vehicles can reach the top of the mountain. There is another steep, beautiful climb over a shoulder of Turrialba Volcano dropping down to the eastern lowland. From the top of that ridge you can see the Caribbean Sea.

Three miles east of Turrialba **CATIE** (Centro Agronomico Tropical de Investigacion y Enseñanza) is a 2,500-acre agricultural research station devoted to the needs of the tropical small farmer. Foreign governments including the United States, Canada, Britain and West Germany support research into high producing, disease-resistant strains of coffee, bananas, and cacao. Aside from pollution dangers, the small farmer can't afford to buy agricultural chemicals. Other projects include improved strains of plantain, palms, and livestock bred to grow on coarse tropical grass with little or no grain supplement. A tissue culture lab grows genetic replicas of each desirable plant for virus-free shipment in small containers all over the tropical world.

Agricultural school instructors and researchers in tropical agriculture from many countries study here, living in quarters on the grounds. The world's largest library of books and papers on tropical agriculture is here, and the card catalog is in English. The station also has a collection of hundreds of palms as well as many other forest species. It's a fascinating place which you can only begin to explore in a day. With over 27,000 acres including riverbanks, its trails (one starting behind the administration center goes to the Reventazón River) offer good birding.

Tissue-cultured orchid plants in sealed vials are sold as souvenirs.

If you live in Costa Rica, you may want to talk to station personnel about nursery stock and seed which they sell at very reasonable prices. They grow and sell sealed vials with tissue-cultured starter plants of the national flower, the *guaria morada* and another endangered orchid. In sealed vials with gel, these pass customs easily on your way home, but are hard to raise in another climate unless you're experienced with orchids. About $4.50, they're in some San Jose gift shops. Dairy products from CATIE are sold in Turrialba, and it's the town's biggest employer.

To tour the station with an English-speaking guide, call 56-6431 and arrange an appointment M-F, 9-4. The bus from San Jose will drop you in town (it leaves from the same station as the Cartago buses), and the locals can direct you to the bus that goes by CATIE or you can take a taxi from Turrialba. Tour agencies in San Jose run tours there, and would be glad to set up special tours for interested small groups. If somehow what is learned here can reach the small farmer, there seems more hope of feeding populations without losing or depleting the world's topsoil.

Turrialba has become an international training center for whitewater kayakers using the Reventazón and Pacuare Rivers, especially in fall and early winter when North American and European rivers have low water. Its restaurants make a good dinner stop after a day on the river on the one day raft tours from San Jose.

Where To Stay

Wagelia: Attractive, modern hotel, surprisingly quiet in center of town, with rooms around plant-filled court. Cool lobby has fish pond and waterfall. Five rooms have refrigerators, all have phone, radio. Safety box. Good food. Recommended.

Pochotel: 11 km southeast of town on hilltop overlooking Turrialba with breeze, open air restaurant (closed Monday except for hotel guests, but hotel is open all week). Roofed sitting area, playground equipment for kids. Pleasant wood cabinas. Quieter mid-week.

Albergue La Calzada: Hospitable, peaceful inn with Costa Rican food, good birdwatching and relaxing, 1/4 mile before entrance to Guayabo National Monument. Message phone 56-0465. Rates with IHYF card.

Rancho Naturalista is in hills above the Tuis Valley south of Turrialba. See our Nature Lodges section, page 80. Birdwatching and tranquility.

Guayabo National Monument

Costa Rica's main archeological site, important in its effort to piece together its pre-Spanish history, is 19 km up the slopes of Volcan Turrialba north of the town. The road is paved for 15 km and OK for 2-wheel drive on the last 4 km from Santa Teresita. A daily bus also goes that far.

Stone mound believed to be foundation of wooden prehistoric building.

Hotel	Address	Telephone (Fax)	No. of Rms	Pvt Bath	Hot Water	In Town	On Waterfront	Courtesy Transp	Recomm Access	Parking	Air Cond or Fan	Restaurant	Bar	Cooking Facil	Elevator	Wheelchair Acc	TV	Pool	English Spoken	Noise Level	Cleanliness	Single Rate	Range
ORÓSI VALLEY:																							
Motel Rio	Apdo. 220-7050 Cartago	73-3128 73-3057	7	All	•		•	Car Taxi	•		•	•						•	•	Exc	Exc	•	D
TURRIALBA:																							
Wagelia	Apdo. 99-7150 Turrialba	56-1566 56-1596	18	All	•	•		Bus Car	•	•	•	•								Exc	Exc	•	D
Pochotel	Apdo. 258-7150 Turrialba	56-0111	4	All	•			Car Taxi	•		•	•						•	•	Exc	Exc	•	E
Albergue La Calzada	Apdo. 260-7150 Turrialba	56-0465 (message)	4					Car Taxi	•		•									Exc	Exc	•	E

Price Range for 2 people in high season, before taxes—A+ Over $80/day, A $60–80, B $45–60, C $30–45, D $20–30, $E $11–20, F up to $11, U.S. $. * = Meals included.

158

From about 1000 B.C. until just before the Spanish arrived, 10,000 people are believed to have lived here. The center of this city has been excavated to show building mounds, foundations, stone walkways, roads, and aqueducts. A trail leads through the rainforest (carry raingear) past bromeliads and other tropical plants identified in a brochure and past excavated gravesites to an overlook with benches above the city center. Besides the view out over valley and mountains, you look down into the site to appreciate its complicated design.

In the site you are escorted by park staff but free to wander among the circular foundations, petroglyphs (drawings carved in rock), and wonder what so many people did here, who they were, and what became of them. In March and April Montezuma Oropendolas fly to and from their woven straw nests hanging from trees between the prehistoric mounds.

The visitor center has exhibits explaining what is known about the site and its people, a picnic ground, and camping area, and a trail to the river. The monument is open from 8 to 4 on holidays and weekends. If you can't come on a weekend, check with the Park Service in San Jose to see if the monument can spare an escort to let you in during the week.

A suggestion: Visit CATIE on Friday as they're not open weekends, stay overnight in Turrialba or at La Calzada, and visit Guayabo early Saturday before most weekend visitors get there.

Route of The Saints

South of San Jose, in the mountains south of the Central Valley, is Costa Rica as she was. Tiny villages cling to steep ridges (note the contour of their soccer fields!) or cluster in narrow canyon bottoms, while the slopes between are a patchwork of small coffee farms. The main road is paved but side roads aren't as they follow stream banks or head up a slope you'd hate to send a mule. Most towns are named for saints, San Pablo, San Pedro, San Marcos, Santa Maria, etc. Up the steep dirt roads that are perhaps better done on foot or with a rented horse, you may hear a quetzal or meet a farmer driving his cows to pasture.

For a day circle you can start around in either direction. If you aren't stopping overnight, you can avoid the afternoon fog on the Interamerican Hwy. crest by driving to Cartago in the morning and south on the highway to Empalme, where you turn right at the Texaco station and head down the Pacific slope. If you're traveling in the other direction, you take the road south from San Jose to Aserrí, and then to Tarbaca, Frailes, etc. This area is at 3-6000 ft altitude, so it's cool and comfortable.

I'd love to spend a few days or a quiet week in a town like Santa Maria de Dota, a delightful, clean village (easily reached by bus from San Jose) de Dota, a delightful, clean village (easily reached by bus from San Jose) exploring the surrounding hills and valleys on foot and horse. Copey is a friendly village 7 km above Santa Maria with apple, trout, and carnation farms nearby. Rooms and horses can be rented.These villages haven't been mobbed by tourists, and probably never will be. What a peaceful way to improve Spanish, meet people, and forget what hurrying is!

Hotel Dota in Santa Maria is sometimes closed for lack of business, but has a great collection of old tools and weapons on the walls downstairs, and would open for a phone call. (74-1193, 9 rooms, about $6 single), half a block from the plaza. If I were staying longer, I'd rent a small house and settle in for a month. That has to be the best reason I've heard for not being glued to a computer for one's writing projects.

The East Coast

The railroad from San Jose to Puerto Limón opened the rest of the world to the Costa Ricans and their exports. More recently a winding road was added, not following the railroad, but connecting all the major towns along the way, Cartago, Turrialba, and Siquirres. By car, bus, or truck, this was much faster than the train but still took three and a half hours. Climbing and dropping down steep grades, it was hard for the heavily loaded trucks coming up from the port on the East Coast. The time and distance limited weekend traffic to the beaches south of Limón.

In 1987 the long-awaited Guápiles Highway opened, shortening driving time from San Jose to two and a quarter hours by going under Cerro Zurquí in a tunnel, down through **Braulio Carrillo National Park**, the most accessible park in the country, to Guápiles and then to Limón.

You can enjoy grand views over the rainforested mountains and canyons, especially in the morning as afternoons are more apt to be foggy and rainy. If you're driving, be sure to park completely off the pavement at the few pullouts as traffic is heavy and fast. One pullout is at the bridge over the Río Sucio (dirty river) whose rusty yellow is caused by volcanic chemicals from Barva Volcano, not man's actions.

Braulio Carrillo preserves 80,000 acres of forested mountains from the development that would have been inevitable after the highway was built. Later a fundraising drive bought the "Zona Protectora", a strip of land connecting Braulio Carrillo Park with La Selva biological Reserve in the northern plain, allowing many birds and animals a vertical migration route from the lowlands to the top of Barva Volcano. There are 20 kilometers of trails, some quite steep and muddy, which you can hike if you pay a small fee for maintenance at either of the ranger stations. One is just inside the entrance near the tunnel. Ask advice and get a trail map.

Suddenly you emerge from the mountains and descend to the Caribbean lowland, and everything changes—topography, plants, and people. The flat land is cut by rivers and most rainforest is gone, replaced by pastures and banana plantations. Many people are blacks, descended from Jamaicans who built the railroad. Houses are mostly wood, often up on poles to avoid water and insects while catching the breeze. Guápiles and Siquirres are the main towns, marketing centers for the area before you reach Limón.

Signs point to smaller villages off the highway with wonderfully presumptuous names—Canadá, México, London, Liverpool, Boston, Bristol, Stratford, Venecia, Cairo, Manila, Batán, Luzon, Suiza, Germania, Francia, Búffalo, Florida, Louisiana, Indiana Dos (and Tres), and Babilonia!

Now the coast has become an easy weekend trip, and can be crowded on weekends and holidays. The facilities will catch up with the crowds eventually. Meanwhile, enjoy the fast, scenic route, but be sure you have reservations if you're staying in hotels or cabinas. There's a toll for using the new road, but you save more than that in gas. You might want to go one way by the old road just for variety in scenery. On the new road the distance from San Jose (go north on Calle 3) is about 165 kilometers, slightly over 100 miles.

Puerto Limón
(pop. 61,620)

Puerto Limón, capital of the province of Limón, is the only port and the only town larger than a village on Costa Rica's East Coast. Throughout this book, we've used Puerto Limón and Limón interchangeably as the people do. After Columbus's landing here in 1502, a permanent Spanish settlement was still delayed for many years by raiding pirates and the lack of obvious wealth. Construction of the railroad to San Jose and the introduction of Jamaican blacks adapted to the climate led to its growth as Costa Rica's eastern port. Today it's a busy town with modern port facilities at Limón and at Moín, its northern suburb.

As it was in Columbus's time. Limón still is hot and humid, and is significant for the tourist mainly as the gateway to attractions north and south and as the end of the road from San Jose. The waterfront central park is a pleasant early morning or late afternoon walk with its ornate bandstand and the chance of seeing some of the resident sloths in its trees (look for a motionless blob that looks as if the tide washed it up there, especially on the south side of the park).

Normally sloths only climb down their trees every 7 or 8 days to defecate, but in the dry season these may come down more often for water

161

from park fountains. Local people who find the sloths in the street set them back on their trees, carefully avoiding their 3-inch claws. You may see them peering myopically above or eating a few leaves between naps. For aerobic exercise a sloth scratches his tummy.

Puerto Limón

There's a small library and roofed open study area for children amid the trees and flowers. Men and boys fish with throw-lines from the stone seawall. (The 1991 earthquake lifted this shore so the sea may not again reach the wall.) Several blocks away the central mercado is interesting and has fresh fruit and other supplies you'll want if you're going to stay in villages like Cahuita and Puerto Viejo to the south or in the basic cabinas at Tortuguero.

Like San Jose, Puerto Limón has numbered calles (north-south) and avenidas (east-west, away from shore), except that there are no signs even on buildings and no one seems to have heard of the system! As the shoreline curves deeply into downtown, it's hard to keep count even if you try. If you ask where a hotel is, people will tell you it's so many meters from the park, mercado, or a small radio station. You head in that direction and ask again, or take a cab. Fortunately, distances in the downtown area are short and many people are blacks who speak English. Frequent public buses to Moín pass through Portete.

Columbus Day, October 12, is Limón's big annual festival with street dancing and parades, calypso and reggae music, Caribbean food, and several days of celebrating. Hotel reservations then are a must, though if you can get them in hotels outside Limón, you'll probably get more

Price Range for 2 people in high season, before taxes—A+ Over $80/day, A $60–80, B $45–60, C $30–45, D $20–30, $E $11–20, F up to $11, U.S. $

Hotel	Address	Telephone (Fax)	No. of Rms	Pvt Bath	Hot Water	In Town	On Waterfront	Recomm Access	Courtesy Transp	Parking	Air Cond or Fan	Restaurant	Bar	Cooking Facil	Elevator	Wheelchair Acc	TV	Pool	English Spoken	Noise Level	Cleanliness	Single Rate	Range
PUERTO LIMÓN:																							
Acón	Apdo. 528-7300 P. Limón	58-1010 (58-2954)	39	All	●	●		Car, Bus	●	●	●	●	●	●				●	Exc	V gd		●	E
Miami	Apdo. 266-7300 P. Limón	58-0490 / 24-8183 (58-1978)	30	All	●	●		Car, Bus	●	●	●							●	Gd	Fair			E
Tete	Apdo. 401-7300 P. Limón	58-1122	14	All	●	●		Car, Bus		●									Exc	High		●	E
Gran Hotel Los Angeles	Apdo. 514-7300 P. Limón	58-2068	28	All	●	●		Car, Bus		●	●	●	●						Gd	Fair		●	F
Las Palmeras	150 mts. w. of park P. Limón	58-0241	20	12	●	●		Bus		●									V gd	V gd			F
Lincoln	Apdo. 888-7300 P. Limón	58-0074	14	All	●	●		Bus		●	●								Gd	Fair			F
Park	Apdo. 147-7300 P. Limón	58-3476	27	All	●	●		Car, Bus											V gd to Bad	V gd		●	F
PORTETE:																							
Matama	Apdo. 686-7300 P. Limón	58-1123 (58-4499)	16	All			●	Taxi, Bus, Car	●	●	●	●	●					●	Exc	Exc		●	A
Maribu Caribe	Apdo. 623-7300 P. Limón	58-4543 / 58-4010 (58-3541)	44	All			●	Car, Taxi, Bus	●	●	●	●	●					●	Exc	Exc		●	B

sleep. In 1992 Limón will celebrate the 500th anniversary of Columbus's arrival in the New World. The celebration in 1991 will be of their own quake survival

Most North Americans staying in Limón require at least a fan moving air to be able to sleep. There are budget and basic hotels in Limón, reviewed below. However, if you can afford more and don't have to catch a 5:30 a.m. bus, it's worth going to one of those at Portete, several miles north. At Moín, the ICT built a picnic and camping area with a swimming pool. Playa Bonita at Portete is Limón's swimming beach.

Where to Stay in Puerto Limón

Acón: Dining room and food are good. Hotel is the best in town, but noisy on weekends when discotheque and casino on second floor swing. Get room on 4th or 5th floor for quiet. All others in town are basic.

Miami: Rooms at back quieter. Soda restaurant serves tipico and Chinese food. Ask for demonstration of air conditioning or fan and hot water on shower head.

Tete: Rooms at back quieter. New bathrooms. Across from mercado. Hotel is on second floor ringed by marble tiled balcony with plants and seats, TV. Night security guard. Helpful manager speaks English.

Gran Hotel Los Angeles: Across from mercado. Rooms with air conditioning slightly higher price. Hot water.

Las Palmeras: Basic but clean hotel on 2nd and 3rd floors of building a block from park. Small rooms, twin beds, table fans. OK neighborhood.

Lincoln: Two blocks north of town center. Some rooms have no windows and only 5 have air conditioning (the rest have table fans), but a good value in a very basic hotel. Pleasant manager.

Park: Stay only if you can get room facing sea with fresh air, view and quiet (fill early). Rooms facing street are on block with traffic, two cantinas and a firehouse, but without air conditioning, you'll want to open window. You can ask for fans. Windows on street side could be entered by agile person from street. Dining room good. Two blocks from park.

Not inspected: **Caribe,** 58-0138, 13 rooms. Having found clean if basic rooms for as little as 400 colones near the market and in the next few blocks north, I avoided the rough neighborhood with basic hotels and cantinas near the railroad station.

Portete

Matama: Deluxe, comfortable concrete cabinas for 6 on shady landscaped grounds across highway from sea. (2 BR plus loft each.) Open air dining room and lounge, attractive.

Maribu Caribe: Most deluxe in area. Large rooms, phones, considerate staff. Some stairs in pool area, but staff will help wheelchairs up. Meeting room. Calypso or mariachis on weekends. Dining room and lounge open air at top of cliff. Tours to Cahuita and Tortuguero. Recommended.

Las Olas: Built over beach rocks with covered open air dining overlooking surf and swimming pool. Wheelchair ramp from parking area, sauna (in Limón!), casino. Corner suites with sea view in two directions, balcony and sitting room. All rooms have ocean-facing balconies. Parking below is limited, guarded, but requires car moving. I've stayed here and liked it. Good value. Damaged in '91 quake. Open?

Cabinas Cocorí: Two bedroom cabinas with cooking facilities for up to 4 on waterfront across from Matama, beside small rocky cove, with swimming. Surfing readers liked.

Puerto Limón has no bus station, but there are several main bus stops with ticket windows for hourly buses to San Jose and others south stopping at Cahuita and Puerto Viejo to Bribri and Sixaola on the Panamanian border, "la frontera." You should buy bus tickets the day before to be sure of getting on and then get there early to get a seat.

Taxis wait along the west side of the mercado, even at 5 a.m. when you want to go to Moín to catch a boat. Sometimes you can arrange a reasonable price for a day tour or drop-off at Cahuita or Puerto Viejo for a small group at the time you want to go .

South of Limón there are beaches all along the coast, some with excellent swimming like Cahuita and Puerto Viejo. To the north there are sharks and muddy water from the rivers emptying into the sea. While some people swim at Tortuguero, it is risky. The sharks follow river channels back into fresh water and some go all the way up the San Juan River to Lake Nicaragua. Surprising even the scientists, these sharks move freely back and forth between fresh and salt water.

North From Puerto Limón

Having already described the canales as an unforgettable experience for any nature-lover (in the Attractions section), I won't go into detail here. Accommodations range from basic cabinas to deluxe fishing lodges, and now also include moderately-priced places—one in Barra and some in Tortuguero. Most fishermen using the lodges book weekly package plans before leaving the U.S. or Europe and fly into the lodge by air taxi.

The very low budget traveler with more time could use basic rooms at Tortuguero or Barra Colorado and hire a boat in the village. At Tortuguero several locals rent dugout *cayucas* ranging from barely big enough to sit in, with perhaps a leak, to more stable dry boats which you may paddle for yourself or hire with a guide. These are for quiet backwaters only, *not* for going out the river mouths. Wildlife viewing or fishing success would then depend on the knowledge of the person you picked.

At Moín, ICT developed a recreation area with pool, camping, and boat dock for the *Gran Delta*, the government boat which runs to Barra once a week on Thursdays, and to Tortuguero on Saturdays, returning Sunday. Check with ICT to see if the boat is running. In dry season it may not be.

SANSA now flies several times weekly from San Jose to Barra (reservations required). **Rio Colorado Lodge** and **Isla de Pesca** run tours the full length of the main canal from Moín to Barra and their lodges there. **Rio Colorado Lodge** offers loop trips using a boat on the canales and another on the Río San Juan and Sarapiquí, connecting with a tour bus at Puerto Viejo de Sarapiquí. **Isla de Pesca** now advertises a similar tour up the San Juan, flying one way to Barra.

Tortuguero's airstrip is shorter and unpaved, used by air taxis only. **Costa Rica Expeditions** runs nature tours in the quiet back channels near Tortuguero with naturalist guides. Shy species such as the manatee are more likely there. Nature tours generally have to be booked well ahead. In 1991 they will run tours from Tortuguero up the Río San Juan all the way to Lake Nicaragua. The **Jungle Lodge, Hotel Ilan Ilan**, and **Mawamba** in Tortuguero run tour boats from Moín to their lodges.

From Moín, **Tortuguero Odysseys**, phones 58-1940, 58-2705, offers boats daily for $60 round trip to Tortuguero. Will arrange rooms or hotel in the village if you want to stay over. Call first. Since the earthquake they may be using the Reventazón River to reach the canales.

Parismina

Parismina Tarpon Rancho: Caters to fishermen only, not nature tours. Open January through October. Fly into local strip, or ride boat short distance from Moín. Rate includes meals, open bar, boat, motor and fishing guide. Offers fishing packages including nights in San Jose and discounted airfare. Some tours include fishing on both coasts using their **Golfito Sailfish Rancho.**

Rio Parismina Lodge: Attractive new lodge across the river from Parismina. Open, screened dining room. Good food. Offers packages for wildlife viewing with boat tour on the canales as well as fishing packages. 50 acres with trails. Pool, jacuzzi, open bar. Reserve with San Antonio office.

Price Range for 2 people in high season, before taxes—A+ Over $80/day, A $60–80, B $45–60, C $30–45, D $20–30, $E $11–20, F up to $11, U.S. $

Hotel	Address	Telephone (Fax)	No. of Rms	Pvt Bath	Hot Water	In Town	On Waterfront	Courtesy Transp	Recomm Access	Parking	Air Cond or Fan	Restaurant	Bar	Cooking Facil	Elevator	Wheelchair Acc	TV	Pool	English Spoken	Noise Level	Cleanliness	Single Rate	Price Range
Las Olas	Apdo. 701-7300 P. Limón	58-1414 (58-1678)	49	All		•			Car, Taxi, Bus	•	•	•	•		•		•	•	Exc	V gd		•	C
Cabinas Cocori	Portete, Limón	58-2930	6	All		•			Car, Taxi, Bus	•				•					V gd	Exc		•	E
PARISMINA:																							
Parismina Tarpon Rancho	Apdo. 149-Moravia, San Jose; P.O. Box 290190 San Antonio, TX 78280	71-2583 35-7766 (35-7766) 1-800-531-7232	20	All	•	•			Boat, Plane	•	•	•	•					•	Exc	Exc			A+*
Rio Parismina Lodge	All Reservations: P.O. Box 460009 San Antonio, TX	22-6633 (21-9127) 1-800-338-5688	12	All		•			Boat, Plane	•	•	•	•				•	•	Exc	Exc			A+*
Parismina Lodge	Parismina Lodge Parismina, Limón	76-8636	9	3		•			Boat, Plane		•	•	•						V gd	V gd			F
TORTUGUERO:																							
Tortuga Lodge	Apdo. 6941 San Jose	71-6861 SJ: 22-0333 (57-1665)	18	•		•	•		Boat, Plane	•	•	•	•					•	Exc	Exc		•	A+*
Jungle Lodge	Apdo. 26-1017 San Jose	33-0155 33-0133 (22-0568)	16	All		•	•		Boat, Plane	•	•	•	•						Exc	Exc		•	A+*

Parismina Lodge: Older, simple two story hotel with good screens, no fans. Fishing from dock in canal or can arrange with boat and guide at higher cost. Quiet mid-week., sometimes has party-time boat weekends.

Tortuguero

Except for fishermen, most people who stop at Tortuguero come to watch wildlife including sea turtle nesting and hatching. Here, adjacent to the national park, the line between nature lodges and village rooms is blurred. Green turtles lay eggs on the beach in July through September with hatching two months later, running into November. Leatherback turtles may nest any time, though March and April are peak months. Note that Tortuga Lodge, Jungle Lodge, and Ilan Ilan are across the river from the village—quieter on weekends but require boat to get to beach, park headquarters and trails, and to airstrip.

Tortuga Lodge: Deluxe lodge owned by Costa Rica Expeditions across channel from village, serves fishermen and *well-guided* nature tours. Nature trail adjacent to lodge. Open all year. Fishing is for tarpon, shark and bass in spring; snook, shark, and bass in fall. Rooms only are Range B, but packages are better value, since airport, turtle beach and all local restaurants are across river requiring several boat trips. Package tours include meals, and transportation by boat or air taxi. Recommended.

Tortuga Lodge manager Eduardo Brown with 217 lb. jewfish he caught.

Price Range for 2 people in high season, before taxes—A+ Over $80/day, A $60–80, B $45–60, C $30–45, D $20–30, $E $11–20, F up to $11, U.S. $. * = Meals included.

Hotel	Address	Telephone (Fax)	No. of Rms	Pvt Bath	Hot Water	In Town	On Waterfront	Courtesy Transp	Recomm Access	Parking	Air Cond or Fan	Restaurant	Bar	Cooking Facil	Elevator	Wheelchair Acc	TV	Pool	English Spoken	Noise Level	Cleanliness	Single Rate Range
Mawamba Lodge	Apdo. x7300 P. Limón	33-9964 58-4915 (25-8613)	12	•		•			Boat Plane	•	•	•	•					·	Exc	Exc	Exc	B
Ilan Ilan	Apdo. 91-1150 La Uruca San Jose	55-2262 55-2031 (55-1946)	20	All		•	•		Boat Plane	•	•	•	•					•	Exc	Exc	Exc	C
Sabina's Cabinas	Tortuguero	71-8099	38	2		•			Boat Plane		•	•	•						V gd	V gd	V gd	E
Cabinas Tortuguero	Cabinas Tortuguero, Tortuguero	71-6716	6	•		•			Boat Plane		•	•	•					•	Gd	Gd	Gd	F
BARRA COLORADO:																						
Casa Mar	Apdo. 825, Centro Colón, San Jose	41-2820, 43-8834 (43-9287)	12	All		•	•		Boat Plane	•	•	•	•					•	Exc	Exc	Exc	A+*
Isla de Pesca	Apdo. 8-4390-1000, San Jose	23-4560 21-6673 (21-5148)	17	All		•	•		Boat Plane	•	•	•	•					•	Exc	Exc	Exc	A+*
Rio Colorado Lodge	Apdo. 5094-1000 San Jose	71-6879 32-4063 (31-5987)	17	All	•	•			Boat Plane	•	•	•	•				•	•	Exc	Exc	Exc	A+*
Tarponland	Barra Colorado del Sud, Limón	71-6917 54-3679	22	All	•	•			Boat Plane	•	•	•	•					•	V gd	Exc	V gd	E

169

Jungle Lodge: Attractive lodge with covered walks, nesting oropendolas in yard, and trail on grounds. Rooms have double and single beds. Price includes meals. Package for 3 days/2 nights, round trip from San Jose, with guided tour to park and the hill for less than $150 is a good value. Owner Cotur, uses their covered boat, *Miss Caribe*. Recommended.

Mawamba Lodge: New 4 room cabinas (the only ones we've seen with electric outlets anywhere you'd want) just north of village, walking distance from beach and park headquarters, which allows you flexibility in arranging your time since you don't need a boat, but perhaps less quiet. Tours include bus and boat to/from San Jose and guided tours in park.

Ilan Ilan: Comfortable row building on opposite side of channel from village and beach. It's a climb up bank from small boats but has hosted guests in wheelchairs, flat once you're up. Run budget tours from San Jose, cruise to hotel with *Colorado Prince*, large motor launch. Good value.

Sabina's Cabinas: In village of Tortuguero near boat landing. Several newer rooms with bath, fans. Basic rooms without fans cheaper, but the ones upstairs have smashing view of beach and catch breeze. Shower and restrooms downstairs. While not always quiet, rooms here are farther from cantina than others in village. Small restaurant. Adjacent to beach.

Cabinas Tortuguero: Basic, clean cabinas with shower and restroom outside, no fans. 4-5 single beds/room. About $4/person. Adjacent to beach, in village, near restaurant. Quieter mid-week.

Additional basic cabinas in and near village, and several small restaurants, some of which require reservations for dinner.

Barra Colorado

Barra Colorado is divided by the Rio Colorado into separate villages, Barra Nord and Barra Sud. The airstrip, Rio Colorado Lodge, and Tarponland are at Barra Sud. At Barra Nord there are basic cabinas, not inspected. High tides and rains can leave both villages soggy and they aren't well lit at night. If you're using basic accommodations, try to avoid a night arrival. The ocean beach at Barra Sud is a steep, wild place, not for swimming, but an inspiring walk with driftwood, surf and birds. Locals fish for snook from the beach at the river mouth. Sunsets here are some of the world's finest.

SANSA flies to Barra Tuesday, Thursday and Saturday. Most fishing package tours are scheduled around those flights to save air charter cost. Outboard boats meet the flight and haul passengers and baggage to all the lodges except Tarponland, adjacent to the airport. *Essential* flight reservations are arranged by lodges when you book a package with them.

Independent travelers should reserve flights well ahead as lodge groups can fill the plane.

Cabina at Casa Mar.

Casa Mar: Deluxe fishing lodge, open Jan. to June for tarpon and late Aug. to Nov. for snook. Package fishing trips include almost everything. Duplex screened cabinas with twin beds, attractive landscaped grounds including orchids. Dining room overlooks river, serves excellent food. Many repeat guests.

Isla de Pesca: Deluxe fishing lodge open all year. Duplex cabins with queen-sized beds on landscaped grounds beside river. Tackle shop with sales, rentals. Lodge is beside quiet channel and forest, away from village and beach. Offers tours up canales with their own boat and packages which offer some fishing as well as nature trips into nearby lagoons. Under same ownership as Hotel Herradura in San Jose and Guanamar, fishing resort in Guanacaste.

Rio Colorado Lodge: Archie Fields's lodge was first to offer tours as well as fishing, open all year. You can add days to tours or join a tour in Limón if you want go to Cahuita first. Tours can fly one way on SANSA or go one way up or down the San Juan and Sarapiquí Rivers doing a loop from San Jose with a bus to Puerto Viejo. Excellent food, hospitable staff. Rooms are in screened duplex cabins connected by wooden walkways over river edge. Roofed deck overlooking river is a great relaxing spot. Walking distance to beach. Caged macaws, monkeys, tapir and deer on grounds. Satellite TV, game room, tackle shop. Fishing boats are specially built for seaworthiness to allow frequent fishing outside river mouth as well as in quiet channels. Recommended.

All gone fishing! Covered dock at Rio Colorado Lodge.

Tarponland: Comfortable, newly remodeled budget hotel with new detached cabinas adjacent to airstrip and village, walking distance to beach. Not deluxe, but a clean alternative for the budget traveler. Owner Guillermo Cunningham can arrange fishing boats, guides, tours to delta lagoons for birdwatching, or boats to Tortuguero or Moín.

Rates at lodges, not Tarponland, include meals. Fishing tours include boats, guides, tackle (though not lures, and you are always welcome to bring your own equipment) and transportation to camp as indicated in package. Some serve liquor extra and with some it's bring your own. Guides are tipped and hotel staff is too if a service charge isn't added.

Terns fly down the Rio Colorado.

South From Puerto Limón

The coastal villages of Cahuita and Puerto Viejo are relaxed places in the Caribbean style of years ago, except for stereos in the cantinas and streetlights in Cahuita. Accommodations range from moderate to basic though clean. Hint—do bring toilet paper and your own towel as basic cabinas don't furnish them. I bring a daypack with a canteen and water drops to treat any water I'm not absolutely sure of. Liquids are essential, and carrying anything in sweaty hands isn't fun. Note also that fruit isn't generally available in town, and you may want to bring hiking food with you. Local stores sometimes sell bread made with coconut by the local women. You'll meet children on the street with baskets of bread, still hot.

You can relax, swim, snorkel (best swimming and snorkeling in calmer water at both villages is in September and October), walk roads and paths to see birds, flowers, monkeys and butterflies, and meet nice people (some of whom are quoted in Paula Palmer's book, *What Happen*). Absorbing the feeling of these villages and understanding what it's like to live here takes time. After 4 days in Cahuita, I began to feel in pace and without a reason to hurry, or any "must-dos".

The new highway from San Jose to Puerto Limón and the paved road to Cahuita are changing the tempo of life here, especially on holidays and weekends when you may prefer to be somewhere else. Come mid-week and enjoy it. With faster roads, tourism is replacing agriculture as the major activity on the coast. So far most new facilities are small scale eating, sleeping and touring operations by local people. I wish it could stay that way.

Living is cheap—especially if you use simple cabinas and bring at least snack food. Recently more mid-priced hotel rooms and cabinas have been built in both towns and big plans are announced. If you want deluxe hotel rooms, you could stay at Portete and make a day trip south.

Cahuita

Cahuita is larger than Puerto Viejo. Cahuita National Park, protecting the only sizeable coral reef on Costa Rica's east coast, adjoins it on the south. Beaches within the park are white coral sand, while the beach at the north end of town is black volcanic sand, Black Beach. A delightful, flat, mostly shady trail runs 7 km through the trees just behind the beach from Cahuita to park headquarters at Puerto Vargas. You can enjoy monkeys, flocks of parrots, huge blue morpho butterflies, and a wonderful variety of flowers. The 1991 earthquake has lifted this shoreline, probably permanently. If you swim, observe any cautions offered by park staff or other locals about rips and underwater rocks. You'll want tennis

173

shoes or beach sandals for walking on exposed coral.

Near the park entrance, a block from the bus stop are a hotel, cabinas, cantinas, and a pulpería, small store with a few groceries and occasional fresh bread. Cabinas are near the park entrance, at the end of the point Cahuita is built on, and near Black Beach—down main street, left at the town power house and follow the road.

Telephone service in Cahuita is to a switchboard, 58-1515, and you give a *live* operator the extension number listed for each establishment.

Aviarios Río Estrella, on the road 10 km north of town, offers boat tours in the river and canals for wildlife and birdwatching. They allow camping in their preserve, and rent rafts and canoes. Phone: 24-7822, Fax: 24-6895.

Two operators now offer tours and rental equipment: **Cahuita Tours,** on the main street, has glass-bottomed boats for tours to the reef, and rents snorkeling and scuba gear and bicycles. They can also arrange car and driver for tours or for an early morning run to Limón. Ext. 232. **Moray's,** near the rural guard station, rents gear, and offers hiking, horseback, boat, and snorkeling tours. Ext. 216.

Where To Eat

At the park entrance are the **Cahuita National Park Restaurante,** featuring Caribbean and Italian food as well as cold drinks and fruit salads enticing after a day on the park beach and trail. **Hotel Cahuita** has a restaurant next door. **Restaurante Sol y Mar** across the street serves reasonably priced tipico food. **Surfside Cabinas** has a new restaurant I haven't tried (but they do everything else well).

Restaurant Edith, one block to right at rural guard station, serves great Caribbean food, has a vegetarian menu, and makes ice cream on weekends from tropical fruit. Breakfast 7-9 a.m. Miss Edith and her family are hospitable and fun. Closed Tuesdays. Highly recommended.

Continuing on the road north along Black Beach, **Cabinas Black Beach** serves lasagna and other Italian food in high season, **Hotel Cahuita Jaguar** has an international restaurant, and **Cabinas Algebra** serves very good Caribbean fare.

Where To Stay

Hotels and cabinas are ranged generally in descending order of price as I found them, and alphabetically within the range, not by area of town. The new Hotel Jaguar and Cabinas Iguana are added at the end.

Club Campestre: Beside highway between Puerto Limón and Cahuita on long exposed beach. Tico-style country club for families takes non-mem-

Stream meets ocean at high tide in Cahuita Park, a quiet walk.

Warning sign at park entrance—rips occur on the reef when water runs out in channels.

bers. Has pool, but beach across road is for walking, not swimming (camping allowed, $3). When inspected, electricity was from generator so didn't run fans at night. Damaged in earthquake. Open?

Cabinas Black Beach: Two story A-frame cabinas with stonework on shaded lawn. Attractive and comfortable, about a mile from the park boundary and nearly that far north of the center of town. Restaurant serves breakfast only in low season, Italian food in high season. Very good value.

Cabinas Sol y Mar: Near park entrance at south end of town. Ground floor wheelchair accessible. Upper floor has breeze through rooms, porch with chairs overlooking park entrance. Fans, some screens. Restaurant below and across street (noisy on weekends).

El Atlantida: Cabinas with fan, twin beds, on lawn adjacent to soccer field north of town, near Black Beach, quiet. Canadian owned.

Hotel Cahuita: Basic rooms above and behind small dining room with TV, loud stereo. Cabinas in backyard quieter, and better than rooms above hotel, higher rate.

Surfside Cabinas: Modern buildings on shady Cahuita Point divided into 2 cabinas for 2-4 people. You can ask for fans. Excellent value. Mr. and Mrs. David Buchanan are pleasant, interesting mainstays of village. They also have modern though not deluxe rooms in row building one block off main street., Range F. Recommended.

Cabinas Jenny: New building, 3 blocks from bus, on Cahuita Point, outdoor cooking area. Canadian owner. Friendly, communal atmosphere.

Cabinas Vaz: Modern concrete cabinas with plain rooms for up to 6 guests around lawn, across from Cahuita Hotel. Owner in Saloon Vaz. No screens. Rooms at back quieter.

Grant's Cabinas: Separate rooms in basic cabins, shared bath. One cabina has private bath. Across road from Black Beach. Owner Letty Grant delightful and helpful, designs the Cahuita T-shirts sold by **Tienda de Artesania**, the women's coop, between rural guard station and Black Beach. The shop also sells coconut shell jewelry and other handcrafts.

Palmer Cabinas: Large cabinas that can sleep up to 4. Fenced backyard. Sell much-needed items such as sunscreen. Manager helpful. 1/2 block from town center.

Cabinas Iguana: New, near Black Beach. Haven't inspected.

Hotel Cahuita Jaguar: New cinder block hotel planning 60 rooms, some still being built, on 17 acres of orchards and forest with paths near Black

Price Range for 2 people in high season, before taxes—A+ Over $80/day, A $60–80, B $45–60, C $30–45, D $20–30, $E $11–20, F up to $11, U.S. $

Hotel	Address	Telephone (Fax)	No. of Rms	Pvt Bath	Hot Water	In Town	On Waterfront	Courtesy Transp	Recomm Access	Parking	Air Cond or Fan	Restaurant	Bar	Cooking Facil	Elevator	Wheelchair Acc	TV	Pool	English Spoken	Noise Level	Cleanliness	Single Rate	Range
CAHUITA:																							
Club Campestre	Apdo. 214 La Uruca, San Jose	55-1676 / 58-2861 (21-5005)	20	All					Bus, Car		•	•						•	Gd	V gd	Gd		D
Black Beach Cabinas	Playa Negra, Cahuita	58-1515 Ext. 251	4	All	•				Bus, Car	•	•	•							Exc	Exc	Exc	•	E
Cabinas Sol y Mar	Cahuita, Limón	58-1515 Ext. 237	8	All	•	•			Bus, Car	•	•								Exc	V gd	V gd		E
El Atlantida	Cahuita, Limón	None	2	All	•	•			Bus, Car	•	•								Exc	Exc	Exc		E
Hotel Cahuita	Hotel Cahuita, Cahuita, Talamanca, Limón	58-1515 Ext. 201	11 cab 13 rms	11	•	•			Bus, Car	•	•	•						•	Exc	Fair	V gd		E
Surfside Cabinas	Apdo. 36-7300 Limón	58-1515 Ext. 246	23	All	•		•		Bus, Car					•					Exc	Exc	Exc	•	E/F
Cabinas Jenny	Apdo. 783 Cahuita, Limón	58-1515 Ext. 256	7	All	•	•			Bus, Car	•									Exc	Exc	Exc		F
Cabinas Vaz	Cahuita, Limón	58-1515 Ext. 218	14	All	•	•			Bus, Car	•	•								V gd	V gd	V gd	•	F
Grant's Cabinas	Apdo. 64, Limón	58-1515 Ext. 206	2 cab 6 rms	2	•		•		Bus, Car										Exc	Exc	Exc	•	F

Beach. When complete will be by far the largest hotel in Cahuita. Queen-sized beds, large breezy rooms. About a mile from the national park, quiet area.

Not in our tables: In town near school, **Cabinas Brisas del Mar,** pvt. bath, Range E. Phone ext. 267. Beside the soccer field and Black Beach are **Cabinas Colibrí,** comfortable cabinas with kitchens, hot water and pvt. bath. Range C. Phone ext. 263. Farther north past Cabinas Black Beach are: **Cabinas Brigitte,** basic rooms in large wooden house. Shared bath. Range F. Can rent horses. **Cabinas Algebra,** on shaded grounds, private bath, restaurant, Range E. Message phone, 58-2623.

Camping is possible at several sites among the palms on the park trail south from Cahuita and there is a 25 space campground three miles south of Cahuita at Puerto Vargas, the park headquarters. You can hike there from Cahuita, but most campers follow the main road south of town and turn in at the park entrance, admission fee $1 plus a small fee for camping. The Sixaola bus will let you off at the entrance, or pick you up there for the ride back to Cahuita if you've hiked one-way. It's less than half a mile to the campground facing the beach—shaded, with trees to hang a hammock. Parking space, picnic tables, firepits, pit toilets. Bring anything you'll need except water which you can hand pump from a well in front of park headquarters.

Puerto Viejo

Puerto Viejo's pace is slow and relaxed despite its recent discovery by surfers. It's built around a lovely bay with calm water for swimming in front of town. You'll find helpful, genial blacks who speak English, Talamanca Indians, Costa Ricans of Spanish descent, and foreigners who've intermarried or moved here for farming or tourism. Long-time residents worry about their town's future with increased traffic. Puerto Viejo is still a wonderful place to enjoy the ocean, walk, bike or ride horses on quiet paths and roads, visit with English-speaking local people, watch birds and monkeys, and not hurry about *anything*.

The Salsa Brava wave breaking on the reef at Puerto Viejo's bay entrance is the big attraction for surfers. Waves are challenging there, even for experts. The peak seasons are December through April and June-July. The sea is calmer in September and October when the rest of Costa Rica has its rainiest season and possibly the "temporal", a rain that lasts for days. However, a Caribbean hurricane passing nearby may raise the surf even then. The 1991 earthquake raised this coast, probably permanently, and its effect on swimming, waves, and snorkeling is?

The twice daily bus from San Jose to Sixaola stops only on the main

Price Range for 2 people in high season, before taxes—A+ Over $80/day, A $60–80, B $45–60, C $30–45, D $20–30, $E $11–20, F up to $11, U.S. $

Hotel	Address	Telephone (Fax)	No. of Rms	Pvt Bath	Hot Water	In Town	On Waterfront	Courtesy Transp	Recom Access	Parking	Air Cond or Fan	Restaurant	Bar	Cooking Facil	Elevator	Wheelchair Acc	TV	Pool	English Spoken	Noise Level	Cleanliness	Single Rate	Range
Palmer Cabinas	Apdo. 865, Limón	58-1515 Ext. 243	5	All	•				Bus / Car	•		•						•	Gd	Gd	•	•	F
Cabinas Iguana		58-1515 Ext. 263	4	All	•				Bus / Car									•	Exc	Exc			
Jaguar	Apdo. 7046-1000 San Jose	58-1515 Ext. 238	22	All	•				Bus / Car	•	•	•				•		•	Exc	Exc	•		C
PUERTO VIEJO:																							
El Pizote Surf Lodge	Puerto Viejo, Talamanca	22-4547 (21-3011)	8 cab / 4	4					Car / Bus	•	•	•						•	Exc	Exc	•	•	C
Cabinas Manuel Leon	Puerto Viejo, Limón	58-0854	5	All	•	•			Car / Bus	•	•	•						•	Poor	Gd	•	•	E
Escape Caribeño	Puerto Viejo, Limón	58-3844 (message)	4	All	•				Car / Bus				•					•	Exc	Exc	•	•	E
Cabinas Black Sands	Puerto Viejo, Limón	58-3844 (message)	3	0		•			Car / Bus				•					•	Exc	Exc		•	F
Cabinas Chimuri	Puerto Viejo, Limón	58-3844 (message)	4	0					Car / Bus				•					•	Exc	Exc			F
Hotel Puerto Viejo	Puerto Viejo, Limón	58-0854 (message)	18		•	•			Car / Bus		•								Vgd	Vgd	•	•	F
Cabinas Ritz	Puerto Viejo, Limón	58-3844 (message)	5	All		•			Car / Bus		•							•	V gd	V gd			F

road 6 km from Puerto Viejo. The Limón-Sixaola bus, several times a day stops near the Maritza Hotel in Puerto Viejo. Most buses have no suitable place for surfboards, so surfers usually rent cars or hire a truck to haul them and their boards from Limón.

Where to Eat

Stanford's Restaurant El Caribe (second floor) was famous for seafood long before travelers found other reasons for coming to Puerto Viejo. It throbs with reggae on weekends. Farther southeast along the shore and the road to Manzanillo are Parquecito, Soda Támara, and Juices, good for breakfast. Our readers like the breakfasts and rave about pizza suppers at the Restaurant Coral where you eat looking out at the jungle. Women in town make coconut bread, jam, biscuits, and other Caribbean goodies—Miss Dolly, Miss Daisy, and others.

Where To Stay

Puerto Viejo has only two public phones which *may* relay messages. The Hotel Maritza has 58-3844, and Cabinas Manuel Leon has 58-0854. Both hotels are basic. Most other hotels and cabinas use the Maritza's phone, except those with an agent in San Jose handling reservations. If you're trying to reserve by phone at any other cabina in Puerto Viejo, you should call the message phone and leave only the message that you want Mr. So-and-so to call you back. Mentioning reservations can make the message relay less likely. This town desperately needs a real reservation phone. I hope ICE, the government electric and phone utility, or the ICT gets another line in *soon*. Unless you're equipped for camping, be sure you have reservations, especially on weekends. Several owners listed here have improved their rooms and built more since the new highway is bringing more travelers. More cabinas are opening soon.

El Pizote Surf Lodge: Comfortable, screened wood cabinas with shared baths, and bungalows with pvt. bath, well separated from dining room on landscaped grounds across from beach before entering town. Has trails, rents bicycles, horses, snorkeling equipment. Good for groups. Recommended.

Cabinas Manuel Leon: *Very* basic rooms in long building. End units have windows on two sides, ones between don't. Rates per room for 1-3.

Cabinas Stanford's: Simple, comfortable rooms in town near Hotel Puerto Viejo. Reserve at Stanford's Restaurant.

Escape Caribeño: On shore road 1 km south of town. New screened rooms, with fridge add $3. Shared cooking facilities. Wheelchair accessible. High season reservation with traveler's check for full amount. Rent bikes, snorkeling gear. Tours to Manzanillo, etc. Recommended.

Cabinas Black Sands: Friendly Canadian-owned place. Simple thatched huts near beach. Communal cooking area. Bathrooms in separate building. Turn left at Violeta's pulpería before village and follow signs.

Cabinas Chimuri: Uphill from the road on the right, 1.5 km before the village. New A-frame cabinas surrounded by forest. Roofed, open-air 'communal cooking area. Mauricio Salazar, Bribri Indian owner, sells crafts and leads 1-day horseback tours in nearby forest reserves with visits to Indian villages and 3-day backpacking trips in La Amistad Park (requires reservations for longer trips). He also rents horses.

Hotel Maritza: Basic rooms on second floor. Five newer rooms in annex are basic but clean and airy. Music in cantina said to be off at 9 p.m.

Hotel Puerto Viejo: Rooms basic, but screened. Downstairs cheaper, but upstairs slightly better. Owner offers snorkeling trips, rents bikes.

Cabinas Ritz: Simple rooms behind pulpería as you enter town. Need fans. Owner Vincente Guthrie is interesting long-timer in region.

Pensión Agaricia, owned by Javier Escobedoand his Belgian wife, is across from the beach as you enter town. Attractive rooms with shared bath, clean, quiet. Great breakfast, optional. Range E. Rent bikes. Readers *rave.* Apdo. 704, Puerto Limón. Message phone 58-3844. Nearby is **Cabinas Grant,**with pvt bath, locked parking, Range D. Same message phone.

Kiskadee Hostel is recommended by readers, up path in forest behind soccer field. Dormitory, with kitchen privileges. North American owned. In town and on the road toward Punta Uva are **Cabinas Támara** (same ownership as Restaurant Támara, Range D, **Cabinas Jacaranda,** basic, Range F and **Cabinas La Salsa Brava,** basic but has pvt. bath, Range F.

Campesino heads for home after shopping in Puerto Viejo store.

181

Hotel	Address	Telephone (Fax)	No. of Rms	Pvt Bath	Hot Water	In Town	On Waterfront	Courtesy Transp	Recomm Access	Parking	Air Cond or Fan	Restaurant	Bar	Cooking Facil	Elevator	Wheelchair Acc	TV	Pool	English Spoken	Noise Level	Cleanliness	Single Rate Range
Cabinas Stanford's	Puerto Viejo, Limón	58-3844 (message)	10	All	•				Car Bus	•	•								•	Exc	Exc	E
Hotel Maritza	Puerto Viejo, Limón	58-3844	16		•				Car Bus	•	•								•	Fair	Gd	E,F

Price Range for 2 people in high season, before taxes—A+ Over $80/day, A $60–80, B $45–60, C $30–45, D $20–30, $E $11–20, F up to $11, U.S. $. * = Meals included.

Punta Uva and Manzanillo

The beaches at Punta Uva have fine swimming, and this area, 7 km south of Puerto Viejo, and the road to it are developing fast for tourism, with new cabinas and more planned. At Manzanillo, still another 7 km, there are only basic cabinas in the village now, but the **Manzanillo-Gandoca Wildlife Refuge** includes coral reefs, a beach with nesting turtles (peak time, January-April), a turtle hatchery, the Gandoca River with manatees, and great birdwatching. Get their birdlist and see how many you can find.

Where To Stay

Accommodations range from basic to very comfortable. **Hotel Punta Cocles**, 4 km past Puerto Viejo, has cabinas with porches where you can sit looking into the forest,.Pool, hot water, and nearby beach. Range B. They rent snorkeling gear and surfboards, horses, and bicycles. Phone 34-0306, Fax 34-0014. **Hotel Play Cocles** is under construction nearby. At Punta Uva is **Hotel Las Palmas** offering 12 comfortable cabinas with bath and hot water, Range B. Phone 55-2650. Fax 55-3737. They have package rates for minimum of 4 people with transportation from San Jose. In between are **Cabinas Dasa, Miraflores Lodge** (b & b), **Selvyn's Cabinas** (basic) and restaurant, and comfortable **Cabina Punta Uva** with pvt. bath and cooking facilities. There will be more by the time you get there!

Limón bus to Manzanillo passes Punta Uva. Leaves Limón at 6.m. and 2 p.m. Leaves Manzanillo at 9 a.m. and 4:30 p.m.

WEST COAST

Puntarenas
(pop. 85,430)

Like Limón on the Caribbean coast, Puntarenas is a port city more important to the tourist as a gateway to the Gulf of Nicoya and the Nicoya Peninsula than as a destination. It was Costa Rica's main trading port at the end of the oxcart trail down from the highlands until the railroad was built to Limón in the 1890's. Most freighters and all visiting cruise ships now stop instead at the new port of Caldera a few miles south. Buses (2 hours, leave hourly) or the electric train (4 hours, once daily in afternoon) from San Jose can get you there. Puntarenas fills a long narrow sandspit out into the gulf, only two blocks wide at the narrowest. To the south is the open end of the gulf with mild surf hitting the beach. On the north is an estuary with yacht moorage and mangrove swamps, important to wildlife and fisheries.

If you look quickly as you pass mangroves (one of few trees that grow with roots in salt water) on the right as you start out on the spit, you'll see storks, roseate spoonbills, and other waterfowl feeding in shallow water a few feet from the busy highway, near the cemetery. If you're driving, this is a good spot to stop for bird photography, especially early in the morning. Farther along in the estuary is the Costa Rica Yacht Club and marina followed by the commercial fishing fleet and the ferry dock. Shrimp fishing is very important here and you may wonder why shrimp is the most expensive item on most menus. Most shrimp are exported and command a high price on the international market.

Calypso Tours (55-3022, 61-0585) gives very popular day tours with refreshments on their comfortable yacht, *Calypso*, and gourmet lunch on a secluded island beach in the Gulf of Nicoya, leaving from near the yacht harbor. You have time to swim and snorkel at Tortuga Island and enjoy passing frigate bird and pelican rookeries. They run a minibus down from San Jose and can pick you up at your hotel, returning you that night. You can combine this tour with a trip to Monteverde, but I think you'll prefer spending the night after the boat trip in Puntarenas *before* going up to Monteverde. The Monteverde road after a day in sun and water would be exhausting. They also offer a sunset cruise with music and a bar on Saturday evenings and recently acquired a larger boat with cabins to offer multi-day trips out to Cocos Island as well as cruises in the gulf.

Pacific Island Adventures (55-0791 and 61-0697) and **Bay Island Cruises** (31-2898) also offer day cruises from Puntarenas and will pick you up at San Jose hotels.

A boat charter service, **Taximar**, (61-0331, 61-1143) based at the yacht harbor, takes individuals or groups fishing or cruising among the islands in the Gulf, with a boat holding 4-6 people. **Sportfishing Costa Rica** (55-0791, 61-0697) offers fishing for marlin and sailfish.

The launch to Paquera on the Nicoya Peninsula departs from just behind the market on the estuary at 6 a.m. and 3 p.m. Mon.–Sat. (From the bus station for San Jose, go north several blocks on the same street.) This boat doesn't carry cars, but the bus to Cóbano meets it at Paquera, stopping at Playa Tambor. The launch no longer goes to San Lucas Island on Sundays since the prison there has closed to make way for tourist development.

The car ferry leaves at 7:30 a.m. and 4 p.m. Mon.–Fri., and 7:30 a.m., 11 a.m., and 4 p.m. Sat. and Sun. for Naranjo on the Nicoya Peninsula. Get in line an hour (or two on weekends and holidays) ahead if you have a car to be sure of getting on. At Naranjo a bus to Nicoya and Santa Cruz meets the ferry, but there is no bus south from there. The ship was built

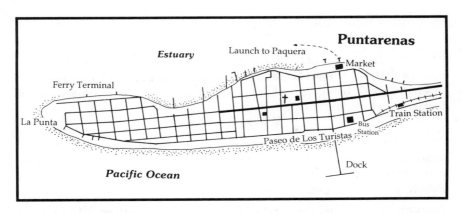

in Denmark with a stormproof lounge, but you can sit out on deck to enjoy the view for the one hour crossing.

The center of town has several pleasant restaurants with good food and a lovely old church. During high season you can enjoy good inexpensive plays and concerts at the Casa de la Cultura. Like Limón, Puntarenas is hot and humid. You'll probably want a fan or air conditioning that really makes the air move if you take a room not on the waterfront. Accordingly, I didn't inspect all the basic hotels in the breezeless center of town. If you're staying there, ask for a demonstration of fans or air conditioning. Check out the **Cayuga** (good restaurant) and the **Ayi Con** (near the market) first.

Along the ocean side of downtown Puntarenas is the Paseo de los Turistas, a tree-lined street and promenade adjoining the beach with many soda stands and several hotels. At the far end there's a public swimming pool, open 9-4:30, closed Mondays, about 50¢. The ocean here isn't as clean as in more remote places, not recommended for swimming. Don't leave anything, including towels, lying unwatched. Several hotels face this beach and most have pools. You definitely need reservations in high season, especially on weekends.

The east or near end of the peninsula if you're coming from San Jose is the Cocal district. There are several deluxe hotels facing the estuary and perhaps a dozen sets of cabinas ranging from basic to deluxe. South of the spit is the ICT recreation area at Doña Ana beach, and farther south is the modern port at Caldera where cruise ships dock to give their passengers a day tour in Costa Rica as far as San Jose.

Hourly bus service from Puntarenas back to San Jose even a day or two after a holiday can require a three hour wait in the sun. I found several other people in line willing to split the cost of a taxi, about $25 a

185

person for 4 to San Jose.

Restaurants

Hotels particularly noted for their food are the **Porto Bello, Colonial,** and **Las Brisas. La Caravelle** and the restaurant at **Cabinas El Joron** on the Paseo are good. Inexpensive Chinese food, pizza, and seafood are served at clean small restaurants downtown.

Where To Stay

Note that most hotels on Costa Rica's west coast have high and low season rates, though their definition of the season varies. Most often it's from early December through April. Discounts may be 10-30% in low season. You can get excellent values in November.

Yadran: Deluxe hotel near end of spit. Rooms have balcony, 1 dbl and 1 sgl bed, TV and phone.

Fiesta: New, deluxe hotel near costanera at base of Puntarenas spit. Has all resort facilities including tennis, casinos, meeting rooms, landscaped grounds. Rents water sports gear. Arranges tours to Monteverde, Carara.

Porto Bello: (Cocal) Deluxe hotel well landscaped, on estuary. Has dock and moorage Excellent food. Has live music on weekends. Can arrange boats and fishing. Helpful manager. Recommended. (Both Porto Bello and Colonial allow free use of their facilities by yachtsmen moored here.)

Colonial: (Cocal) Deluxe hotel adjacent to Porto Bello, has dock. Attractive landscaped grounds, shaded parking. Good food. Mid-week rates. Helpful staff, can arrange boats and fishing. Casino. Recommended.

Las Brisas: Modern hotel near west end of waterfront. Large rooms with desk and table, acoustical tile ceiling. two story building with 4 rooms on ground level. *Excellent* international food. Guarded parking. Hospitable owners. Recommended.

Los Chalets:(Chacarita) Very attractive separate cabinas for 8 on shaded ground facing beach at east end of Puntarenas spit. Kitchen facilities. Shaded sitting area for each cabina. Rate is per cabina, a good value for a group. Recommended.

Cabinas Los Joron: Pleasant, roomy cabinas with two single or one double bed, refrigerator and sink. Clean thatched open restaurant overlooking waterfront. Ask for demo of air conditioning.

Cabinas San Isidro: (Cocal) Attractive, same ownership as Los Chalets. Less expensive and across back street from beach but has beach access. Has rate for youth hostel members.

Costa Rica Yacht Club: (Cocal) Private yacht club catering to members

Yachts moored in the Puntarenas estuary, some from California.

of their club and others, even from other countries. Rooms have twin beds or bunks. Faces marina on estuary; ocean beach one block.

Tioga: Popular hotel facing beach. Reservations a must. Price includes full American breakfast, the only meal served. Snack bar. Less expensive rooms have cold water only—but that isn't very cold in Puntarenas! Check-out is late, 2 p.m., which may mean you can't get into rooms early in afternoon if coming from San Jose. Hotel has night parking guard. Pool beautiful. Some rooms have ocean view. Recommended.

Las Hamacas: On waterfront downtown. Simple rooms less expensive without air conditioning but well lined up with ocean breeze on 2nd floor. Dance floor and bar on 3rd floor are *noisy* and have speakers going day and night.

La Punta: Pleasant, simple hotel very near ferry to Naranjo. Rooms have sitting area or balcony. Second floor preferred, breezy. Pingpong tables.

There are additional cabinas in the Cocal and Chacarita areas at the east end of the Puntarenas spit, a few hundred meters east of the big hospital. Some are deluxe and others quite basic. Not inspected: **Cabinas Orlando** has a pool and **Villas Palmas** also is attractive. All are much quieter mid-week and in low season than on weekends or holidays.

Esparza

Esparza is several miles before you get to Puntarenas, near the junction of the Interamerican Highway and the road to Puntarenas. Big fruit stands

Price Range for 2 people in high season, before taxes—A+ Over $80/day, A $60–80, B $45–60, C $30–45, D $20–30, $E $11–20, F up to $11, U.S. $. * = Meals included.

PUNTARENAS:

Feature	Yadran	Fiesta	Porto Bello	Colonial	Las Brisas	Los Chalets	Cabinas El Joron
Price Range	A+	A+	B	C	C	C	D
Single Rate			•	•	•		•
Cleanliness	Exc	Exc	Exc	Exc	Exc	Exc	V gd
Noise Level	Exc	Exc	Exc	V gd	Exc	Exc	Exc
English Spoken	Exc	Exc	Exc	Exc	Exc	Exc	V gd
Pool	•	•	•	•	•		
TV	•	•	•	•	•	•	
Wheelchair Acc	•	•					
Elevator		•				•	
Cooking Facil		•					
Bar							•
Restaurant	•	•	•	•	•		•
Air Cond or Fan	•	•	•	•	•		
Parking	•	•	•	•	•	•	•
Recomm Access	•	•	•	•	•	•	•
Courtesy Transp	Car Bus Train	Car Bus Taxi Train	Car Bus Train	Bus Train Car	Bus Train Car	Car Bus Train	Train Car Bus
On Waterfront		•					
In Town	•		•	•	•	•	•
Hot Water	•		•	•	•	•	•
Pvt Bath	All	All	All	All	All	All	•
No. of Rms	30	174	34	34	9	18	4
Telephone (Fax)	61-2662 (61-1944)	63-0185 39-4266 (63-1516)	61-2122 61-1322 (61-0036)	61-1833	61-2120	63-0150 25-3520	61-0467
Address	Apdo. 14-5400 Puntarenas	Apdo. 171-5400 Puntarenas	Apdo. 108-5400 Puntarenas	Apdo. 368-5400 Puntarenas	Apdo. 83-5400 Puntarenas	Apdo. 1287 San Jose	Paseo de los Turistas, Puntarenas

Price Range for 2 people in high season, before taxes—A+ Over $80/day, A $60–80, B $45–60, C $30–45, D $20–30, $E $11–20, F up to $11, U.S. $. * = Meals included.

Hotel	Address	Telephone (Fax)	No. of Rms	Pvt Bath	Hot Water	In Town	On Waterfront	Courtesy Transp	Recomm Access	Parking	Air Cond or Fan	Restaurant	Bar	Cooking Facil	Elevator	Wheelchair Acc	TV	Pool	English Spoken	Noise Level	Cleanliness	Single Rate	Range
Cabinas San Isidro	Apdo. 4674 San Jose	21-1225 63-0031	54	All	•			Train Car Bus	•	•									V gd	V gd	•		D
Costa Rica Yacht Club	Apdo. 2530-1000 San Jose	61-0784 (21-5958)	28	All	•	•		Train Bus Car Boat	•	•	•	•					•	•	Exc	V gd	•		D
Tioga	Apdo. 96-5400 Puntarenas	61-0271 (61-0127)	46	All	•	•		Car Train Bus	•	•	●						•	•	Exc	Exc	•		D
Las Hamacas	Paseo de los Turistas, Puntarenas	61-0398	30	All	•	•		Bus Car Train									•		Fair	Fair	•		B
La Punta	Apdo. 228 Puntarenas	61-0696	8	All	•			Bus Car Train		•	•	•					•		Exc	V gd			E
Castañuelas	Esparza, Punt.	63-5105	13	All				Bus Car	•		•				•				Exc	V gd	•		F
Rio Mar (SOUTHWEST COAST:)	Apdo. 250 Puntarenas	63-0158 63-0550	52	All				Car Bus	•	•	•	•						•	V gd	V gd	•		E

ESPARZA:

SOUTHWEST COAST:

189

along the highway serve cold melon juice and have many kinds of low-land fruits and melons, nice to take with you to the coast and back to San Jose where they're more expensive with less variety.

Castañuelas: Altitude a bit higher and cooler than Puntarenas, an option if hotels in Puntarenas are full. Large ground floor rooms with table, twin beds, trees set back from highway. Price varies whether room has fan or a.c., (ask for demo). Coffee shops nearby. Good value. Restaurant under same ownership nearby.

South From Puntarenas

Each village in Costa Rica has at least basic hotels used by the locals. South of Puntarenas there are more tourist facilities, some new and some old, between Puntarenas and Jacó Beach.

The *costanera* is Costa Rica's priority road project, the highway down the southwest coast. It's a wide, two-lane road with gentle grades and good gravel where it isn't paved, that now runs from just outside Puntarenas south past Doña Ana beach, Mata Limón, the modern port of Caldera, Playas Tarcoles and Herradura, Carara Biological Reserve, Jacó Beach, Esterillos, Quepos (with its spur road to Manuel Antonio), south across a dozen or more Bailey bridges built in 1987 by U.S. Army engineers as a gift to Costa Rica, past Playa Dominical. Eventually it will be extended to Palmar Norte on the Interamerican Highway, but now the main road cuts inland through the hills to San Isidro de General. Resorts and hotels are listed here in the order you'll find them driving south.

Starting from the east end of the Puntarenas spit and continuing down the coast past Jacó, there are several good surfing beaches with very consistent waves. River mouths with estuaries and mangrove swamps just upstream attract many birds, caimans, and even crocodiles. Several older hotels and cabinas offer simple rooms often overlooking the estuaries. By road (car, taxi or bus from Puntarenas) or the electric train, this is a quiet area for budget birdwatching if you avoid weekends and holidays with crowds and tape recorders. At Mata Limón you could rent a boat or pay a local guide with one to take you birding in the mangrove channels.

Rio Mar: Older hotel north of highway. All rooms have shaded sitting area, recent paint and good screens. Rooms behind, particularly on breezy second floor, look out on mangroves and water. **Surfers** stay here to use long left waves at mouth of the Barranca River. Puntarenas–Quepos bus will stop at entrance.

Doña Ana Recreation area on your right is a sheltered beach with shade between rocky points. Safe swimming, shaded picnic area with tables. Surfing nearby. Small soda bar restaurant, dressing rooms. No camping. Admission 25 colones/adult.

Mata Limón

Mata Limón was one of Costa Rica's early beach resorts, on an estuary across from the port of Caldera. The village is divided by the river, with entrances to both parts of it from the highway. The north side is also an electric train stop. On the north side are one older hotel, basic cabinas, a cantina and a few houses. A high wooden footbridge (use flashlight at night to avoid missing planks) crosses the river, giving a fine view of the whole area. On the south side is main village with several basic cabinas, and restaurant, **Costa El Sol**, owned by Ringo Lastro, who can answer anything, arrange for boats, guides, etc. (67-4008). Deep sea fishing available. Ornithologist Paul Slud did some early work here. Ask at restaurant to find local with skiff to explore mangrove and river.

Manglares: Older basic hotel on north side. Portable fans available. Balcony and open air restaurant overlook estuary. Dance floor. Adjacent to train stop. Severely damaged in 1990 earthquake,. Rebuilt?

Cabinas Las Santas: Rate is for simple cabina with cooking facilities, 3 small bedrooms and bathroom. Good value for family.

Hotel Viña del Mar: Basic hotel, with 1 dbl and 1 sgl bed per room. Some breeze, not all windows screened.

Villas Fanny, Cabinas Maria Cecelia, Villas America look basic, OK.

Playas Tarcoles, Herradura

Crocodile napping on Tarcoles River bank, taken from the bridge.

The highway bridge crossing the Rio Tarcoles has a pullout for cars at the south end. One of the best spots in Costa Rica for roadside wildlife viewing, it's well worth a stop any time, to look for crocodiles up to 12 feet long on the river banks and shore birds, including wood storks and roseate spoonbills. Early morning and late afternoon you may see flights

Hotel	Address	Telephone (Fax)	No. of Rms	Pvt Bath	Hot Water	In Town	On Waterfront	Courtesy Transp	Recomm Access	Parking	Air Cond or Fan	Restaurant	Bar	Cooking Facil	Elevator	Wheelchair Acc	TV	Pool	English Spoken	Noise Level	Cleanliness	Single Rate	Range
MATA LIMÓN, NORTH SIDE:																							
Manglares	Esparza, Puntarenas	63-4010 63-4013	14	All	•	•		Train Bus	•	•	•	•							V gd	Fair		•	F
SOUTH SIDE:																							
Cabinas Las Santas	Mata Limón, Esparza, Puntarenas	41-0510	6	All	•	•		Car Bus	•										Gd	Gd			C
Viña de Mar	Mata Limón, Esparza, Puntarenas	63-4030	8	All	•			Bus Car	•	•	•	•							Gd	Gd		•	E
TARCOLES:																							
Las Palmas	Tarcoles, Garabito, Punt.	61-0455	17	All	•	•		Car Bus	•		•								Exc	Gd		•	E
PUNTA LEONA:																							
Punta Leona	Apdo. 8592-1000 San Jose	31-3131 (32-3074)	69	All			•	Car	•	•	•	•	•	•		•	•	•	Exc	Exc			A+

Price Range for 2 people in high season, before taxes—A+ Over $80/day, A $60–80, B $45–60, C $30–45, D $20–30, $E $11–20, F up to $11, U.S. $. * = Meals included.

of scarlet macaws. **Carara Biological Reserve** starts just south of the bridge. A kilometer down the road there's a ranger station and short nature trail through the forest. Tours with special permission go farther inside the reserve.

Playa Tarcoles is a gravel beach but with calm sea, near Carara Biological Reserve. Nearby are lagoons with birds including storks. I saw 2 scarlet macaws on the 2 km gravel road leading in from the highway. Camping is OK on the beach, with some shade. Bar. restaurant, ice. I wouldn't swim near the river mouth due to pollution.

Las Palmas: Two story building across from church. Plain rooms with 1 dbl and 2 bunk beds. No screens. Older cheaper rooms have shared bath.

Cabinas Viña del Mar is a shaded 2 story building, across from park and not right on the beach. Upper level looks OK.

Playa Herradura is a sheltered black sand beach with safe swimming 3 km from highway. Swimming is safer than Jacó just to the south, and possibly not as crowded on weekends since bus doesn't come in from highway. Several basic cabinas, restaurants and bars. Shaded camping along beach. Despite signs about keeping sites clean, there are few trash cans. Be prepared to clean up site initially. One private campground on lawn with trees just back from beach and another about two blocks from the beach on the road in.

Punta Leona : Complete resort that was until recently a private club but now serves guests with hotel rooms and cabinas ranging from mobilehomes to deluxe chalets, on shaded grounds with private beach. Restaurant, bar, disco, pool, and game room facing beach. Horse rentals. *Note:* trailer and camper sites, some with hookups.

Jacó Beach

This long beach is easily reached from San Jose and usually crowded on weekends and holidays, as the bus goes there and it's only a 2-hour drive from San Jose via Atenas, San Mateo and Orotina on a scenic hilly paved road that joins the costanera just below Orotina. You can also drive from San Jose to the outskirts of Puntarenas and turn south on the costanera at its beginning. This way is less scenic, but the road is wider and route simpler. If you have time and want to avoid crowds in the dry season, you'll probably go farther.

Jacó Beach has surf enjoyed by board surfers but also has dangerous rips. Only strong, knowledgeable swimmers should swim in the ocean here. If you are caught in a rip, which may appear as a muddy streak leading out from shore where the surf is lower, you should not fight it, but swim parallel to shore until you are free of the current and then swim in. Swimmers drown every year when they exhaust themselves trying to swim to shore against the rip current. Most hotels have pools. Hotels here encourage surfers with low rates during low season, May through November, and surfers have a wide choice of nearby beaches. Playa Hermosa, 3 km south, is well known for surfing with very consistent waves, the site of surfing contests. (See photo is Safety section.)

Jacó has restaurants, bars, discos, 2 small grocery stores, a bank, and several camping areas. Canadian air charters from Montreal. Toronto, and Vancouver fill several hotels here during high season. Some hotels even fly the Canadian maple leaf beside the Costa Rican flag! Menus are often printed in French as well as English, Spanish and German.

Several places rent bicycles—bring your own flashlight and lock. With many black, unlit bikes on road at night, I'd take a roll of reflective tape and donate a piece to the back fender of anything I rented! If you're driving at night, be very careful. Surf and body boards also rented here.

The ICT has built a beach facility near the Pizzeria Bribri, south of the Jacó Beach Hotel for day users, with dressing rooms, showers, and lockers for clothes.

Restaurants

For a splurge for dinner, try the **El Jardin**. The **Cocal** is excellent. Less expensively, the family-run soda restaurant on the beach side of the main road, 150 m. south of the Jacó Beach Hotel has good tipico food and great refrescos. I drank the latter in pairs, especially the maracuyá, while inspecting hotels in the summer heat. **El Bosque**, near the gas station on the costanera at the south end of Jacó. has mango shade trees, good, moderately priced food, refrescos, breakfasts, seafood.

Children in pool at Jac'ø Beach Hotel.

Where To Stay

Jacó Beach Hotel: Deluxe hotel under same ownership as Irazú in San Jose with a courtesy bus from San Jose. Canadian charters use during high season. Grounds landscaped adjoining beach. Big, clean pool, 1 meter deep, has island in middle. Lighted tennis courts. Large rooms with tub and shower, marble floors and sinks from Guatemala and El Salvador. Balconies face pool. Suites have refrigerator, sitting room. Good food, breakfast. Moped and sports equipment rentals. Variety of bus tours. Recently added condo units across street.

Apartotel Gaviotas: Very attractive rooms with kitchenettes, laundry sinks, small patio, and settees as well as beds. Very good value for 3 or more. 100 m north of Banco Nacional and 50 m east of the road in quiet neighborhood. Recommended.

Cabinas Tangerí: Modern buildings catering to families, shaded, landscaped, attractive. Rate is per cabina with up to 3 bedrooms, kitchen with 2 burner stove, roofed outside eating area. Adding some hotel-style rooms. Pool, pingpong and refreshment area well-separated from rooms.

Rooms at Jacó Fiesta Hotel.

Jacó Fiesta: At south end of Jacó. *Very* attractive, well-designed, large new hotel, with trees, creek estuary. Rooms are large and cool, 2 dbl beds, some with kitchens, all with fridge, satellite TV. Bathrooms big with door wide enough for wheelchair (may add ramp to room door). Covered sitting area or balcony for each room. Rate is per room for 1-4. Tennis. Recommended.

Club Marparaiso: Attractive modern 3 story facing beach. Large rooms

Price Range for 2 people in high season, before taxes—A+ Over $80/day, A $60–80, B $45–60, C $30–45, D $20–30, $E $11–20, F up to $11, U.S. $. * = Meals included.

Hotel	Address	Telephone (Fax)	No. of Rms	Pvt Bath	Hot Water	In Town	On Waterfront	Courtesy Transp	Recomm Access	Parking	Air Cond or Fan	Restaurant	Bar	Cooking Facil	Elevator	Wheelchair Acc	TV	Pool	English Spoken	Noise Level	Cleanliness	Single Rate	Range
JACÓ BEACH:																							
Jacó Beach	Apdo. 962-1000, San Jose	32-5627 64-3032 (32-3159)	120	All	•		•	Car / Bus	•	•	•	•		•	•	•	•	•	Exc	V gd	Exc	•	A
Apartotel Gaviotas	Playa Jacó, Puntarenas	64-3092	12	All	•	•		Car / Bus	•	•	•	•		•			•			Exc	Exc		B
Chalet Tangeri	Apdo. 622, Alajuela	64-3001	10	All	•	•		Car / Bus	•	•			•	•			•		V gd				A
Jacó Fiesta	Apdo. 38, Jacó, Garabito, Punt.	64-3147 (64-3148)	82	All	•	•		Car / Bus	•	•	•	•	•				•	•		Exc	Exc		B
Club Marparaiso	Apdo. 6699-1000, San Jose	64-3025	26	All •	•	•		Car / Bus	•	•	•	•			•	•	•	•		V gd	Exc		B
Cocal	Hotel Cocal, Jacó, Garabito, Puntarenas	64-3067	26	All	•	•		Car / Bus	•	•	•	•					•	•		Exc	Exc	•	C
Villas Miramar	Apdo. 018 Jacó, Garabito, Punt.	64-3003	10	All	•	•		Car / Bus	•	•			•	•	•		•	•		Exc	Exc	•	C
Cabinas Las Brisas	Apdo. 8 Jacó, Garabito, Punt.	64-3074	12	2	•	•		Car / Bus	•	•				•						Exc	Exc	•	D/F
Cabinas Antonio	Playa Jacó, Garabito, Punt.	64-3043	11	?	•	•		Car / Bus	•	•	•									V gd	Gd		E

196

have sitting area, sink, 2 double beds (low). Wading pool. Pool table. Caters to Tico families, quiet early part of week.

Cocal: Very pleasant, small hotel on beach south part of town. 8 rooms face beach with outside decks. No children under 16. Deluxe dining room, good food. Shaded, breezy sitting area with hammocks in trees. 2 pools. Hotel on ground level. German spoken. Recommended. Reservations essential.

Villas Miramar: Very attractive, quiet grounds shaded by mango trees. 1 and 2 bedroom units (have 2 dbl + 2 sgl beds), kitchens, big refrigerators. Recommended.

Cabinas Playa Las Brisas: Two modern very pleasant bungalows are Range D. Basic rooms tbeing remodeled and may have price increase. Attractive grounds facing beach. North American owner. Recommended.

Cabinas Antonio: At north end of Jacó resort area, first cabinas you pass. Lawn, landscaping, pleasant rooms. Ground level. Shaded sitting area.

Chalets Santa Ana: New two story building across from Jacó Fiesta. No one there when we stopped. Looks OK.

El Jardin: North end of Jacó. Shaded sitting area near pool and beach. Attractive rooms. Belgian owner. Restaurant excellent, not cheap. Breakfast included. Recommended.

Cabinas Las Palmas: Large tile floored rooms, some with with 2 dbl beds, some with kitchens and laundry sinks. Lawn, landscaping with barbecue, a block from beach. Many North Americans stay here. Rate is per cabina for 1 or 2. Simple, cool, clean. On first right after you pass Cabinas Antonio at north end of Jacó.

Cabinas Heredia: Freshly painted. Bunk beds. Rooms screened on side facing landscaped yard. Some have no opening at back so no breeze through. Need fans, OK otherwise. No single rate.

At north end of town, **Hotel Pochote Grande Jacó**, 24 rooms, kitchenettes, fans, facing beach, pool, bar and restaurant. German owned. Range B. Phone 64-3236 (200 m north of El Jardin, not inspected). **Cabinas Chelo:** has basic cheap cabinas, clean, shaded, friendly. Also camping. Not inspected, but look OK if basic: **Cabinas Super Tica** near main road, **Cabinas Cindy** and **Cabinas El Bohio** on the beach. Near the south end of town, **Tropical Camping** is a private campground facing beach with showers, picnic tables and palms, inexpensive, but peace depends on crowd. **Madrigal** is a camping area facing the beach at the quieter south end. Has a restaurant. More hotels and cabinas are being built.

Price Range for 2 people in high season, before taxes—A+ Over $80/day; A $60–80, B $45–60, C $30–45, D $20–30, $E $11–20, F up to $11, U.S. $. * = Meals included.

Hotel	Address	Telephone (Fax)	No. of Rms	Pvt Bath	Hot Water	In Town	On Waterfront	Courtesy Transp	Recomm Access	Parking	Air Cond or Fan	Restaurant	Bar	Cooking Facil	Elevator	Wheelchair Acc	TV	Pool	English Spoken	Noise Level	Cleanliness	Single Rate	Range
Heredia	Playa Jacó	64-3131	12	All		•		Car, Bus											•	Exc	Vgd		C
El Jardin	Playa Jacó	64-3050	7	All	•	•	•	Car, Bus	•	•	•	•						•	Exc	Vgd		C
Cabinas Las Palmas	Apdo. 5 Playa Jacó	64-3005	14	All		•		Car, Bus	•	•								•	Exc	Exc		C
Chalets Santa Ana	Playa Jacó Garabito, Punt.	64-3233	8	All		•		Bus, Car	•	•									not inspected	not inspected		
ESTERILLOS:																						
Delfin	Apdo.37, Parrita, Puntarenas	71-1640	16	All	•		•	Car	•	•	•	•						•	•	V gd	Exc	•	B
Cabinas Los Angeles	Apdo. 5329 Esterillos, Punt.	22-8503	8	All				Car	•	•	•	•		•						Gd	Exc		C
QUEPOS:																						
Viña del Mar	Apdo. 5527 San Jose	77-0077	20	All		•	•	Bus, Car, Plane	•		•	•								Exc	V gd	•	D
Ceciliano	(1 block from Plaza), Quepos	77-0192	20	14		•		Bus, Plane	•											Exc	V gd	•	F

Esterillos

Esterillos is a seven-mile-long beach with virtually no one on it though it's less than a mile from the main highway. Note signs to the west and east ends. Be careful of rips. Good surfing, walking, horseback riding. Turtles still hatch on beach. All facilities on this beach seem priced high for what is offered, but even at the beginning of Easter Week (*semana santa*) it was quiet.

Esterillos Oeste is the northwest end of the beach, with some surf, but looks OK for strong swimmers or waders. Quiet laid back area with a few houses and several sets of cabinas. **Cabinas Fernando Mora** is new and looks basic, but OK. Have never found owner here. Bring padlock to add to theirs. **Cabinas Caletas** is too basic with bare mattresses and no breeze. Some camping on lawn with tents.

Esterillos Este:

El Delfin: Very well designed beach hotel building. Each room has balcony catching every breeze. Secluded, attractive spot.

Cabinas Los Angeles: Back road parallel to beach, too basic for Range C, no single rate. Rooms filled with 4-6 cots, bare mattresses. 2 burner stove.

Cabinas El Pelicano: Basic cabinas near beach. Refused inspection.

The costanera continues south (some still unpaved at presstime) through palm nut plantations and several villages, including Parrita, which has a beach and basic accommodations. Note that beaches near river mouths, as this is, have muddy water.

Quepos

Quepos was a banana port, but now is a marketing center and gateway to Manuel Antonio resorts, beaches and national park. Daily buses, including twice daily express buses from San Jose, and SANSA flights from San Jose reach Quepos, while local buses (6 a.m.–10 a.m.) and taxis run regularly the few miles on to Manuel Antonio. Public transportation makes a rental car unnecessary for 1-2 people.

Quepos has a beach used mostly by locals and a dock area plus budget hotels that are perhaps a better value than ones nearer the park. The town also has cantinas, and the groceries those cooking for themselves at Manuel Antonio need. A mangrove area at the north end of town has good birdwatching morning and night.

Deep-sea fishing from Quepos has grown with several operators chartering boats and selling package tours. Some run multi-day trips from Quepos to fish off Caño Island and Drake Bay for sailfish and other

species. **Sportfishing Costa Rica,** 37-8312, Fax 38-4434, and **Costa Rican Dreams,** 39-3387, Fax 39-3383.

A major development, **Pueblo,** is being built just north of Quepos and will include a hotel, golf course and condos. Started in 1991.

La Buena Nota is a beachwear shop on your left just after you cross the bridge entering Quepos from the north. Owner Anita Myketuk is a good person to ask about longer term rentals, rip currents, diving spots, guides and tours. Phone 77-0345. She's really the area's information bureau. Her shop has souvenirs and U.S. newspapers.

Soda Isabel, El Kiosko, and **Soda Ana** are all in the blocks beyond La Buena Nota on the waterfront street. Clean, inexpensive.

Viña del Mar: Hotel on right side entering Quepos from north. Faces one estuary with another across road. Simple rooms for 15 people, light, airy, with hardwood.

Ceciliano: Clean, light, hospitable budget hotel a block from SANSA office. Rooms all at ground level, Family owned and run. Recommended.

Quepos: Very clean basic rooms with fans on second floor near SANSA office. Peace Corps members use. Good value.

Manuel Antonio

The three beaches, separated by headlands, at Manuel Antonio are as beautiful as any in the world. The road ends at the south end of First Beach (Espadilla), long and open with strong rip currents. You can wade a creek, pay the admission fee at the ranger station, and walk to Second and Third Beaches inside Manuel Antonio National Park. These are more sheltered and much safer swimming. In the early morning and late afternoon here you may see 3-toed sloths, white-faced (capuchin) mon-keys, and the rare marmoset or squirrel monkey (smallest of the four kinds in Costa Rica), as well as many birds. Troops of monkeys often swing through the trees even outside the park near hotels.

Punta Catedral separates Second and Third Beaches. A nature trail leads up and around it, with fine views and good birdwatching early or late in the day. Second Beach offers good swimming and snorkeling when the waves aren't up, and Third Beach is a sheltered white sand crescent with some rocks for snorkeling. Both beaches have freshwater showers.

Park rangers sometimes lead walks on other trails open only to escort-ed groups—including to Fourth Beach which has the best snorkeling in the park, a big variety of bright fish and clear water. At park head-

Children and pelican enjoy quiet Third Beach.

quarters on Third Beach you can see exhibits of the plants and wildlife of the park and learn what may be scheduled that day.

Camping is not allowed in the park. Some accommodations are adjacent to Espadilla and others are on the hills above. You need reservations during high season, and any time you want to stay in a particular hotel. or cabina

Especially during holidays, you should be concerned about the safety of your valuables while you swim. The park entrance station may keep a day pack for you. When I've been swimming alone here on Third Beach, I've left my day pack with friendly family groups sitting nearby.

For horseback nature tours on forested trails with birds and monkeys, stopping for lunch and swimming in a secluded cove, and visiting the solar-powered lighthouse at Pt. Quepos, **Unicorn Adventures**, Apdo. 158, Quepos. Phone 77-0489 from inside Costa Rica. **Rios Tropicales** runs kayaking tours, 33-6655.

Shopping

For groceries, **Super Mas** in Quepos has what you'll need. (If you drive via the main road through Esparza, there are great fruit stands with melons along the highway. By the scenic route, Orotina is a good place to buy fruit.) Any time you go to the coast, it's worth bringing hiking food, fresh fruit and a canteen for water. There is *nothing* for sale in the park, and the nearest refreshments are nearly a mile behind you when you're on Third Beach. For beachwear, Manuel Antonio T-shirts, and other souvenirs, try **La Buena Nota** in Quepos and the gift shop in front of Mar y

Sombra Restaurant at First Beach. For Costa Rican arts and crafts, **Mamiya** above the Barba Roja has a good selection.

Restaurants

Your choices here starting from the most expensive and working down, include well-done French cuisine at **El Byblos,** fine dinners at the **Mariposa** (requires reservations 24 hours in advance—they told me the one time I tried to make reservations 4 hours ahead). Uruguayan-style beef and seafood are specialties at the **Karahé**, the **Uruguayan Steak House** (good breakfasts too). **Vela Bar** serves very good seafood and Spanish/ Costa Rican dishes. Full menu may not be available, especially in low season. The popular **Hotel Plinio** serves moderately priced Italian food and homemade bread, recommended, (breakfast and dinner, make reservations, closed Wed.). **Bahias,** south of the Plinio, dinners all year, lunch and dinner in high season, bar/restaurant with music, tropical drinks, seafood specialties. The **Barba Roja** is a popular bar/restaurant, and gathering place with North American style sandwiches, breakfast, dinners, moderately priced. **Mar Y Sombra** has good, inexpensive Costa Rican food for all 3 meals, including refreshing fruit plates after a day on the beach. **Del Mar Bar** on beach just south of Mar y Sombra serves casados, hamburgers, pizza (and rents beach chairs and sports equipment). Readers liked food at **Los Almendros.** Most are closed at least one day a week, so you have to move around.

Where to Stay

El Byblos: Deluxe cabins in forested area on uphill side of road. French owned. Fine international food in restaurant with ocean view. Breakfast and dinner included.

Mariposa: On ridge above beach with smashing views from every room including the bathrooms. Luxurious, exclusive. Price includes breakfast and dinner, but a 20% tax and service charge is additional. Credit cards not accepted. Noted for food. Adult guests only. North American owned.

Villas Nicolas: Condo units with balconies and hammocks overlooking wooded ravine and ocean. Kitchens. Each unit different, most with stairs. Friendly management. Recommended.

Colibrí: On uphill side of road 125 m from Barba Roja restaurant. Attractive, separate cabinas with kitchens, hammocks, barbecue. Pond and trees attract birds. No children under 10. Helpful manager even lends a blender! Recommended.

Costa Verde: On road before beach. Shaded porch with rocking chairs and great view, kitchen. Rate is for 1-3 people. Also has villas for 4-6.

Price Range for 2 people in high season, before taxes—A+ Over $80/day, A $60–80, B $45–60, C $30–45, D $20–30, $E $11–20, F up to $11, U.S. $. * = Meals included.

Hotel	Price Range	Single Rate	Cleanliness	Noise Level	English Spoken	Pool	TV	Wheelchair Acc	Elevator	Cooking Facil	Bar	Restaurant	Air Cond or Fan	Parking	Recomm Access	Courtesy Transp	On Waterfront	In Town	Hot Water	Pvt Bath	No. of Rms	Telephone (Fax)	Address
Quepos	F	•	Exc	V gd			•						•	•	Bus, Car, Plane			•		13	22	77-0274	Apdo. 79, Quepos
MANUEL ANTONIO:																							
El Byblos	A+	•	Exc	Exc	•	•					•	•	•	•	Plane, Car				•	All	7	77-0411 (77-0009)	Apdo. 112 Quepos
Mariposa	A+	•	Exc	Exc	•	•					•	•	•	•	Plane, Car				•	All	10	77-0355 (77-0456)	Apdo. 4, Quepos
Villas Nicolas	A+		Exc	Exc	•	•								•	Plane, Car		•		•	All	19	77-0538	Apdo. 26, Quepos
Colibri	B	•	Exc	Exc	•					•				•	Car, Plane, Bus				•	All	8	77-0432	Apdo. 94, Quepos
Costa Verde	B	•	Exc	Exc	•					•				•	Bus, Car, Plane				•	All	10	77-0584 23-7946 (23-9446)	Apdo. 6944, San Jose
El Lirio	B	•	Exc	Exc	•					•				•	Car, Bus, Plane				•	All	4	77-0403	Apdo. 123 Quepos
Karahé	B		V gd	V gd	•	•					•	•	•	•	Car, Bus, Plane				•	All	10	77-0170 (77-0152)	Apdo. 100-6350 Quepos

El Lirio: Small, Canadian-owned hotel with big, light rooms, some with queen-sized beds. Ample continental breakfast included. Shady, attractive grounds, on uphill side of main road. Hospitable. Short walk to restaurants. Recommended.

Apartotel Karahé: Cabinas on hill above highway with path down to beach. Cooking facilities, hammock in private area with view, attractive stonework. Stair climb to cabinas. Rate is per cabina whether 1 or 2 people (can be crowded with 4). Weekly, monthly rates especially in off season. Manager helpful, fluent English. Good food. Recommended.

La Quinta: On hilltop north of Manuel Antonio, it has deluxe separate cabinas with balconies, fine view, screens and fans. Some have kitchen. Can serve breakfast. Readers like. Recommended.

Los Mogotes: On right side of road, with view over jungle to sea. Light and airy. Quieter rooms on second floor have no one walking overhead. Rate includes full breakfast.

Cabinas Espadillas: Modern, ground level buildings with little shade on road uphill to left as you approach park (across from Vela Bar). Large room with 1 dbl and 2 bunk beds. Shaded sitting area. Kitchen has 2 burner plate, refrigerator, sink.

La Arboleda: Attractive stone cabinas on hillside above beach, with path down. Covered sitting area. 2 restaurants. Owner speaks German. Tape recorders, radios not allowed. Also basic rooms with shared bath next to bar/restaurant at beach level. Readers report overbooking.

Cabinas Los Almendros: Comfortable, modern ground-floor rooms with sitting area, on road uphill from beach. In high season, Dec. through Easter, rate is per room. Low season, Range E. Recommended.

Plinio: On hill north of beach. Porch with hammocks and view over beach. Well known and recommended for food, music, talk. Friendly, attracts young international group. Third floor rooms simple, pleasant.

Vela Bar: Large cool rooms in Spanish style wood and tile with safety boxes, on road uphill above First Beach. Shaded porch with hammock. One house has kitchen. Hospitable manager. Good food. Recommended.

Cabinas Divisamar: Friendly place caters to families, can be noisy when full. Rooms have 2 dbl beds. Courtesy transportation to beach. Boat tours to offshore islands. Can arrange horses, guide. Doesn't take credit cards.

Costa Linda: Basic simple rooms, screened but without fans. Hostel style.

Hotel Manuel Antonio: Pleasant, airy rooms. Upstairs balcony and lounge, not deluxe but nice use of wood. At end of road next to park,

Price Range for 2 people in high season, before taxes—A+ Over $80/day, A $60–80, B $45–60, C $30–45, D $20–30, $E $11–20, F up to $11, U.S. $. * = Meals included.

Hotel	Address	Telephone (Fax)	No. of Rms	Pvt Bath	Hot Water	In Town	On Waterfront	Courtesy Transp	Recomm Access	Parking	Air Cond or Fan	Restaurant	Bar	Cooking Facil	Elevator	Wheelchair Acc	TV	Pool	English Spoken	Noise Level	Cleanliness	Single Rate Range
La Quinta	Apdo. 76, Quepos	77-0434	4	All	•			Car Bus Plane	•	•				•			•	•	Exc	Exc		B
Los Mogotes	Apdo. 120, Quepos	77-0582 (Fax same)	5	All	•			Car Bus Plane	•	•								•	Exc	Exc	•	B
Cabinas Espadillas	Playa Manuel Antonio, Quepos	77-0416	16	All	•		•	Car Bus Plane	•	•				•					Exc	Exc	•	C
La Arboleda	Apdo. 55, Quepos	77-0414 (Fax same)	36	All	•			Car Bus Plane	•	•	•	•						•	Exc	Exc	•	C
Los Almendros	Apdo. 68, Quepos	77-0225	15	All	•			Car Bus Plane	•	•	•	•							Exc	Exc		D
Plinio	Apdo. 71, Quepos	77-0055	8	All				Car Bus Plane	•	•	•	•						•	Exc	Vgd	•	D
Vela Bar	Apdo. 13, Quepos	77-0413	6	All	•			Car Bus Plane	•	•	•	•				•	•	•	Exc	Exc	•	D

handy to better swimming beaches. (Closed at presstime.)

Costa Linda: Basic simple rooms, screened but without fans. Hostel style.

Cabinas Manuel Antonio: Simple rooms with bunk beds, single story with sitting area in front, on beach. Popular with young set. Very good value for 4-5 people per cabina. Adjacent to national park at end of road.

Cabinas Pedro Miguel: Basic, clean, quiet rooms with effective fan on top of hill before reaching Manuel Antonio.

Cabinas Ramirez: Formerly called Mar y Sombra (still name of restaurant in front). Pleasant, ground-level rooms, some on beach, some in building behind. Price higher with fans which most people will need. Shaded sitting area for each room and on grounds fronting beach.

Visitor stalks a butterfly with her camera at Third Beach.

Bungalows: Bamboo huts near Cabinas Ramirez on beach with 2 bunks. Small, very basic shelters with showers, toilets in separate building.

Condos: there are several condos here and more will be built at the big resort development just north of Quepos. Presently, besides the Villas Nicolas in our hotel list, John Biesanz has 2-bedroom units with space for 4 or more in each, on the ridge near the Mariposa Hotel. A tram hauls baggage up from the road. Modern, attractive, hot water, fully furnished, including linen. *Part* of the view is on our back cover. Good birding and a quiet cove in walking distance. Range A+. Low season and long term rates. Apdo. 47, 6100 Ciudad Colón, San Jose. Phone 49-1507. You could also leave a message for Jesse at this number for the beach shelters listed below or for horseback tours.

Price Range for 2 people in high season, before taxes—A+ Over $80/day, A $60–80, B $45–60, C $30–45, D $20–30, $E $11–20, F up to $11, U.S. $. * = Meals included.

Hotel	Address	Telephone (Fax)	No. of Rms	Pvt Bath	Range	Single Rate	Cleanliness	Noise Level	English Spoken	Pool	Bar	Restaurant	Air Cond or Fan	Parking	Recomm Access	In Town	Hot Water
Cabinas Divisamar	Apdo. 7857 San Jose	77-0371 25-0785 (77-0525)	9	All	D	•	Exc	Exc	Exc	•	•	•	•	•	Car Bus Plane		
Manuel Antonio	Apdo. 88, Quepos	77-0290	5	All	E		Gd	Exc	Gd		•	•	•	•	Car Bus Plane		
Costa Linda	Apdo. 62, Quepos	77-0307	11	2	F		Exc	Exc	Exc						Car Bus Plane	•	
Cabinas Manuel Antonio	Playa Manuel Antonio, Quepos	77-0212	18	All	F		Gd	V gd	Gd						Bus Car Plane	•	
Cabinas Pedro Miguel	Carretara Manuel Antonio	77-0035	5	All	F		Exc	Exc	Exc					•	Car Bus Plane		
Cabinas Ramirez	Playa Manuel Antonio, Quepos	77-0510 77-0003	16	All	F		Exc	V gd	Exc					•	Car Bus Plane		
PLAYA DOMINICAL: Cabinas Punta Dominical	Apdo. 176-8000 San Isidro de General	71-0866 25-5328	4	All	D	•	Exc	Exc	Exc		•	•	•	•	Car	•	•

El Salto: Not inspected. Cabinas on hill south of Hotel Plinio, 60 acres with forest trails, pool, gardens, bar/restaurant. English spoken. Range A. Apdo. 119, Quepos. (phone 77-0130, fax 41-2938)

For rustic living away from it all on a quiet cove just north of Manuel Antonio, you can call Jesse Biesanz at 77-04-89 from inside Costa Rica. He has two cabins without electricity but with a caretaker, birds, monkeys and good snorkeling. We did not inspect. If you can live primitively, this is one way to beat the crowds on weekends.

White-face or capuchin monkeys swing through the trees in Manuel Antonio Park.

Driftwood "animal" gazes out to sea on Third Beach.

Playa Dominical

Driving south from Quepos 45 km on the costanera, good gravel, (or 36 km west of San Isidro, paved) you reach Playa Dominical. This long beach has surf and rips for most of its several miles. At low tide *only*, the reefs north and south of Punta Dominical are good for tidepooling, and the north side offers good swimming. Watch the tide here as the reefed areas are dangerous when the tide is up. The beach is never crowded.

Cabinas Punta Dominical: 4 km south of the village. Separate, very attractive screened wood cabinas with balcony, hammock and smashing view from clifftop over beach. Great spot to read or write, good breeze. Bar, restaurant, fishing, horseback riding. Good value. Recommended.

There are several sets of cabinas in the village. **Cabinas Coco,** 71-2555, **Cabinas Narayit,** 71-1878, and **Cabinas Wili** are clean, Range E/F. The latter two have private bath. Horses can be rented to ride on the beach. Bring fruit with you. Buses run here from Quepos, and buses from San Isidro to Uvita, the next coastal village to the south, stop at Dominical.

Golfito

Golfito is a small town filling a narrow strip of land several miles long between a jungle-covered cliff and the Golfo Dulce. It was a busy banana port where United Fruit Company loaded fruit hauled by train from its plantations, until 1985 when the company left due to strikes and the economics of the banana trade, including Costa Rica's export tax on bananas (while competing countries subsidized theirs).

Near the docks at Golfito's north end, the flat area widens out. Here, in an effort to provide an economy for the town, the Costa Rican government in 1990 built a mall with shops and opened a "duty-free" port where Costa Ricans can buy $400 worth of imported goods taxed much less than standard duties every 6 months. Electrical appliances are a big attraction. Tourists can buy here too, but won't find great bargains. Besides the new freeport, at the north end of town you'll find the landscaped former banana company housing, a mangrove lagoon, the airport and the overgrown golf course.

The road to Golfito is good. It's a 7-hour bus ride over the scenic Talamanca Mountains on the Interamerican Highway or a half-hour flight on SANSA.(Monday through Saturday, twice some days, about $20, fully paid reservations essential.) Riding the bus down and flying back can make a good loop trip. While Golfito is not a primary destination, if you have time, coming here adds another dimension to what you'll see of Costa Rica. The climate is humid and you'll probably want a fan at night.

There are comfortable but no deluxe hotels in town. Golfito is crowded with traffic and, since the freeport opened, suffers a bad shortage of hotels and restaurants. More are being built, but with only one street running the full length of town, traffic will stay congested. Golfito has local buses and taxis, including jeeps. The taxis are "collectivos," picking up and dropping off passengers along the way.

Freeport buildings at north end of town opened in 1990.

Birdwatching, especially north of town, is excellent. Most hotels can arrange boats, fishing, snorkeling, or visits to nearby fincas with wildlife. A good gravel road leads up from the first soccer field about 7 km to a microwave station on the ridge above town, a forest reserve protecting Golfito's water supply. High enough to be cooler than town, and covered with flowering trees, vines, and tree ferns, the ridge offers beautiful views over the gulf and south to coastal bays and islands. Many birds, including toucans, live in this forest. If you don't want to hike up from town, a taxi could give you a tour up there and, if you like, drop you off to hike back down whatever distance you choose. The early morning quiet breeze and bird calls are unforgettable.

Restaurants—the restaurant at Las Gaviotas is the best I've found in Golfito, moderately priced. The small restaurant under the Hotel Golfito and the service station in town serves good tipico food at budget prices, and is OK for breakfast. You can hire a skiff at the municipal dock to run to the **Jungle Club** on the shore across from Las Gaviotas; readers like.

Cabinas at Las Gaviotas.

Where To Stay

Hotel Las Gaviotas: Very pleasant landscaped grounds with orchids overlooking bay. Cabinas have small patio. Excellent bar/restaurant. Offers facilities, including laundry, to yachts using its dock and moorage. Best in town and a good value. Recommended.

Costa Rica Surf: Older hotel above central district. Some rooms have skylight instead of windows. Upstairs lounge. North American owned. Can arrange surfing, nature trips, snorkeling, fill air tanks.

Golfito: Clean, budget hotel on bay across from service station halfway through town. Government employees stay here. Waterfront rooms preferred. Good restaurant downstairs. Very good value. Recommended.

Visiting yachts moored at Las Gaviotas marina.

Hotel	Address	Telephone (Fax)	No. of Rms	Pvt Bath	Hot Water	In Town	On Waterfront	Courtesy Transp	Recomm Access	Parking	Air Cond or Fan	Restaurant	Bar	Cooking Facil	Elevator	Wheelchair Acc	TV	Pool	English Spoken	Noise Level	Cleanliness	Single Rate Range
GOLFITO:																						
Las Gaviotas	Apdo. 12-8201 Golfito	75-0062 (75-0544)	12	All	•	•		Car Bus Plane	•	•	•	•	•				•	•	Exc	Exc	•	C
Costa Rica Surf	Apdo. 7-8201, Golfito	75-0034	20	15	•			Car Plane Bus	•	•	•	•	•					•	Fair	Gd	•	D
Golfito	Golfito	75-0047	16	All	•	•		Plane Car Bus	•	•	•								V gd	Exc		E
Delfina	Golfito	75-0043	26	7	•	•		Plane Car Bus	•	•									Gd	V gd		F

Price Range for 2 people in high season, before taxes—A+ Over $80/day, A $60–80, B $45–60, C $30–45, D $20–30, $E $11–20, F up to $11, U.S. $. * = Meals included.

Cabinas Delfina: Two styles—basic rooms with partitions not all the way up, shared bath. More modern rooms with bath (cold water), ones facing away from street are quiet, OK

Outlying From Golfito, The Osa Peninsula

Across the bay from Golfito is **Captain Tom's Place,** where Captain Tom and his wife serve meals, allow camping and will rent tents, and rent rooms (about $10/person) in a trawler drawn up on the beach. Basic, clean, friendly, and memorable.

A short boat ride from Golfito is **Golfito Sailfish Rancho,** under same ownership as Parismina Sailfish Rancho. Package tours start in San Jose, include hotel, transportation, lodge with meals, open bar, boat and guide for marlin, sailfish, roosterfish. Tours available combined with their other lodge to fish both coasts in a single trip! On trip of 3 or more days they guarantee each angler a sailfish or marlin–or a free return trip! P. O. Box 290190, San Antonio, TX. 78280. 1-800-531-7232. In C. R. phone 35-7766.

North of Golfito is **Rainbow Adventures Lodge.** Very comfortable lodge (includes third floor penthouse) and cabinas on Playa Cativo, a secluded beach with 1000 acres of rainforest. Range A includes all meals for 2 people and round trip by boat from Golfito. For 3 or 4 people in 2 bed-room cabinas, they only add $20 for each add'l. person, including meals. Reduced rate for children, under 4 free. Guided walk included. Guide for more extensive hikes, fishing, snorkeling and water skiing available. Quiet, get away from the world place with good food. In U.S. (503) 690-7750. Rainbow Adventures, Apdo. 63, Golfito. Phone 75-0220 on Mondays and Fridays 8-9 a.m. CST when lodge manager is in Golfito.

Tiskita Lodge, on a cliff-top over the ocean south of Golfito by jeep taxi or plane, is described in Nature Lodges, page 80.

An air taxi, **Aeronaves de Costa Rica,** 75-0278, flies from Golfito pro-viding the shortest air charters (5 passenger plane for about $110) into **Corcovado National Park.** A launch runs from town daily at noon to the Osa Peninsula at Puerto Jiménez, which has several basic cabinas and the park's main office 78-5036). Independent travelers not in tour groups must check in with them or with national park headquarters in San Jose for permission to visit. Getting to the park from there involves hitchhiking plus at least a day of hot, humid hiking uphill or around the south end on beaches. You can get to Puerto Jiménez by road, and buses run there from San Isidro de El General and Ciudad Nielly. Chartered skiffs to the park from Sierpe running around the peninsula from the outside have to go over the Sierpe River bar, a very dangerous spot unless the tide is right and the operator skillful. Your best choices are flying into park research center at Sirena in a chartered plane, flying to Carate to **Costa Rica Expeditions'** new tent camp, or going in by boat or horse from **Drake Bay Wilderness Lodge, La Paloma,** or **Marenco Biological Station** (all reached by boat or plane) on the north side of the Osa Peninsula. See our Nature Lodges chapter, page 80.

Wild beach near Llorona in Corcovado Nat'l. Park.

Ferry crossing Río Coto.

Playa Zancudo.

Zancudo

Playa Zancudo is a long black sand beach south of Golfito with good fishing, fine swimming and easy surf. It's a quiet place, especially in the rainy season. Readers liked: **Los Almendros**, cabinas with private bath, restaurant, Range E. 75-0515. Has charter fishing boats. **Sol y Mar**, Has suites, rooms with bath (Range E), restaurant. 75-0353. Friendly, quiet, south of Zancudo, picks up guests by boat in Golfito. Other places, some with private bath, Range F, are **Cabinas Zancudo**, 77-3027, **El Coquito**, and **Rio Mar**, near river as well as beach. More are being built.

You can get there by bus or jeep taxi in about 2 1/2 hours when the road isn't bad. Several cabina owners will pick you up by boat in Golfito. A public boat leaves Golfito's city dock at noon on Mondays and Fridays. Local boats are available other days, and boats are available in Zancudo for the return.

Pavones

Pavones, 2 1/2 hours by bus (2 p.m. near Golfito's city dock) or jeep taxi south of Golfito when the road is "good", offers world class surfing on unbelievably *long* waves. During the rainy season the surf is best, but the road isn't good. Some surfers bring tents and camp on the point. **Bahia Pavones Lodge** has screened rooms and cabinas for about $20 per person, including breakfast. Reserve at Tsunami Surf Shop in San Jose's eastern suburb, Los Yoses, Ave. Central. Basic rooms are available near the cantina and pulpería.

Note: There have been problems, including violence and drug trafficking, between landowners and squatters here. Police were stationed in Pavones but may not be permanent. Heed local warnings (leave or stay away if that's prudent) and don't get involved.

215

Northwest Region
(Nicoya Peninsula, Guanacaste, Monteverde)

This region has the majority of Costa Rica's beach resorts, several of its volcanoes, and the biological preserve of Monteverde. Access by air is to several resort strips or the regional airport at Liberia.

A big car ferry crosses the Gulf of Nicoya from Puntarenas twice a day to Naranjo and a very small one shuttles many times a day across the head of the gulf near the mouth of the Tempisque River. A bridge with new access roads is planned to replace the Tempisque ferry, shortening the driving time from San Jose to Nicoya and many beaches. The Interamerican Highway runs from San Jose down to the western coastal plain and north through Liberia to the Nicaraguan border.

A good two-lane road, mostly paved, leads from the Puntarenas ferry terminal north through Jicaral, Nicoya, and Santa Cruz to Liberia. A bus meets the ferry and runs north, though you may have to change buses at Santa Cruz. There is no bus service south or west from this terminal.

Smaller roads, some of them 4-wheel drive all year and some only during the wet season, run from these towns out to the coast. All-weather roads run with bus service to Playas Tamarindo and Coco. While there's daily bus service to Nosara and Sámara, it can be an adventure in the wet season. Some buses go to the coast and stay overnight, coming back the next day. Their main purpose is to let the coastal people come to town to shop. It's a fascinating area, and bus riding is one way to see it cheaply. Some resorts have transportation all the way from San Jose, while others will pick you up at the local airstrip or at the Liberia or Tamarindo airports, reached by SANSA several days a week. If there are several of you, or you're going to be on the coast for some days, a taxi ride from Liberia or Santa Cruz may be reasonable.

Santa Cruz, Nicoya and Liberia have festivals, rodeos and bullfights that are worth a trip from San Jose or a day in town from the beach. Remember that in Costa Rican bullfights, the bull chases the people in the arena and isn't killed. During festivals, you'll need hotel reservations, and your best chance of getting them is in Liberia, which has several large reasonably-priced hotels. It's centrally located for a wide range of interesting day trips to mountains, beaches, rodeos, and national parks.

Guanacaste is the driest part of Costa Rica and most cattle land is burned off during the dry season, producing smoke and dust, especially in March and April. The rainy season, however, isn't very rainy here, and I *like* November, when the grass is green, hotels and rental cars still

have off-season rates, there are no crowds, and the frequent high overcast somewhat limits heat and sunburn.

ICT is pushing for more road signs and paving to tourist areas, but
particularly around Sámara, Garza, and Nosara, the dirt tracks are presently quite anonymous and easy to get lost on, especially after dark. Do
fill a car with gas in the main towns as most beach resorts don't have
service stations.

Most villages have basic rooms or hotels at rock-bottom prices, generally
cleaner than you'd expect from the outside, but possibly at a lower level
than you'll want unless you're on a bare survival budget. There are some
of the "we'd rather sleep on the beach" sort, though few of those are
listed here. I once stayed in a basic hotel at Nosara when daylight ran out
and there was a closed hotel nearby to inspect the next day. The room
was clean, but I had to be careful not to trip over the black pig in the
backyard en route to the privy in the dark! Remember a flashlight. Costa
Rica has hundreds of hotels far above that level, but it has the full range.

On the coast, you'll want a building carefully aligned with the pre-
vailing breeze or a fan, often more comfortable than air conditioning,
and considerably more common. Starting with the southern end of the
Nicoya Peninsula, actually in Puntarenas province, we'll work our way
generally north, covering Monteverde and Lake Arenal after the west.
Remember the 20-30% low season discounts offered by most hotels.

South Coast of the Nicoya Peninsula

Playa Naranjo is near the ferry terminal, and there are several other
beaches, including one at Bahia Gigante. In the order you come to them:

De Paso: up hill and to right from terminal. Clean, modern, large pool.
Breakfast included. Taxis meeting ferry try for longer fares to Nicoya.

Playa Oasis Pacifico: On your left as the ferry from Puntarenas nears the
dock. Courtesy transfer from ferry. Attractive, landscaped grounds facing gravel beach with shells. Waterfront bar, music, dancing. Screened
open-air dining room, thatched shelters with hammocks, large pool,
wading pool, tennis. Adjacent woods for birdwatchers. Guided fishing
(bait, tackle, ice included) and horses available. Boat moorage. VHF
channel 68. Day rate for use of pool and other facilities while waiting for
ferry, $3. Reserved room is free any day the sun doesn't shine!

Bahia Gigante: Large rooms with dbl and sgl beds in each. Shaded walk
with hammocks. Hotel is near the road, a short walk through trees and
brush with howler monkeys and other wildlife. The sheltered, secluded
bay has good snorkeling, location for launching kayaks to paddle to

Bahia Gigante. Hotel is left of photo.

nearby islands. Boat tours available to Tortuga Island. Nature trails. Canadian -owned. In Canada phone (604) 926-8087. Recommended.

Paquera is the first village southwest of Naranjo and the port for the passenger launch from Puntarenas, not a resort but a center for the area. **Soda Crimaya** serves excellent tipico food. Nearby, **Cabinas Ginana**, 61-1444, ext. 119, is probably the best in town. **Cabinas Rosita**, 61-1444, ext. 102, on the west side of town, is small and attractive.

Curú National Wildlife Refuge is on a private farm with a sheltered, curved beach good for swimming and snorkeling, facing nearby islands off-shore. Turtles nest on the beach. Monkeys, snakes, mountain lions, and ocelots are among the wildlife, and 115 species of birds are recorded. Nature trails cross the reserve. (Bring insect repellant.) It's 7 km south of Paquera, behind an unmarked gate that's locked if you're not with an organized tour group, or have not called ahead. Phone: 61-6392 or 61-2392 for permission.

Playa Tambor

Playa Tambor is a calm black sand beach with safe swimming on the southeast coast of the Nicoya Peninsula. You can drive from the Puntarenas ferry on good gravel road or ride the bus that meets the Paquera ferry and goes to Cóbano. Charter planes land on the lawn airstrip at the hacienda. It is a quiet area now. **Soda Restaurant Cristina** is clean, attractive, serves good food. Open 7 a.m.–8 p.m.

La Hacienda: Deluxe hotel in rustic style on working cattle ranch with

Price Range for 2 people in high season, before taxes—A+ Over $80/day, A $60–80, B $45–60, C $30–45, D $20–30, $E $11–20, F up to $11, U.S. $. * = Meals included.

Hotel	Address	Telephone (Fax)	No. of Rms	Pvt Bath	Hot Water	In Town	On Waterfront	Courtesy Transp	Recomm Access	Parking	Air Cond or Fan	Restaurant	Bar	Cooking Facil	Elevator	Wheelchair Acc	TV	Pool	English Spoken	Noise Level	Cleanliness	Single Rate	Range
PLAYA NARANJO:																							
De Paso	Apdo. 2320-2120 Calle Blanco	61-2610	14	10					Car Bus Ferry	•	•	•					•			V gd	Exc	•	E
Oasis del Pacifico	Apdo. 200-5400 Puntarenas	61-1555 (22-8385)	36	All		•			Car Bus Ferry	•	•	•					•			Exc	Exc	•	C
Bahia Gigante	Apdo. 1866-1000 San Jose	22-9557 61-2442 US (800) 331-0485	11 rms 2 cnd	All					Car Bus Ferry	•	•	•					•		•	Exc	Exc		E
PLAYA TAMBOR:																							
Tango Mar	Apdo. 3877-1000 San Jose	23-1864 61-2798 (55-2697)	10	All		•	•		Plane Car	•	•	•	•	•			•	•	•	Exc	Exc		A+
La Hacienda	Apdo. 458-1150 La Uruca San Jose	61-2980 (20-2036)	25	All		•	•		Plane Car Bus	•	•	•					•	•	•	Exc	Exc	•	B
Dos Logartos	Apdo. 5602-1000 San Jose	61-1122 Ext. 236	26	4	•	•			Plane Bus Car	•	•									V gd	V gd	•	E

airstrip. Shaded veranda overlooks corrals. Beautifully landscaped, sepa-rated thatched bungalows besides rooms. Attractive pool. Excellent food. Recommended. Enjoy it now before the Spanish company that recently bought it builds 4 planned hotels with 1000 rooms!

Dos Logartos: Rustic, simple hotel on landscaped grounds facing beach. Rooms with bath Range E. Quiet mid-week.

Southwest of Playa Tambor:

Tango Mar: Attractive, well designed new resort with airstrip and 9-hole golf course, on quiet beach. Horses, surfboards, snorkeling gear, golfcarts for rent. Sailing (Hobie Cats), windsurfing. Fishing for sailfish, marlin. Very good restaurant. Hotel rooms and 1-2 bedroom cottages, condos on wooded hillside overlooking beach. Well-screened units have balconies with hammocks. Sells memberships. Recommended.

Playa Montezuma.

Playa Montezuma

 Playa Montezuma is a group of Costa Rica's nicest beaches, reachable by taxi from Cóbano if the Paquera bus doesn't come all the way, or by car. This is as far as you should go with 2-wheel drive (may be farther if much recent rain on the muddy hill leading down to the beach). You can walk or ride rental horses along the beaches in either direction, even as far as Cabo Blanco Biological Reserve, 9 km south Good snorkeling in rocky coves south of the village. South of the village 1 km, the road crosses a creek worth walking up to see a beautiful waterfall and pool. Do watch for snakes—we saw a fer-de-lance run over on the road though we didn't see any in the woods.

You can walk beaches for miles to the north and find good camping with fresh water about half an hour from the village. Monkeys are the camp robbers here. Swimming can be quiet or rough, depending on the tide and wind.

Restaurants

El Sano Banano is a natural food restaurant with non-greasy food, a real find at a tropical beach. Has yogurt and granola breakfast, vegetarian menu, bag lunches, safe water, fruit, refrescos. Some nights they show nature films (small admission charge). Also have cabinas.

If you see children carrying live lobsters and fresh-caught fish in from that direction, you might follow along to see which restaurant buys them while you decide where to have dinner! The lobster dinner we had at **Chico's Bar and Restaurant** (location of the village message phone, 61-2472) was great. **Hotel Moctezuma** has good food including breakfast. **Montezuma Pacific** serves Italian food including pizza, seafood.

Where to Stay

Electricity recently reached the village and more cabinas are being built, some around the point south Rooms range from budget to basic, none deluxe, appealing generally to a younger crowd and families who don't require luxury. Groups leaving at 4-5 a.m. to catch the Paquera launch can make early morning sleeping difficult in the hotels. Basic cabinas that cost 500 colones/person in high season may be 300 colones in low season. Both rates will probably rise. Holidays can be busy, so you should call for reservations.

Cabinas Mar y Cielo: Attractive rooms on beach with balcony and shaded sitting area. Rooms have 1 dbl and several sgl beds. Ask for upstairs rooms for most breeze. Recommended.

Casa de Huespedes Alfaro: South of village center. Rate per room, pvt. or shared bath. Better rooms are large, have 1 dbl and 2 sgl beds.

Hotel Moctezuma: Upper level sitting area with hammocks. Most rooms have 1 dbl and several sgl beds. Portable fans. Rooms on ocean side have breeze. New building across street doesn't have view but is quieter.

Cabinas Karen: Basic clean rooms in white house next door to Sano Banano. Light and clean, have outlet in room so you could bring fan. Bath in separate building, laundry sink, cooking facilities. *Note:* Owner Karen Wessberg has a nature reserve and farm, 170 acres, a mile walk

Price Range for 2 people in high season, before taxes—A+ Over $80/day, A $60–80, B $45–60, C $30–45, D $20–30, $E $11–20, F up to $11, U.S. $. * = Meals included.

PLAYA MONTEZUMA:

Attribute	Cabinas Mar y Cielo	Casa de Huespedes Alfaro	Moctezuma	Cabinas Karen	Cabinas Las Praderas	Cabinas Lucy	Casa Blanca	Montezuma Pacific
Range	E	E	E	F	F	F	F	D
Single Rate				•	•	•	•	
Cleanliness	V gd	Exc	V gd	Exc	Exc	Exc	V gd	V gd
Noise Level	Exc	V gd	Exc	V gd	V gd	V gd	V gd	V gd
English Spoken								
Pool	•	•		•				
TV								
Wheelchair Acc								
Elevator								
Cooking Facil								
Bar								
Restaurant	•		•					
Air Cond or Fan	•	•	•					•
Parking	•	•	•			•	•	•
Recomm Access	Car / Taxi	Car / Taxi	Car / Taxi	Car / Taxi	Car / Taxi	Car / Taxi	Car / Taxi	Car / Bus
Courtesy Transp								
On Waterfront								
In Town	•		•			•		
Hot Water	•	•	•	•	•	•	•	
Pvt Bath	All	6	10	All				•
No. of Rms	8+ hs	10	19	6	4	9	3	7
Telephone (Fax)	61-2472	61-1122 Ext. 259	61-2472	61-2472 (message)	61-1122 Ext. 284	61-1122 Ext. 273	61-1122 Ext. 284	37-2518 61-1122 Ext. 200 (37-2547)
Address	536 Cóbano Puntarenas	Oscar Alfaro Montezuma, Cóbano, Punt.	Montezuma, Cóbano, Punt.	Montezuma, Cóbano, Punt.	Montezuma, Cóbano, Punt.	Montezuma, Cóbano, Punt.	Montezuma, Cóbano, Punt.	Apdo. 496-3000 Heredia

from the village. Attractive simple cabins, no electricity, face the beach, have kitchen facilities. White-faced and howler monkeys and agoutis are there—an idyllic retreat for those into simple living. Range F. Karen and her late husband, Nils Olaf Wessberg, saved Cabo Blanco Reserve before Costa Rica's park system was established.

Cabinas Las Praderas: Cinder block buildings with sitting area above town center. Rooms are simple, have 1 dbl or 1-4 sgl beds.

Cabinas Lucy: South of town center, in attractive 2 story, friendly place. Small unscreened rooms, but light and airy, overlooking rocky beach. Waves are the main sound here. Very good value, especially for two.

Casa Blanca: White house as you enter village. Upper two rooms have roofed porch with fan. No fans in rooms. Unscreened window openings with shutters.

Montezuma Pacific: New units in 2 story building. Has balconies on both floors, common room, air conditioning.

The road to Cabo Blanco Reserve becomes a single track crossing a stream. En route are: **Restaurant El Ancla De Oro** with basic rooms, outside bathroom and laundry sink, camping, boat, horses. **Pension Arenas** has rooms, restaurant, camping on shaded lawn overlooking beach. **Restaurant Cabuya** (only 2.5 km from reserve), has rooms, Range F, horses. 61-1122, ext. 201. Building cabinas.

Cabo Blanco Wildlife Reserve

Established as a strict nature reserve, the nearly 3000 acres on the cape until recently required an advance permit from the park service in San Jose for entry. Now you can reach it by horse, car (4-wheel drive recommended) or on foot from Montezuma (parking the former two at the entrance), pay a 100 colon entrance fee at the visitor center, and hike its trails, open 8-4. The visitor center has exhibits of the biology and prehistoric Indian residents. Monkeys and seabirds as well as other forest creatures are easy to see here. These trails offer the easiest wildlife viewing I've seen in a low rainfall setting. If you hike out on the trail and want to come back by beach to the visitor center, you need low tide. Swimming is allowed, but no snorkeling gear (rangers say it saves arguing about lobster and coral poaching). Picnic facilities. You can also hike in from Mal País, paying at the ranger station just inside that entrance.

Mal País

Mal País is about as far as you can go in Costa Rica, 4-wheel drive most of the year from Cóbano due to a stream crossing. It's a quiet, tipico village with a miles-long light sand beach and surf extending north from Cabo Blanco. Oxcarts and horses are the main local transport. From the village you can walk or ride horses 4 km to Cabo Blanco Reserve. The ranger station just inside can sell you the daily permit, $1. Beaches on this side of the point are the best in the reserve. Surfing, especially at Playa Hermosa 10 km north, snorkeling and tidepooling near the restaurant, and riding on the beach are recommended.

Restaurante Mar Azul: Hospitable owner Otto Angulo has 8 new, simple cabinas, with 2 beds each. Shared bath. Trees shade hammocks and beach chairs. Tipico meals. Range E/F. Otto Angulo, Mal País de Cóbano, Puntarenas. Phone 61-1122, extension 203. Can arrange horses.

Driving north from Cóbano up the coast to Playa Carrillo and Sámara is possible in dry season with 4-wheel drive and some Spanish for asking directions, about 6 hours if you don't get lost and the road is entirely passable. Cabinas at Playa San Miguel north of Punta Coyote are less than basic—thatch with resident bugs and a two inch crawl space under the ground level door for *anything* (midnight scratching noise on floor was land crab). Shared toilets had been shared for years since cleaning. The jeep's alternator went out after dark so we had no choice.

North from the Puntarenas ferry:

Guamalé: In village of Jicaral across from back of church, first village north of ferry. Not resort area, but budget travelers could need a night here to make ferry schedule. Clean, with cold water, and has small, clean tipico restaurant.

Ox cart, often with auto tires, is still working transportation in rural Costa Rica.

Nicoya

Nicoya is a government and marketing center for the southern peninsula and has a colonial church built in 1644, being restored, open 8-12 and 2-6 every day except Sun. and Wed. A museum in the church has pre-Columbian artifacts. Nicoya is your last chance for gas and most groceries if you're headed west to beaches.

Many people here are Chorotega Indians, some working on cattle haciendas or rice fincas. In the villages of Guaitil and San Vicente, 19 and 21 km northeast of Nicoya respectively, men and women make Chortegan natural red clay pottery without potter's wheel or added colors. They use the old patterns and create new ones. In both villages there's a shop selling their work and more is sold from private houses in the villages. Peace Corp volunteers are helping with organization and marketing. The villagers are friendly and glad to show you what they do as well as the much greater selection available here than in San Jose.

Workers rake salt in evaporation ponds near Nicoya.

Where To Stay

Curime: The only resort hotel in town is actually a set of cabinas for 4 on landscaped grounds outside of town—well done. Each has 2 single and 1 double bed, sitting room, bar, refrigerator. Rate is for each cabina. Large pool. TV.

Jenny: Large open style. TV in rooms; cold water, but very good value. Fenced parking. Ask for demo of air conditioning.

Cabinas Loma Bonita: As you enter Nicoya, on left, above level of road. Shaded parking. Basic but may be quietest in town.

Price Range for 2 people in high season, before taxes—A+ Over $80/day, A $60–80, B $45–60, C $30–45, D $20–30, $E $11–20, F up to $11, U.S. $. * = Meals included.

Hotel	Address	Telephone (Fax)	No. of Rms	Pvt Bath	Hot Water	In Town	On Waterfront	Courtesy Transp	Recomm Access	Parking	Air Cond or Fan	Restaurant	Bar	Cooking Facil	Elevator	Wheelchair Acc	TV	Pool	English Spoken	Noise Level	Cleanliness	Single Rate	Range
MAL PAÍS: Restaurante Mar Azul	Mal Pais, Punt.	61-1122 Ext. 203	8				•	Car Jeep Taxi	•		•	•	•							V gd	Exc	•	F
JICARAL: Guamalé	Jicaral, Punt.	64-0073	13	6		•		Car Bus	•	•	•	•	•							V gd	V gd		E
NICOYA: Curime	Apdo. 51, Nicoya	68-5269	20	All	•	•		Car Bus	•	•	•	•	•					•		V gd	Exc		C
Jenny	50 N. Repetidora Columbia, Nicoya	68-5050	24	All		•		Car Bus	•	•	•									Exc	Exc		D
Cabinas Loma Bonita	Nicoya	68-5269	11	All		•		Car Bus	•	•	•	•	•							V gd	V gd		E
Chorotega	Chorotega, Nicoya	68-5245	24	All		•		Car Bus		•	•									Exc	Exc		E
Las Tinajas	Nicoya	68-5081	20	All		•		Car Bus	•	•	•	•								Exc	Exc		E

Chorotega: Simple rooms with tile floors. Back rooms open to court, light and airy. Good value at this level.

Las Tinajas: Rooms larger than most. Quieter at back away from bus station. Enclosed parking behind. Hospitable manager speaks no English. Recommended at this level.

Cattle hacienda and beach south of Playa Carillo.

Playas Carrillo, Sámara, Garza, and Nosara

These are beautiful, light sand beaches reached from Nicoya, listed here from south to north. Playa Carrillo is undeveloped, but the owners have big plans, starting with Guanamar, a fishing lodge built on the ridge above. The villages of Sámara and Garza are at the beach, while Nosara is inland. All are rather basic coastal villages without a resort atmosphere, though near Nosara there's a real estate development with many retired North Americans. Part of the development is a natural area with trees and some wildlife.

The beaches have gentle surf and headlands at the ends. Except at Guanamar you see little sign of fishing and boating, and no real harbor or marina. At Garza a boatbuilder builds fishing boats beside the road. Sámara and Nosara have very basic accommodations in town, but all have some tourist facilities outside. Playa Sámara has a reef offshore so waves are small and swimming safe from the white sand beach. If you're avoiding crowds during holidays and make reservations for the limited tourist rooms, or camp, these would be a good choice. There's daily bus

Price Range for 2 people in high season, before taxes—A+ Over $80/day, A $60–80, B $45–60, C $30–45, D $20–30, $E $11–20, F up to $11, U.S. $. * = Meals included.

Hotel	Address	Telephone (Fax)	No. of Rms	Pvt Bath	Hot Water	In Town	On Waterfront	Courtesy Transp	Recomm Access	Parking	Air Cond or Fan	Restaurant	Pool	TV	English Spoken	Noise Level	Cleanliness	Single Rate	Range
PLAYAS CARRILLO & SÁMARA:																			
Campo de Pesca Guanamar	Apdo. 7-1880 1000 San Jose	39-4433 39-4544 39-2405	30	All			•	Car	•	•	•	•	•	•	Exc	Exc		•	A+
Las Brisas del Pacifico	Apdo. 129-6100 Centro Colón San Jose	68-0876 (55-2380)	14	All		•		Car Bus	•		•	•	•	•	Exc	Exc			B
Los Almendros	Sámara, Gste.	68-0022 68-0773	30	All	•	•		Car Bus	•		•	•			V gd	Gd		•	D
Cabinas Punta Sámara	Sámara, Gste.	68-0022	10	All	•	•		Car Bus	•		•	•			Fair	High			E
PLAYAS GARZA, NOSARA:																			
Villagio La Guaria Morada	Apdo. 860-6100 Centro Colón San Jose	33-2476 68-0784 (22-4073)	30	All		•		Car Bus	•		•	•		•	Exc	Exc		•	A+
Playa de Nosara	Apdo. 4-5233 Nosara, Gste.	68-0495 (68-0495)	16	All				Car Bus	•	•	•	•	•		Exc	Exc			C

service from Nicoya though the road may be impassable in rainy season. SANSA has flown weekly to the airstrip, but it may not be useable at presstime. Don't count on being able to drive north from Nosara in the wet season even with 4-wheel-drive. Ask the locals about current road conditions.

Campo de Pesca Guanamar.

Guanamar: Deluxe fishing lodge on top of a ridge above Playa Carrillo. Rooms are big, carpeted, with shaded deck overlooking the beach—in several rows across the hill below the restaurant and bar, reached by stairs. Some have kitchen. Has *excellent* fishing, boats and guides. Designer replaced natural shade with concrete and small palms.

Las Brisas del Pacifico: Very attractive hotel with pool fronting beach. Large rooms with high ceilings, nice woodwork. Shaded sitting area for each cabina. Children to 14 free in same room. German manager, food and guests. Can arrange surfing, diving, horses, jet skiing.

Los Almendros: Simple new rooms with 1 dbl and 1-2 sgl beds, no screens, in 2 story concrete building at north end of soccer field in Sámara. Quieter and better than next.

Cabinas Punta Sámara: Very basic budget rooms.

Near Garza:

Villaggio La Guaria Morada: Deluxe cabinas and resort with pool, horseback riding, deep-sea fishing, and snorkeling. Big rooms, 2 per separate building, but no fans or screens—they depend on breeze. Shaded sitting area. Italian restaurant.

At Playa Nosara:

Playa Nosara: Attractive cabinas, all with view, on ridge overlooking beach. Rate is per cabina. Tennis, fishing, snorkeling. Landscaping chosen to attract birds. Recommended.

Condos and foreign residents' houses are rented here. Camping is allowed in some beach areas.

North of Playa Nosara is **Playa Ostional**, a biological preserve for nesting ridley turtles. Huge *arribadas* of turtles come ashore during the rainy season (August and September are the peak months) to lay eggs. In Costa Rica's best example of a compromise between preservation and local poaching, the villagers are allowed to take all the eggs laid in the first 36 hours of the *arribada* as as they would be dug up and smashed by later turtles anyway. Then the villagers and some Boy Scouts protect the turtles and remaining eggs. Bars selling turtle eggs for bocas are supposed to have a certificate indicating the eggs are legal.

Playa Junquillal

Surf is usually up here. Swimming requires caution for rips though long scenic beach is good walking or riding. Locals catch big fish from rocks on the south point. There's no snorkeling here, but some body surfing. Turtles nest on the beach. Camping is OK on north part and would be improved with some shade. There are 3 deluxe hotels and a set of cabinas here, but no village. It's hard to imagine this area crowded!

You can drive on all-weather road 28 km southwest from Santa Cruz or drive south from Tamarindo to meet the same road. Buses go several times a day from San Jose to Santa Cruz from which you could take a taxi. A direct (Tralapa) bus from San Jose to Junquillal leaves at 2 p.m. for the 6 hour drive,from Ave. 3, Calle 20.

Villa Serena: Price includes meals. Good food. Sauna, tennis. VCR films. Children are allowed if parents are responsible for them. Ownership changed recently—ask about this policy. Popular as honeymoon spot. Large rooms. Dine on balcony overlooking beach and landscaped grounds. May not take singles during high season Dec.—April with limited room.

Hotel Autumalal: Open all year with high season Dec.—Mar. Deluxe duplex cabinas, brick floors, good beds. Thatched roof over dining room on terrace. Rate includes meals. Attractive pool. Fishing (surf in front of hotel, or in boats from Tamarindo), tennis, horses. Howler monkeys live nearby and are seen on the grounds. Hotel is in trees above the south

Price Range for 2 people in high season, before taxes—A+ Over $80/day, A $60–80, B $45–60, C $30–45, D $20–30, $E $11–20, F up to $11, U.S. $. * = Meals included.

PLAYAS JUNQUILLAL, BLANCA:

Hotel	Address	Telephone (Fax)	No. of Rms	Pvt Bath	Hot Water	In Town	On Waterfront	Courtesy Transp	Recomm Access	Parking	Air Cond or Fan	Restaurant	Bar	Cooking Facil	Elevator	Wheelchair Acc	TV	Pool	English Spoken	Noise Level	Cleanliness	Single Rate	Range
Villa Serena	Apdo. 17, Santa Cruz, Gste.	68-0737 (31-5043)	6	All				Car, Bus	•	•	•	•	•					•	•	Exc	Exc		A+*
Autumalal	Apdo. 49-5150, Santa Cruz, Gste.	68-0506 (Fax same)	20	All				Car, Bus	•	•	•	•	•					•	•	Exc	Exc		A-
Iguanazul	Apdo. 130-5150, Santa Cruz	32-1423 (Fax same)	24	All				Car, Bus	•	•	•	•	•					•	•	Exc	Exc		A

PLAYA TAMARINDO:

Hotel	Address	Telephone (Fax)	No. of Rms	Pvt Bath	Hot Water	In Town	On Waterfront	Courtesy Transp	Recomm Access	Parking	Air Cond or Fan	Restaurant	Bar	Cooking Facil	Elevator	Wheelchair Acc	TV	Pool	English Spoken	Noise Level	Cleanliness	Single Rate	Range
Tamarindo Diria	Apdo. 4211-1000, San José	68-0652, 33-0530 (22-0568)	60	All	•	•		Car, Bus, Plane	•	•	•	•	•		•	•		•	•	•	Exc	Exc		A+
Pueblo Dorado	Apdo. 1711-1002, San José	22-5741 (Fax same)	22	All	•	•	•	Car, Bus, Plane	•	•	•							•	•	•	Exc	Exc	•	B
Tamarindo Resort Club	Apdo. 73-5150, Santa Cruz, Gste.	68-0883 (55-3785)	44	All	•	•	•	Car, Bus, Plane	•	•	•	•	•	•				•	•	•	Exc	Exc	•	B
Cabinas Pozo Azul	Playa Tamarindo, Santa Cruz, Gste.	68-0147	27	All	•	•		Car, Bus, Plane	•	•	•								•	Exc	Exc	•	C

end of beach.

Hotel Playa Junquillal: Is actually 3 very basic cabinas and a restaurant where the road reaches the beach. Range E. Also known as Pablo's. Sometimes closed. Camping allowed, fee.

At Playa Blanca, 3 km north of Junquillal:

Iguanazul: New deluxe hotel for active couples and groups, overlooking white sand beach. Tours and transportation arranged. Diving, fishing, horses, nature trail. Turtles nest on beach. Primarily for adults, does not have kid's pool or day care.

Playa Tamarindo

Playa Tamarindo is one of the Guanacaste beaches most easily reached by public bus and all-year roads from San Jose with a full price range of accommodations. It has a resort atmosphere, food and drink stands, and sometimes crowds and litter. Avoid weekends and holidays. Fortunately, the price of imported bottles saves Costa Rican beaches from broken glass, as the bottle being worth more than its contents usually means you have to drink it where you get it. Unfortunately, plastic bottles have recently come to Costa Rica.

Swimming is safe in front of the village, and there's good snorkeling within walking distance. Tamarindo is famous for deep-sea fishing for sailfish and marlin. Seafood, freshly caught, is excellent in restaurants here. The estuary with mangroves just to the north is a biological reserve with good birding and has leatherback turtles nesting, September–February. **Papagayo Excursions** (68-0859, 68-0652) offers tours of the estuary and turtle nesting as well as sportfishing.

Besides bus and car, leaving the Nicoya Peninsula highway just south of Belén and turning south at Huacas (lots of signs), you can fly via SANSA Monday, Wednesday, Friday, and Saturday from San Jose to the Tamarindo strip.

Johan's Bakery, at the beach, is a good stop for continental breakfast, lunch or snack—great pastries, breads, and pizza.

Tamarindo Diria: Deluxe hotel very well done, Canadian-owned. Rooms comfortable, cool. Suites have sitting room, refrigerator, bar, dbl and sgl bed. Game room with pool table and "foosball". Third floor has ocean view. Landscaped, shaded terrace between pools and ocean, tennis.

Pueblo Dorado: At the north edge of town, new, comfortable.

Tamarindo Resort Club: New cinder block cabinas, row on row, with trees, 2 blocks from beach. Separate buildings, but density of people and kids would be high if all were occupied.

Cabinas Pozo Azúl: Modern cabinas on left of road as you enter resort. Large light rooms with shaded sitting area in front. Across road from mangroves, beach and river. No single rate.

Cabinas Zully Mar: Simple, comfortable large rooms with tile floors. Across street from beach, bar, and restaurant. Rooms have individually carved doors illustrating Costa Rican legends. Excellent value.

Doly: Simple, inexpensive rooms, but clean, OK. Ask for room facing beach. On beach and well-aligned for breeze without a/c. Great view. Shaded open air restaurant on ground floor.

Boatyard at Tamarindo builds sailboats for people in many countries.

Playa Grande, north of the Tamarindo estuary, has surf, nesting turtles, and the threat of major tourist development, already advertised. You get to it by driving on to Matapalo from Huacas instead of turning north or south. **Cabinas Playa Grande**, with kitchen facilities, Range D (37-2552).

Playas Conchal, Brasilito, Flamingo, Potrero, Pan de Azucar

North of Tamarindo, across lagoon and river mouth is Brasilito, a small village on a dark sand beach. If you go through Brasilito onto its beach and half a mile south (4-wheel drive at low tide, or walk), you reach **Conchal,** a sheltered white sand and shell beach surrounded by cattle fincas. There's camping under the trees there and water available from the local ranch hands, some of whose children can be paid to watch your gear if you leave camp. The trees are good for hanging hammocks. You need a tent to keep out crawlies at night. Snorkeling is good, swimming safe.

At the south end there's a small estuary. Two bar/restaurants have been built recently, one owned by the Condor Club, see below. Here the sand is darker and, when I inspected, trash had accumulated around both facilities and on the beach, once one of Costa Rica's loveliest.

Condor Club: Resort on hilltop one km back from the beach. Small rooms and bathrooms in hexagonal buildings. Tennis, volleyball. Van to beach. Condos and lots for sale.

Brasilito has small stores, basic cabinas, and fishermen who sell their catch. Two buses a day come from Santa Cruz or a group can use a cab for about $20 one-way.

Las Palmas: (renamed Villas Pacifica?) On a hilltop inland from Brasilito, with ocean view. Huge, deluxe suites with cooking facilities, shaded veranda. Satellite TV from U.S. Excellent food in restaurant

Cabinas Mi Posada: Basic cabinas with bath in village next to beach and soda. Upstairs rooms are above dust, have breeze.

Flamingo Beach, north of Brasilito, is somewhat sheltered and usually safe for swimming. If it's rough, just wait for tide and wind to change. Private airstrip is owned by the development. There's a marina, the only private one north of Puntarenas, restaurants, several hotels, condos, and houses for rent. Fishing boats and guides. Mangroves behind have birds and caimans.

Flamingo Beach Hotel and Presidential Suites: Luxury hotel at beach has several higher priced rooms facing ocean and breeze. Other rooms face either a mangrove swamp to south (nice view from balcony) or hill with restaurants and suites to north. TV, phone, balcony with chairs, poolside bar. Luxury suites on headland overlook Flamingo Beach, have all facilities, including complete kitchens, large swimming pool. Tennis. Satellite TV from U.S. Pvt. bus ($40 r-t) runs from San Jose, M-W-F, Sun.

Marina Hotel (Club Playa Flamingo): Deluxe new hotel on headland between Flamingo and Potrero beaches. overlooking Potrero. Balcony, TV, phone, fridge, 1 dbl and 1 sgl bed. Tennis, jacuzzi.

Playa Potrero is just north with a long sheltered beach and good swimming. Behind is a creek with woods, birds, and monkeys.

Bahia Flamingo Resort: Quiet, pleasant beach hotel with large rooms in local hardwoods, some with kitchen facilities. Good food. Can arrange snorkeling, scuba rentals, sportfishing, boat trips to reef. Good value.

Price Range for 2 people in high season, before taxes—A+ Over $80/day, A $60–80, B $45–60, C $30–45, D $20–30, $E $11–20, F up to $11, U.S. $. * = Meals included.

Feature	Cabinas Zully Mar	Doly	Condor Club	Las Palmas	Cabinas Mi Posada	Flamingo Beach Hotel & Presidential Suites
Range	E	E	B	B	E	A+
Single Rate	•	•	•	•		•
Cleanliness	Exc	Exc	Exc	Exc	V gd	V gd
Noise Level						
English Spoken	Exc	Exc	Exc	V gd	gd	Exc
Pool			•	•		•
TV			•	•		•
Wheelchair Acc						•
Elevator						•
Cooking Facil						•
Bar					•	•
Restaurant		•	•	•		•
Air Cond or Fan	•	•	•	•		•
Parking	•	•	•	•		•
Recomm Access	Car, Bus, Plane	Car, Bus, Plane	Car, Bus, Plane	Car, Bus, Plane	Car, Bus, Plane	Car, Bus, Plane
Courtesy Transp						
On Waterfront			•	•		•
In Town		•			•	
Hot Water	•	•			•	•
Pvt Bath	All	6	All	All	·	All
No. of Rms	20	12	30 rms (2 hs)	5	6	111
Telephone (Fax)	26-4732	68-0174	68-0920 (68-0944)	68-0932 22-1126	68-0953	39-1584 68-0620 (39-0257)
Address	Playa Tamarindo Santa Cruz, Gste.	Playa Tamarindo Santa Cruz, Gste.	Apdo. 102-2300 Curridabat San Jose	Apdo. 3565-1000 San Jose	Playa Brasilito Santa Cruz, Gste.	Apdo. 692-4050 Alajuela

PLAYAS CONCHAL, BRASILITO: (Condor Club, Las Palmas, Cabinas Mi Posada)

PLAYA FLAMINGO: (Flamingo Beach Hotel & Presidential Suites)

Flamingo Beach Hotel.

Cabinas Cristina: Quiet, pleasant cabinas with good fans, kitchens, small pool, shade, 300 m from beach. Restaurant nearby. Recommended.

Playa Potrero Trailer Park: 2 apartments and 2 trailers with cooking facilities in well-shaded yard a block from the beach. Have own well and good water. Monthly rates.

At Playa Pan de Azucar, at the end of the road, 15 km north of Huacas:

Sugar Beach: Comfortable rooms, 2 dbl beds, on shaded grounds overlooking beach. Dining room on terrace, done with taste. Attractive, never crowded. Good birding. Sheltered cove offers safe swimming and snorkeling. Boats, fishing available. Highly recommended.

Sugar Beach Hotel.

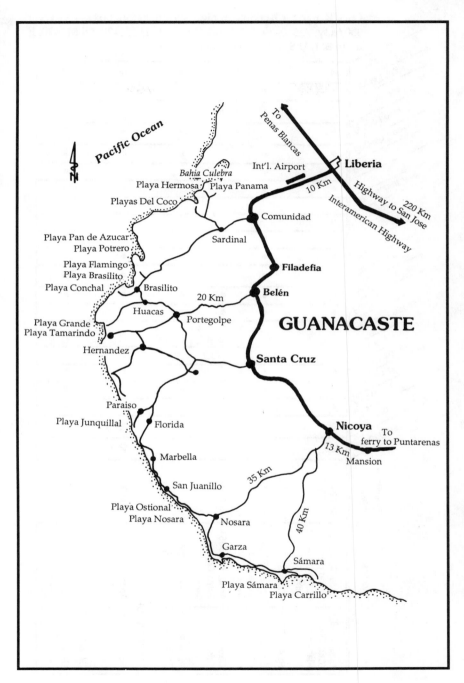

Price Range for 2 people in high season, before taxes—A+ Over $80/day, A $60–80, B $45–60, C $30–45, D $20–30, $E $11–20, F up to $11, U.S. $. * = Meals included.

	Marina Hotel (Club Playa Flamingo)	Bahia Flamingo Resort	Cabinas Cristina	Playa Potrero Trailer Park	Sugar Beach	Diria
Range	A	B	E	E	C	B
Single Rate	•	•	•	•	•	•
Cleanliness	Exc	Exc	Exc	Exc	Exc	Exc
Noise Level	Exc	V gd	Exc	Exc	Exc	Exc
English Spoken	Exc	Exc	Exc	Exc	Exc	Exc
Pool	•	•			•	•
TV	•	•	•			•
Wheelchair Acc	•	•				
Elevator						
Cooking Facil	•					
Bar		•	•			
Restaurant	•	•			•	•
Air Cond or Fan	•	•			•	•
Parking	•	•	•	•	•	•
Recomm Access	•	•	•	•	•	•
Courtesy Transp	Car Bus Plane	Car Bus Plane	Car Bus Plane	Car Bus Plane	Car Taxi Plane	Car Bus Plane
On Waterfront	•	•			•	
In Town	•	•			•	
Hot Water	•	•	•			•
Pvt Bath					•	•
No. of Rms	All	All	All	All	All	All
	45	14	3	4	10	36
Telephone (Fax)	68-0996 (68-0928)	68-0976	68-0997		68-0959	68-0442 68-0080
Address	Apdo. 321-1002 Paseo des Estudiantes San Jose	Apdo. 45-5051 Santa Cruz, Gste.	Apdo. 121-5051 Santa Cruz, Gste.	Apdo. 61-5051 Santa Cruz, Gste.	Apdo. 90-5051 Santa Cruz, Gste.	Apdo. 58-5051 Santa Cruz, Gste.

PLAYA POTRERO: (Bahia Flamingo Resort, Cabinas Cristina, Playa Potrero Trailer Park)

PLAYA PAN DE AZUCAR: (Sugar Beach)

SANTA CRUZ: (Diria)

Santa Cruz

If you've gotten to any of the beaches above, you've probably come through this marketing and cattle town before now—if not, the coastal roads and trails will fail you and you'll have to bounce back to the arterial two-lane highway near Santa Cruz to head out to the coast on another road. As roads are improved and bridges built, other beaches such as Playa Ostional north of Nosara (with huge turtle arribadas) will be more accessible. Santa Cruz is an attractive town with two good hotels and several very basic places. If you come for festival or rodeo, make reservations here or in Liberia as all rooms will be full.

Santa Cruz has a restaurant serving such good cheap food for lunch that it is busy despite being a sooty sheet metal shed three stories high, the hangar at the former airport! A dozen women inside make excellent tipico food and breads of all kinds, for less than $3 for lunch. Costa Rican government employees stop off here and U.S. TV crews taken to the **Tortilla Factory** for lunch at the long tables have raved about both the food and the ethnic experience. You can ask anyone for directions, but it's only a couple of blocks from the main square on a back alley.

Diriá: Very attractive hotel with large clean pool. Landscaping, hanging plants. Best in Santa Cruz and excellent value.

Sharatoga: Cool, attractive, simple rooms with shaded center court, deer, monkey, parrots.

Pension Isabel: Basic, clean.

Playas Coco, Ocotal, Bahia Pez Vela

These beaches are the nearest to Liberia, leaving the highway 26 km southwest. All have good swimming, some snorkeling. Playa Del Coco is hectic on weekends and holidays with cantinas, basic cabinas, busloads. At Playa Ocotal and the cove just south:

El Ocotal: Deluxe resort done in excellent taste. Rooms in duplex cabinas along steep drive (not for new hip replacements!) with great view, satellite TV. Dining room on hilltop with view in all directions, good food. Tennis, horses, snorkeling, boat rentals, fuel. Have two coves & marina. Deep sea fishing is serious sport here.

Bahia Pez Vela: Deluxe small fishing camp for deep sea fishing enthusiasts, on small cove just south of Playa Ocotal. Boats, guides. It is a very attractive resort with sheltered swimming and snorkeling. Good value. Recommended.

Santa Cruz, Coco

Price Range for 2 people in high season, before taxes—A+ Over $80/day, A $60–80, B $45–60, C $30–45, D $20–30, $E $11–20, F up to $11, U.S. $. * = Meals included.

Hotel	Address	Telephone (Fax)	Single Rate Range	Cleanliness	Noise Level	English Spoken	Pool	TV	Restaurant	Air Cond or Fan	Parking	Recomm Access	Courtesy Transp	On Waterfront	In Town	Hot Water	Pvt Bath	No. of Rms
Sharatoga	Apdo. 33-5051 Santa Cruz, Gste.	68-0011	E	•	Exc	V gd					•	•	Car Bus Plane			•	All	39
Pension Isabel	Santa Cruz, Gste.	68-0173	F	•	Gd	Gd			•	•	•	•	Car Bus Plane					22
OCOTAL:																		
El Ocotal	Apdo. 1013-1002 San Jose	67-0230, 22-4259 (23-8483)	A	•	Exc	Exc	•		•	•	•	•	Car Bus	•	•		All	32
Bahia Pez Vela	Apdo. 7758-1000 San Jose	67-0129, 21-1586	C	•	Gd	Exc	•		•	•	•	•	Car Bus	•	•		All	6
PLAYA DE COCO:																		
Flor de Itabo	Apdo. 32 Playa del Coco, Gste.	67-0011, 67-0292 (67-0003)	B	•	Gd	Exc	•	•	•	•	•	•	Car Bus	•			All	18
Aldea Keystone	Apdo. 10 Playa del Coco, Gste.	32-0210	C	•	Exc	V gd						•	Car Bus				All	7
Cabinas Chale	Playa del Coco, Gste.		D	•	Exc	Exc		•	•	•	•	•	Car Bus			•	All	18

At Playa Coco:

Flor de Itabo: Well-done with hardwoods, big bathrooms, pleasant rooms, very attractive pool area. Nice landscaping. Also have 2-story bungalows with cooking facilities. Quiet, well removed from crowds at beach. German spoken. On north side of main road entering town about 1/2 mile from beach. Recommended.

Aldea Keystone: 2 and 3 room very basic single cabinas with stove, refrigerator, among trees back from beach. Shaded sitting area with hammock. Bring own linen. North American owner.

Cabinas Chale: Attractive cabinas in quiet northeastern outskirts of town still have short walk to beach. Rate is per cabina, for 1 or 2. Private walled courts behind cabinas. Very good value. Recommended.

Casino Playa de Coco: Good value with rates varying according to season and whether they face sea. Front rooms facing sea are well worth it. Portable fans for rent (you need them). Ask for rooms at far end away from bar. Food good.

Cabinas Luna Tica: Rooms for 4 or 6, not properly aligned to catch breeze. Too basic.

Playa Hermosa

Playa Hermosa is a fine curved beach several miles long just north of Playa del Coco, with good swimming, and deep sea fishing and water sports available. There are widely differing hotels at opposite ends of the beach—you can definitely pick your style here. **Aqua Sport,** near north end, rents just about any gear you might want and can arrange boats and guides to dive or fish off the Islas Murciélago, where the water is *clear*. Good seafood restaurant. There's a bus from Liberia twice a day.

Condovac La Costa: Large group of condos on hill behind guarded gate with unoccupied rooms for rent. Kitchen facilities. Scuba, fishing, water skiing, horses, tennis, discotheque. Golf carts transport guests to rooms. Offer van from San Jose, for charge.

Cabinas Playa Hermosa: Small attractive hotel among the trees at the south end of the beach. Owned by former Oregon couple who say "We sell tranquillity." Does considerable repeat business. Guests can visit the north end of the beach for water sports or an evening out. Small, reasonable restaurants nearby.

Los Corales is a group of new block cabinas with kitchens just below Condovac. Needs shade.

Price Range for 2 people in high season, before taxes—A+ Over $80/day, A $60–80, B $45–60, C $30–45, D $20–30, $E $11–20, F up to $11, U.S. $. * = Meals included.

Hotel	Address	Telephone (Fax)	No. of Rms	Pvt Bath	Hot Water	In Town	On Waterfront	Courtesy Transp	Recomm Access	Parking	Air Cond or Fan	Restaurant	Bar	Cooking Facil	Elevator	Wheelchair Acc	TV	Pool	English Spoken	Noise Level	Cleanliness	Single Rate	Price Range
Cabinas Luna Tica	Apdo. 67-5059 Playa del Coco, Gste.	67-0127 / 67-0279	35	All		•			Car Bus	•	•	•								Poor	V gd	•	F
Cabinas, El Coco	Apdo. 2-5059 Playa del Coco, Gste.	67-0167	61	All		•			Car Bus	•	•	•							Gd		V gd	•	F
PLAYA HERMOSA:																							
Condovac La Costa	Apdo. 55-1001 Playa Viquez San Jose	67-0267 21-8949 (22-5637)	101	All	•	•	•		Car Bus	•	•	•	•					•	Exc	Exc	Exc	•	A+
Los Corales	Apdo. 1158-1000 San Jose	57-0259 67-0255 (55-4978)	12	All	•		•		Bus Car	•	•		•					•	V gd	V gd	V gd	•	A
Cabinas Playa Hermosa	Apdo. 112 Liberia, Gste.	67-0136	20	All	•	•			Car Bus	•	•	•						•	Exc	Exc	Exc	•	D

Playa Panama

Beaches are increasingly sheltered by Punta Mala as you head north here so surf is gone and water calm. Bahia Culebra is named for sea snakes sometimes found here. Be careful. ICT has major plans in this area with the Papagayo Project to encourage tourist development and take advantage of maximum good weather. Due to cost, most results are years off. There's a pulpería where the road reaches the shore, in otherwise rural area. No accommodations here though camping is allowed on beach and across the bay. Bring water and anything you need.

Liberia
(pop. 40,0000)

Liberia is the provincial capital of Guanacaste, a clean, busy town on the Interamerican Highway at its junction with the road to Santa Cruz and Nicoya. As I previously mentioned, it has excellent, reasonably-priced hotels, mostly with large cool swimming pools you'll appreciate in the heat, and an amazing variety of interesting day trips available. Most can be reached by bus, but the round trip may not be practical in a day with current bus schedules. There are several buses daily between Liberia and San José. From Liberia you can drive to northern Guanacaste beaches, Santa Rosa and Rincon de la Vieja National Parks, Lake Arenal and Arenal Volcano with moving lava flows, Barra Honda and Palo Verde National Parks, and festivals at Nicoya and Santa Cruz, returning to Liberia at night. I've found Liberia a good overnight spot to rest and clean up between camping trips to parks and beaches.

The Casa de Cultura, three blocks from Central Park, provides tourist information and exhibits artifact of Guanacaste history including saddles, lariats, and clothing used by workers and hacienda owners. Gift shop sells hand-made crafts including woven horsehair belts. Latest information on haciendas offering horseback tours and accommodations. Open Tues–Sun., 9–12 and 2–6. Phone, 66-0122.

Guanacaste Tours, in the Hotel Bramadero, offers a wide variety of day tours in a van to national parks, haciendas, beaches, and fiestas. Some tours include boat trips on the Tempisque River for wildlife viewing. Phone: 66-0306, Fax: 66-0307. **Aventura Rent a Car**, also in the Bramadero, has both cars and jeeps. Phone: 39-4821. Fax: 66-2885. You could ride a bus or SANSA to Liberia and rent a car and/or go on tours from there, perhaps with rest days at the hotel pool.

The nearby national parks and refuges are discussed in our National Parks chapter. **Hacienda Los Inocentes** and **Rincon De La Vieja Mountain Lodge**, also on a hacienda, are discussed under Nature Tours and

Price Range for 2 people in high season, before taxes—A+ Over $80/day, A $60–80, B $45–60, C $30–45, D $20–30, $E $11–20, F up to $11, U.S. $. * = Meals included.

Hotel	Address	Telephone (Fax)	No. of Rms	Pvt Bath	Hot Water	In Town	On Waterfront	Courtesy Transp	Recomm Access	Parking	Air Cond or Fan	Restaurant	Bar	Cooking Facil	Elevator	Wheelchair Acc	TV	Pool	English Spoken	Noise Level	Cleanliness	Single Rate	Range
LIBERIA:																							
Las Espuelas	Apdo. 88, Liberia, Gste.	66-0144	44	All				•	Car / Bus	•	•	•	•			•	•	•	Exc	Exc	•	•	C
Bramadero	Apdo. 70, Liberia, Gste.	66-0371 / 66-0203	24	All	•			•	Car / Bus	•	•	•	•				•	•	Exc	Exc	•	•	D
El Sitio	Apdo. 785-1007 Centro Colón, San Jose	66-1211 (66-2059)	52	All	•				Car / Bus	•	•	•	•				•		Exc	Exc	•	•	D
Nuevo Boyeros	Apdo. 85, Liberia, Gste.	66-0995 / 66-0722	62	All	•				Car / Bus	•	•	•	•				•		Exc	Exc	•	•	D
La Siesta	Apdo. 15-5000, Liberia, Gste.	66-0678 / 24-5419	24	All	•				Car / Bus	•	•	•	•				•		Exc	Exc	•	•	E
La Ronda	Apdo. 81, Liberia, Gste.	66-0417	23	All					Car / Bus	•	•	•	•				•		V gd	Exc	•	•	F
Oriental	Liberia	66-0085	28	All	•				Car / Bus	•	•	•	•				•		Fair	Gd	•	•	F
CAÑAS:																							
Hacienda La Pacifica	Apdo. 8-5700 Cañas, Gste.	69-0050 (69-0555)	32	All			•		Car / Bus	•	•	•	•				•	•	Exc	Exc	•	•	C

Lodges, page 80.

Where To Stay

Las Espuelas: Very attractive hotel with entrance shaded by huge guanacaste tree. Interior courts with pond and pre-Columbian figures. Planted breezeways, hardwood furniture in Spanish style. Low season discount. Conference room. Wheelchair accessible. Central air conditioning. Has tour to working hacienda, horseback riding, wildlife. Recommended.

Motel Bramadero: Rooms comfortable and quiet, with shaded sitting area and distinctive Nicaraguan rocking chairs. All rooms have fans or a.c. Pool filled and clean. Restaurant good. Good value. Recommended.

El Sitio: Large attractive hotel with architecture, decoration and planting all in Guanacaste cattle country theme. Wheelchair ramp even for 3 steps from lobby to pool level. Rooms without a.c. are oriented to breeze. Recommended. Low season rates and honeymoon discount.

Nuevo Boyeros: Big clean 2-story hotel around court with large clean swimming pool and wading pool with cascade. Cool rooms with good beds. Small restaurant serves good food, super fruit refrescos. Popular with truckdrivers and government employees. Dance floor in front—on weekends, ask for room at back for quiet. Recommended.

La Siesta: Modern, pleasant hotel with good beds downtown. Second floor rooms bigger, worth asking for. Small clean pool. Manager helpful.

La Ronda: Named for round dining room on second floor with good breeze. Rooms big with tile floors. Pool small. Ask for air conditioning demo. Open?

Oriental: Very basic. Chinese operated. Rooms without a.c. very hot. Ask for demo of a.c. to be sure it's effective.

Rice processing plant near Liberia.

Watch for wildlife at any creek or river you cross. Wood storks rest in tree.

Cañas

Cañas, on the Interamerican Highway, marks the turnoff to Tilarán and Lake Arenal. While not as cool as Tilarán, it's a central spot for trips to Arenal and a good base for birdwatching in Palo Verde National Park, Lomas Barbudal Biological Reserve, and the Gulf of Nicoya. Birds and other animals are usually more approachable by boat or raft than on foot. Note that to drive to Palo Verde, you must go north to Bagaces and turn left. Lomas Barbudal, near Bagaces, has great birdwatching and is involving local people including children in its development—the best way to protect its resources.

The Corobicí River, which runs into the Bebedero River, carries water released by the Lake Arenal powerhouse, making it the only full stream in this area all year. It's an oasis for birds, monkeys and other wildlife in otherwise dry cattle haciendas. **Rios Tropicales** runs raft trips lasting an hour to a whole day long from here to Bebedero or all the way to the gulf from December through April. They can transport you from San Jose or you can start from Cañas where they operate from Hacienda La Pacifica. River is sparkling, perfect for swimming. Not a whitewater trip, this one is calm enough to keep your camera out and take pictures of the wildlife you can easily spot, perfect for families, and even wheelchair accessible! (33-6455)

Hacienda La Pacifica: Older,hardwood cabinas and new, well-designed units. Both good value. Very good food. New tiled pool. Wildlife and the Corobicí River adjacent. 5 km. north of Cañas on Interamerican Highway. Recommended. Horses available to ride on extensive trails on the hacienda.

El Corral, north edge of Cañas, has 12 clean rooms with a/c. Range E. (69-0622). Very good value. In central Cañas there are several good, hospitable budget hotels.

Good food: **Rincón Corobicí** is an open air restaurant overlooking the river at the south end of the bridge over the Interamerican Highway, 6 km. north of Cañas. Food is excellent, prices reasonable, and site lovely. Has several tent camping sites on lawn just north of restaurant. They offer reasonably priced mountain biking and river tours. (69-0303)

Baling hay by hand on small farm. Haciendas have baling machines.

Tilarán

This small town is high on hills above the Guanacaste plain, near Lake Arenal. It's clean, with a cool breeze, and doesn't feel tropical. The country around the lake is lovely rolling upland with dairy cattle. Many of Costa Rica's finest criollo horses are raised and trained here. Tilarán's fiesta in April features an important rodeo and livestock show. The lake is famous for guapote fishing. Afternoon breezes across the lake are usually strong and have recently been discovered by windsurfers.

Hotels in town are simple and clean. The restaurant at **The Spot** is very good and the one downstairs from **Cabinas El Sueño** serves good tipico food, great ceviche and refrescos.

Where To Stay

The Spot: Small rooms on ground floor, but light, pleasant. Has friendly bar/restaurant. Offers day tours, including hiking, birding, horseback riding, visiting farms and hot springs, water skiing, and fishing.

Cabinas El Sueño: Light, airy, small hotel with rooms arranged around central court with fountain on second floor. Hot water. Manager very pleasant. Recommended.

Cabinas Mary: Hotel is upstairs, light airy, friendly. TV in living room. Excellent value. Hint: tall people should duck when going upstairs.

Central: Rooms on first and second floors, back from street. Good value.

Lodges around Lake Arenal are discussed in our North Central region.

Criollo stock horse prances in Tilarán parade during festival held in April.

Hotel	Address	Telephone (Fax)	No. of Rms	Pvt Bath	Hot Water	In Town	On Waterfront	Courtesy Transp	Recomm Access	Parking	Air Cond or Fan	Restaurant	Bar	Cooking Facil	Elevator	Wheelchair Acc	TV	Pool	English Spoken	Noise Level	Cleanliness	Single Rate Range	Range
TILARÁN:																							
The Spot	Apdo. 6398-1000 San Jose	23-2811 (23-1916)	16	All	•	•		Car Bus	•	•	•	•	•				•	•	Exc	V gd	•		C
Cabinas Mary	Tilarán, Gste.	69-5470	6	4	•	•		Car Bus	•										Exc	V gd	•		E
Cabinas El Sueño	Tilarán, Gste.	69-5347	20	All	•	•		Car Bus	•		•	•							Exc	Exc	•		E
Central	Tilarán, Gste.	69-5363	19	8		•		Car Bus											V gd	Exc	•		F

Price Range for 2 people in high season, before taxes—A+ Over $80/day, A $60–80, B $45–60, C $30–45, D $20–30, $E $11–20, F up to $11, U.S. $. * = Meals included.

249

From the winding road to Monteverde you can see the forested ridges above cow pastures.

 Monteverde

Monteverde is a community and a biological reserve administered by the Tropical Science Center in San Jose. For nature lovers it's a major destination, as anyone who watches international nature programs on TV knows. From December through April tour groups and independent travelers come by busloads to see the cloud forest and its wildlife. Tourism, particularly during high season, has cost Monteverde some of its former tranquility.

A group of Quakers mostly from the United States founded the colony 40 years ago, choosing Costa Rica for its peace and tolerance. Monteverde is just below the cloud forest, far from tropical heat—up a winding unpaved road (1.5 –2 hours) from the Interamerican Highway. Today the people raise dairy cattle and goats on the steep slopes above the village of Santa Elena. Their cooperative makes very fine cheeses sold locally and in San Jose. Artists paint Christmas cards, calendars and gifts.

The reserve, partially donated by the Quakers, covers the upper slopes on both sides of the continental divide. It has definite wet and dry seasons, though the upper levels have fog or rain much of the year. Paths wind for miles through the reserve. There's more here than you can see in a day, even if you rent a horse (not allowed on many trails). Many rare species, including the quetzal, three-wattled bellbird, and the golden toad (found nowhere else), are here among the several forest zones. You can come on a nature tour or on your own.

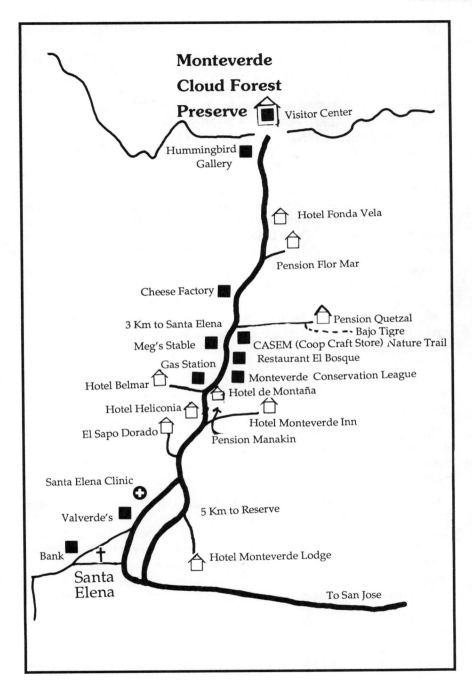

The reserve visitor center, at the end of the road, sells passes for $6 per day but only allows 100 people at a time into the reserve. If you're on a tour, you will have reservations. Traveling independently, you may sign up 24 hours in advance. While most people only walk the nearest trail, perhaps as far as the waterfall, you may have to wait until a tour group leaves to enter. The **Reserve Field Station** has a basic dormitory with kitchen facilities, Range F, priority for researchers and students, often has student groups and classes. Reservations at least 45 days in advance, with deposit 30%, phone 61-2655. Offers guided walks, 8:15 a.m., for $12, call ahead.

There are several hotels and pensions as well as rooms for rent by local people if you're staying longer and living simply. You *need* reservations here, as all hotels are sometimes full, with Christmas and Easter booked many months ahead. While there is camping at the Flor Mar and the Fonda Vela, I think you'd be damp and cold rather soon.

Light rain gear or Goretex, and polyester bunting clothes that dry quickly are welcome. You'll want an umbrella in your day pack, which should be waterproof if you're going to walk far. Hiking boots are a must, though they can be light. Most hotels rent rubber boots. Bring binoculars, a bird book, and plastic bags to keep these dry. You can get bird and animal checklists as well as trail maps at the reserve's visitor center and the Monteverde Conservation League office. You'll see more in less time with a guide on a nature tour, but quiet walking on your own is a memorable experience and the local people are friendly and helpful. Guides are available as are horses to rent.

Note that while November through January is best for hummingbirds and amphibians, it's easiest to see quetzals, three-wattled bellbirds, and possibly the bare-necked umbrella bird in March and April when they're mating and nesting, too busy to be as cautious as usual.

The **Monteverde Conservation League**, started by local people but open to anyone, is raising funds to buy more land for the reserve. **The Children's Rainforest** is an international project, started in a Swedish school, in which children in many countries have contributed and raised money to buy thousands of acres on the eastern slope adjacent to the reserve and managed by it, the **Bosque Eterno de Los Niños**. Former pasture land is now returning to cloudforest on some of this acreage.

There is a very scenic road to Tilarán from Santa Elena so it is possible to make a circuit instead of going up and back on the main road, if you're prepared for even slower going than you had on the direct road. In rainy season ask in Santa Elena before going even with 4-wheel drive.

Besides the Puntarenas–Santa Elena daily bus, there is a bus from San Jose (Tilarán terminal, Calle 12, Ave. 9/11, phone 22-3854) to the cheese factory at Monteverde. Get tickets in advance, $4, and get there early, especially in high season. Leaves San Jose at 2:30 p.m. Mon.–Thurs. and 6:30 a.m. Sat. Leaves Monteverde at 6:30 a.m. Tues.–Thurs. and 3 p.m. Fri., Sun. (and 3 p.m. Sat. in high season).

Where To Stay

Belmar: Very attractive chalet with balconies, fine view, large rooms, woods close by. Hospitable staff. Excellent food. Recommended.

Hotel Belmar.

Hotel de la Montaña Monteverde: First class hotel with 16 modern rooms overlooking the Gulf of Nicoya in the distance. Box lunches, guides and rental horses available. Will pick up guests from bus in Santa Elena. Tours from San Jose can include day on Calypso yacht in gulf.

Monteverde Lodge: New hotel built by Costa Rica Expeditions for their tours and independent travelers on ridge above Santa Elena, 5 km to reserve. Very comfortable and attractive. Jacuzzi to soak away cold of the cloud forest. Good food. Taxi to reserve $4/ea. one way. Recommended.

El Sapo Dorado: Cabins have balconies, fireplace, view. Friendly place with good bar/restaurant. Offers live or taped music for dancing, some vegetarian entrees. Readers enjoyed.

Monteverde Inn: Simple, North American-owned hotel on 28 acres, down steep hill from road, 4 km from reserve. Rate includes American-style meals (sack lunch for trip to reserve). Rooms have twin beds. Also has dormitory, Range F per person with meals. Excellent value.

Pension Manakin: Clean, basic inn on right before Hotel de Montaña. Rate includes 3 meals. Most rooms have bunks, shared bath. Rents boots.

Fonda Vela: New hotel on 35 acre farm, is nearest the reserve, a half hour walk uphill. Very attractive cabins with common room and balcony. fine view. Good food. Rents boots, horses. Camping area. Recommended.

Heliconia: Pleasant modern inn with two lobbies, electric organ. Covered porch with hummingbird feeders. Meals served family style. Good food. Offers horseback tours to view of Arenal Volcano. Recommended.

Pension Quetzal: Very attractive modern pension with pleasant rooms, beautiful wood. New cabinas with queen-size bed, in separate building, higher. Bird bath at edge of woods attracts many and provides a good photo spot. Biologists often stay here. Rate includes 3 meals (box lunch is available when needed). Recommended.

Pension Flor Mar: Rustic inn, pleasant, friendly. Price includes 3 meals, good food. Can provide box lunch. Rooms have bunk beds for 3 or 4. Three km from reserve. Camping area adjacent.

Taxi from Santa Elena to the Quetzal and Flor Mar is about $6 each way. **Restaurant El Bosque** is recommended.

Pension Santa Elena is in the village of Santa Elena, near the bus, but miles from reserve. Basic, Range F. (61-1151)

To see and do, besides visiting the reserve:

Birdwatch along the roads. Quetzals feed in trees along the last grade before the reserve. Walking the side roads allows you to enjoy the pastures and views of Monteverde without tour buses. Please do respect the residents' privacy and stay off their farms unless you're invited. Guides **Gary Diller,** 61-0903, and **Richard Laval** (besides birds, his specialty is bats), 61-0952, offer walks that can add greatly to your experience.

Rent horses, available from several owners, to explore with or without a guide. **Meg's Stables** (call 61-0952 to reserve) are near CASEM, the women's crafts coop.

Walk the **Bajo Tigre Nature Trail** owned by the Monteverde Conservation League. Admission is $1, including map, a contribution to the League. The trail starts on the road leading to the Pension Quetzal.

Price Range for 2 people in high season, before taxes—A+ Over $80/day, A $60–80, B $45–60, C $30–45, D $20–30, $E $11–20, F up to $11, U.S. $. * = Meals included.

Hotel	Range	Single Rate	Cleanliness	Noise Level	English Spoken	Pool	TV	Wheelchair Acc	Elevator	Cooking Facil	Bar	Restaurant	Air Cond or Fan	Parking	Recomm Access	Courtesy Transp	On Waterfront	In Town	Hot Water	Pvt Bath	No. of Rms	Telephone (Fax)	Address
Belmar	B	•	Exc	Exc	Exc	•						•	•		•	Car / Bus			•	All	18	61-1001 (Fax same)	Monteverde, Punt.
De Montaña Monteverde	B	•	Exc	Exc	Exc	•						•	•		•	Car / Bus	•		•	All	19	61-1846 / 33-7078 (22-6184)	Apdo. Box 70 Plaza Gonzales Viques, San Jose
Monteverde Lodge	B		Exc	Exc	Exc											Car / Bus				All	27	57-0766 (57-1665)	Apdo. 6941-1000 San Jose
El Sapo Dorado	B	•	Exc	Exc	Exc	•						•	•		•	Car / Bus	•		•	All	10	61-2952 (Fax same)	Apdo. 10165-1000, San Jose
Monteverde Inn	C	•	Exc	Exc	Exc	•						•	•		•	Car / Bus	•		•	5	10	61-2756	Apdo. 10165-1000, San Jose
Pension Manakin	C	•	Exc	Exc	Exc	•							•		•	Car / Taxi	•			2	9	61-2854	Monteverde, Punt.
Fonda Vela	D	•	Exc	Exc	Exc								•		•	Bus / Taxi			•	3	10	61-2551	Apdo. 10165-1000, San Jose
Heliconia	D	•	Exc	Exc	Exc	•							•		•	Bus / Car			•	All	15	61-1009	Apdo. 10165-1000, San Jose
Pension Quetzal	D	•	Exc	Exc	Exc	•							•		•	Bus / Car			•	7	10	61-0955	Apdo. 10165-1000, San Jose
Pension Flor Mar	E	•	Exc	Exc	Exc	•							•		•	Bus / Car			•	3	7	61-0909	Apdo. 10165-1000, San Jose

Monteverde family walks home while a boy drives the cows to pasture. Residents walk everywhere unless they're hauling a truckload of freight. On foot or horseback, you too can enjoy this pace of life.

See the **slideshow** of Patricia and Michael Fogden's wildlife slides at 6 p.m. nightly at the Fonda Vela for $3 admission, a contribution to the Monteverde Conservation League. Monteverde Lodge offers a slideshow with sounds of the rainforest some nights.

Tour the **Cheese Factory** and buy a variety of great cheeses, milk fudge, and homemade rolls and bread. Tours 9–11 a.m. and 1:30–3 p.m. Mon.–Sat, and 9–11 a.m. Sun. Open 7:30–12 m and 1–3:30 p.m. Mon–Sat and Sunday 7:30 a.m.–12:30 p.m.

Choose gifts from the arts and crafts produced by Monteverde women at **CASEM,** and the paintings exhibited by artists **Sara Dowell** at her studio and mother-daughter **Stella Wallace** and **Meg Laval** at their studio near Meg's Stables. Don't miss Patricia and Michael Fogden's **Hummingbird Gallery** with their slides and prints (plus Guatemalan fabrics, Monteverde T-shirts and trail snacks) just below the reserve entrance. Adjacent to the reserve, their hummingbird feeders outside attract many species including the violet sabrewing, iridescent purple and green, over 5 inches long!

For a gift or souvenir you don't have to pack, stop by the **Monteverde Conservation League** office across from the gas station and make a contribution. $25 gets a subscription to their newsletter, *Tapir Tracks*. $50 buys an acre of forest along a creek the quetzal and other species need for their seasonal migrations.

Costa Rica is a place to absorb and feel, not to dash through. Monte-verde, with its natural scene and wildlife, its hard-working and resource-ful people, and its tiring road before and after your visit, can only be appreciated with time—two nights seem to me the minimum.

North and South Central

These separate areas, the "everywhere else" after we've discussed the areas with better-known tourist attractions. They are interesting and beautiful areas with important sites for ecotourists, but no beaches and little urban or night life. Several good two-lane roads, including the Interamerican Highway in the south, cross these areas, but most secondary roads are rough. Some are impassable after heavy rains. More roads and road improvements are planned, and we have seen changes in recent years. Most hotels are basic, but several better ones and some nature lodges have recently been added. More are planned. Nature tours travel by bus, boat, kayak, and raft on its roads and rivers. These are covered in our Nature Lodges chapter, page 80.

North Central

North and east of the volcano chain including the Cordilleras de Guanacaste, Tilarán, and Central is a rolling to hilly area that flattens out to the Caribbean lowland Roads lead from the Meseta Central to this region via Sarchí to Ciudad Quesada and via Heredia to Puerto Viejo on the Sarapiquí River. There are buses to both towns. The road to Puerto Viejo climbs the saddle between Poás and Barva Volcanoes and passes two of Costa Rica's finest waterfalls, offering a great view over the northern region. Rainfall and humidity are higher on this side of the mountains, and rain can last all day. If you're staying over, bring a dry set of clothes to change into at night.

You may want to do a loop trip through part of the north central plain, driving or riding a bus from Tilarán around Lake Arenal through Fortuna to Ciudad Quesada and back via Zarcero and Sarchí to San Jose. It's the scenic route back from Guanacaste and a great contrast to the dryness there.

You'll be driving around the north end of Lake Arenal, passing first the pump station that sends water west to Guanacaste and then the dam that forms the lake and keeps the water from flowing to the Caribbean. In between is the only bad road of the whole trip, about 10 km of mud and potholes—OK for 2-wheel drive if you take it slowly. Shortly you drive through some beautiful multi-story rainforest near the lake that makes it all worthwhile.

Lake Arenal offers world class windsurfing and guapote fishing.

Near Lake Arenal you'll find several cabinas and lodges, primarily for fishing, volcano watching, or windsurfing. Several houses rent rooms.

Arenal Lodge: Very well designed, comfortable fishing lodge on a hill with great view of the volcano. The lobby and dining area has an orchid garden and many hanging plants. Offers guapote fishing on the lake with guide and boat, tours to hot springs, and Caño Negro Biological Reserve to the north. Rents horses. Friendly, hospitable. Recommended.

Cabinas Puerto San Luis: Cabinas across tree shaded lawn from restaurant on the southwest shore of Lake Arenal, just below Tilarán, well located for fishing and windsurfing. Light, airy, comfortable rooms. Midweek rate is Range F, an excellent value. Recommended.

Albergue Lago Arenal: Hostel with bunk beds on 20 acres with woods, fruit trees and howler monkeys on hill northeast of Lake Arenal, 1 km. from Arenal village. Rate includes breakfast (IYHF discount). Groceries available in village, cooking facilities at lodge. Tabacón bus passes entrance. Friendly, relaxed, youthful place. Trees with hammocks, fishing poles available. Rent canoe, mountain bikes, tents. Recommended.

Check the Nature Lodges chapter, page 80, for more description of **Arenal Observatory**, owned by Costa Rica Sun Tours, atop a ridge part way up the volcano, and **Lago Cote Ecoadventure Camp** on the southeastern side of Lake Arenal, with package tours through Tikal Tours.

Children play in Tabacón creek fed by hot springs from Arenal Volcano.

At Tabacón, about 4 km beyond the lake, you can enjoy hot spring water from the Volcano Arenal in a swimming pool with water slide adjacent to the restaurant or soak in the warm stream with cascade and boulders in the meadow behind. Anywhere you stop along the highway you'll hear an occasional rumble from the volcano, and if you're here at night, you can see bright ash and rock thrown up in the air—if it's one of the mountain's active periods and not clouded over.

In Fortuna, **Hotel Central,** facing the park, wasn't inspected but looked OK. It's on a corner in the center of town, second floor. Every Costa Rican town must have a Hotel Central.)

At Ciudad Quesada, the largest town in the region, a cooperative sells local arts and crafts on the north side of the square. In and near Ciudad Quesada are:

El Tucano: Deluxe resort beside creek fed by hot springs, on 400 acre reserve with forest trails, 8 km north of Ciudad Quesada (and bus). Large carpeted rooms, phone, 1–2 dbl beds, some overlook creek. Olympic-size unchlorinated spring water pool plus hot mineral pool (no kids under 15 allowed in mineral pool). Sauna, spa and massage room. Hiking trails, horseback riding (have riding ring), mini golf, tennis, small zoo, meeting room for 600. International restaurant. English, German and Italian spoken. Quieter mid-week. Recommended.

La Central: Clean tipico business hotel with tile floors, hardwood ceiling, facing west side of central park. Rooms at front and back have balconies, rooms at back quieter, have view if clear. Very good value.

Hotel	Address	Telephone (Fax)	No. of Rms	Pvt Bath	Hot Water	In Town	On Waterfront	Courtesy Transp	Recomm Access	Parking	Air Cond or Fan	Restaurant	Bar	Cooking Facil	Elevator	Wheelchair Acc	TV	Pool	English Spoken	Noise Level	Cleanliness	Single Rate Range
LAKE ARENAL AREA:																						
Arenal Lodge	Apdo. 1139-1250 Escazú, San Jose	28-2588 46-1881 (28-2798)	5	All	•		•	Car Bus	•		•	•						•	Exc	Exc	•	B
Cabinas Puerto San Luis	San Luis de Tilarán	69-5444 Ext. 152	12	All	•	•		Car Bus	•	•	•	•							Exc	Exc	•	D
Albergue Lago Arenal	Apdo. 147-6150 Santa Ana, San Jose	82-7555	16		•			Car Bus	•		•	•	•						Exc	Exc	•	F
CIUDAD QUESADA:																						
El Tucano	Agua Caliente, San Carlos	46-1822 (46-1692)	33	All	•		•	Car Bus	•	•	•	•					•	•	Exc	Exc	•	B
La Central	Cuidad Quesada, San Carlos	46-0766 46-0301	50	All	•			Car Bus											Exc	V gd	•	E
La Mirada	Cuidad Quesada, San Carlos	46-2222	13	All	•			Car Bus	•		•	•							Exc	Exc		E

Price Range for 2 people in high season, before taxes—A+ Over $80/day, A $60–80, B $45–60, C $30–45, D $20–30, $E $11–20, F up to $11, U.S. $. * = Meals included.

La Mirada: New hotel on hilltop 4 km north of Ciudad Quesada with view over most of the northern plain and including Arenal when clear. Phone and radio in rooms, private entrance from carport. Recommended.

While some maps show a straight highway south to the Interamerican Highway, it hasn't been built, and you will have a winding road with many trucks from Ciudad Quesada back through Zarcero and Sarchí to the main road. This traffic may be better on weekends than mid-week. Don't let it stop you from exploring Costa Rica!

Paz Waterfall tumbles out of the rainforest beside the road north of Zarcero.

In this area farther east, are **La Selva Biological Reserve** (reservation absolutely required even to enter) and the nature lodges **El Gavilan** near Puerto Viejo and its camp on the Sarapiquí River at **Oro Verde, Selva Verde Lodge** at Chilamate, and **Rara Avis** above Horquetas—all described in our Nature Lodges chapter, page 80. In Water Sports, page 35, is rustic **Rancho Leona**, offering kayak tours on the Sarapiquí River.

Pair of topiary rabbits in Zarcero's central square, part of collection of animal and human figures worth a trip.

South Central

South central here includes the Talamanca Mountains south of Cerro de La Muerte (the summit on the Interamerican Highway) and the Valles de General and Coto Brus. From the east, you can ride buses from Puerto Limón to Bribri near the base of these mountains. From there into the Indian reserves or up into the mountains requires 4-wheel drive until roads run out entirely and you're on foot. Especially in wet season, even the locals have trouble getting around. Several thousand Indians, remnants of pre-Columbian tribes, live in reserves granted by the government on the eastern slopes of the Talamancas. These bound the national parks of Chirripó and La Amistad.

Statue of Christ above cliff overlooks the Interamerican Highway.

On the west side, the Valles de General and Coto Brus are a developing farming area, with miles of pineapple fields. The Interamerican Highway drops (often suddenly in the wet season or during earthquakes!) from the mountains down to San Isidro, the largest town and government center. Accommodations here are basic to good, and reasonably priced.

Del Sur: Very attractive hotel, the best here, a few miles south of town

263

Hotel	Address	Telephone (Fax)	No. of Rms	Pvt Bath	Hot Water	In Town	On Waterfront	Courtesy Transp	Recomm Access	Parking	Air Cond or Fan	Restaurant	Bar	Cooking Facil	Elevator	Wheelchair Acc	TV	Pool	English Spoken	Noise Level	Cleanliness	Single Rate	Range
SAN ISIDRO DE GENERAL:																							
Del Sur	Apdo. 4 San Isidro, Punt.	71-0233	60	All	•			Bus Car	•	•	•	•	•					•	Exc	V gd	•	•	E
Amaneli	San Isidro, Punt.	71-0352	41	All		•		Bus Car		•	•	•	•						Gd	Exc	•	•	F
Iguazu	San Isidro, Punt.	71-2571	21	16		•		Bus Car	•	•									V gd	Exc	•	•	F

Price Range for 2 people in high season, before taxes—A+ Over $80/day, A $60–80, B $45–60, C $30–45, D $20–30, $E $11–20, F up to $11, U.S. $. * = Meals included.

264

with big pool. During *semana santa* I found many Costa Rican families from San Jose here, enjoying themselves and avoiding crowds at the beach! Excellent value. Recommended.

Amaneli: Clean budget hotel with tipico restaurant below, on highway going through town. Get room at back for quiet. Good value.

Iguazu: Spotless hotel on quiet street behind Amaneli. Recommended.

Nature inns here are **Genesis II** and **Finca Chacon**, in the northern Talamancas, rustic, hospitable, and quiet, uncrowded places to watch quetzals. Description in the Nature Lodges chapter, page 80.

Oxen grind sugar cane in old-style trapiche, beside the Interamerican Highway.

From San Isidro you can take buses to Playa Dominical on the coast or up to Chirripó National Park headquarters on the edge of San Gerardo de Rivas. The Interamerican Highway continues down the valley, down the river to Palmar and on to the Panamanian border. Buses to the border are crowded in December before Christmas as Costa Ricans ride down from San Jose to shop in stores just over the border. Near Palmar the basaltic spheres of all sizes carved by prehistoric peoples are found.

In this area Costa Ricans and foreigners are developing fincas, usually well off the main road. If you meet some of these people and can visit, you'll see pioneer life in the modern tropics and probably some wildlife.

La Amistad National Park covers the top and both sides of the Talamanca Mountains and adjoins a park in Panama. It protects habitat for all of Costa Rica's high and mid-altitude animals, including the jaguar, which need large undeveloped areas. You can now drive to the park entrance at Las Mellizas or take a bus to San Vito from San Jose and the La Lucha 30 km, from which you hike 6 km to Las Mellizas. You should discuss this with the park authorities in San Jose first as you need permission and should get advice on routes from Las Mellizas, as well as what to bring (22-7911, 33-4118). There's camping inside the park entrance and hiking on trails in the adjacent forest reserve. More trails are being added and there are rooms available nearby, but this is a steep, mountainous wilderness park. Except for the trails, some areas with bamboo thicket are impassable.

The **Wilson Botanical Gardens,** maintained by the Organization For Tropical Studies, fill 30 acres, buffered by over 300 acres of forest reserve, with miles of trails, and one of the world's finest collections of ferns, bromeliads, heliconias, and other tropical plants. They've counted 278 bird.species on the grounds. This isn't a place to rush through. You must call the OTS office in San Jose for a reservation (they advise calling two weeks ahead) even to walk their trails for the day. Phone 40-6696, Fax: 40-6783. However, since fewer people come here than to La Selva, reservations are easier to get. You may also be able to reserve space in their dormitory or their two rooms and meals ($45 including meals). They have beds for 30, but may allow more people in for the day. If you're not driving, you can take the San Vito bus from San Jose, a six hour ride. You can then take the Villa Neilly bus or taxi the last 6 km. There are several simple, not deluxe cabinas in San Vito.

While this is an extensive description of Costa Rican tourist attractions and accommodations, more are being planned or built as we go to press. I would appreciate reports of your experiences with facilities described here or new ones you find. You will find a lot to explore and enjoy in this small friendly country!

Crater of Irazú, an earthly moonscape you can reach by car or bus.

NATIONAL PARKS

You've already heard of the significance of Costa Rica's park system. Recently the system of national parks and biological reserves was organized into nine conservation units, for better coordination. Here's a brief outline of the attractions of individual parks and how you can visit. If you're not on a guided tour and are going to see more than Irazú, Poás, Braulio Carrillo, and Manuel Antonio, which are heavily used and organized to handle crowds, you need to stop in at Park Service headquarters, Calle 25, Ave. 8/10, San Jose. Tel. 23-6963, and 33-5473.

Permission is required to visit most other parks and biological reserves. Park headquarters has a 24 hour radio net with the parks, often the only way of getting assistance in an emergency. At headquarters there is bilingual staff who can get you the latest info on roads and conditions in the park. Out at the parks, Spanish may be the only language. Staff at some parks is so limited that they must know when to expect visitors and whether you will need meals, camping areas or bunkrooms (if they have them), guides, information, or horses (which may be available at reasonable cost, but only if the park can spare them and tack, and only by prior arrangement). If you will be eating with the rangers, meals wi;; be inexpensive and basic. Any goodies such as sausage or cheese you can bring to share are much appreciated. This stop at the San Jose office your best chance to find out what to bring and what to expect.

The Park Service has a useful guide to the parks listing the significance of each and some facilities, though more have been added. It has bus info for reaching the parks. You'll soon note that buses getting closest to the remote parks go to villages that aren't on maps and let you off 10 or 15 km. from the park entrance—not what you may be used to! Maps and wildlife checklists may be bought at the CIDA office in the National Zoo in San Jose. Often the nearest food is sold 20 or more miles from the park. Topographic maps are available at bookstores or the National Geographic Institute near Plaza Viquez, east of the Pacific Railroad station.

Costa Rica's national parks need and depend on international support as they've only been established a few years and the country has been unable to build needed facilities or, more important, to buy all the private land within them—in some cases a large proportion of the park. Information on where and how you can help is given in our "So You'd Like to Help" chapter.

Dimensions of the parks are given in hectares, equal to 2.5 acres. Parks we haven't discussed in detail include:

Tortuguero: This is the green turtle nesting site you've probably seen on TV. July through September is the peak nesting season, with hatching two months later. The park has nature trails as well as river channels you can explore by boat to see many land and sea birds, monkeys, and even the rare manatee. Several tour agencies come here, and **Costa Rica Expeditions** runs tours to Tortuga Lodge on which you may fly one way, using the air strip. **The Jungle Lodge, Ilan Ilan,** and **Mawamba Lodge** also run tours using their own boats. Tours to Barra Colorado pass through the park on the main canal only.Note that government boat from Moín gives priority to locals needing transport, so room isn't always available to tourists.

Park headquarters at the south end of the village and the Green Turtle Research Station started by Archie Carr, about a mile north, are worth visiting. There are two tipico restaurants in the village, both good. You may be able to rent a dugout to do your own exploring, or hire a local guide with a boat if you're traveling independently. Beach-walking is fun even by day to see turtle tracks from the night before as well as what washed up.

Guayabo National Monument: 19 km. north of Turrialba on gravel road, discussed at end of Turrialba chapter.

Tree fern shades nature trail at Poás National Park.

Braulio Carrillo: On road from San Jose to Guápiles, starting 12 km from San Jose. Wildlife, several forest zones stretching from the eastern lowlands to the top of Barva Volcano. orchids. The eastern slope has rain and clouds much of the year. It's a beautiful ride even by public bus on the way to Limón, but fascinating if you can stop to look or hike some of its trails (check with ranger stations for maps, trail fee, and directions).

Coco Island: 360 miles offshore with reputed vast pirate and Inca treasure never found, including life-size solid gold statues of the Twelve Apostles. Some tours available. Otherwise reachable only by chartered boat. Some species of flora & fauna are found only there. There are hundreds of waterfalls on the island. With no facilities ashore, you do have to live on the boat. Fishing is not allowed within 15 miles of the island, but it has the best underwater visibility in Costa Rica. (See scuba section.)

La Amistad: Huge, straddling the upper slopes of the Talamanca Mountains, adjoining a park on Panamanian side. Its establishment more than doubled size of Costa Rican park system. New park, with no facilities or services, and few trails. Ask the Park Service in San Jose for latest info and current road conditions.

Chirripó: 43,700 hectares. It includes Cerro Chirripó, 12,530 ft., the highest point in Costa Rica, and is famous for its paramo, a high, treeless zone which has frost but no snow. From San Isidro de El General there's a bus at 5 a.m. and 2 p.m. to San Gerardo de Rivas and park headquarters. The hike takes two or more strenuous days, using shelters on the mountain, so you don't have to carry a tent. Ask the Park Service in San Jose for current conditions.

Ranger station at San Pedrillo in Corcovado Park. Tour groups land here to hike to Llorona.

Corcovado: 41,789 hectares, occupying most of the Osa Peninsula on Costa Rica's southwest coast. In an area 1/7 the size of Yosemite National Park are 285 species of birds (more than in the U.S. and Canada), 139 species of mammals, and 116 reptiles and amphibians! The park was threatened by placer gold miners in its rivers, but the Costa Rican government recently removed them and the park is again open. You can get to the west side and park headquarters by chartered plane, or to the east side via bus or boat to Puerto Jiménez and several days of hot hiking from there. Tours from nature lodges on the Osa Peninsula (see Nature Tours and Lodges, page 80) land by boat at San Pedrillo and hike in the park with rangers. This, or going with a group by plane is easiest. **Costa Rica Expeditions** leads tours from park headquarters, organized months ahead by nature tours in the U.S.

Pre-Columbian grinding stones on Caño Island.

Caño Island: 20 km. northwest of the Osa Peninsula, it has 740 forested acres with few mammal species but many birds, prehistoric burial sites, a ranger station, and coral reefs with a variety of colorful fish. In the rainiest months of September and October, it has one of the world's highest rates of lightning strikes! It was made a national park to save it from developers who wanted to make a gambling resort out of it. Nature lodges on the Osa Peninsula offer day trips.

Barra Honda: Caverns 50 to 600 feet deep with beautiful limestone formations you can visit with a ranger guide. Also dry lowland forest and the low volcanic cone, Barra Honda Volcano, near Gulf of Nicoya. Water and hiking trails are the only facilities nearer than town of Nicoya, 14 km. **Rios Tropicales** runs adventure tours into some caverns otherwise closed to public. The bus from Nicoya to Santa Ana passes about 1 km from the park.

Palo Verde: The park and adjacent wildlife preserve fill the V formed by the Tempisque and Bebedero Rivers at the head of the gulf of Nicoya. During the rainy season most of the park is flooded or swampy, except for limestone ridges in the north. It's the winter or permanent home for hundreds of species of waterfowl, including the rare jabiru stork. Camping is possible at park headquarters. Access is from Bagaces which can be reached by bus from Cañas, or you can take a cab all the way to the park from Cañas. If you're not roughing it, you may want to go with a nature tour, or rent a car and stay in Cañas, driving out to the park. If you use the ranger's bunkroom by reservation, bring a bug net for sleeping. During dry season birds are concentrated along the rivers, and the easiest way to see and photograph them would be from raft or boat. The park has a nature trail on a dike which gives good early morning views of birds in the surrounding swamp.

Rincon de la Vieja: Hike to summit is only advised during dry season due to visibility. One shelter en route. There's also a bunkroom at park headquarters and use of a kitchen by arrangement at headquarters in San Jose. On trails there are several lovely single campsites at lower elevations. Don't camp or even stand longer than you have to on tick-infested lawn in front of park headquarters. Wildlife and volcanic features are spectacular. Bus from Liberia is unreliable in wet season. More comfortable rustic accommodations, horses, and guides are offered by Rincon de la Vieja Mountain Lodge on adjoining hacienda with tours through the park. See Nature Tours and Lodges chapter, page 80.

Tropical forest with a volcanic aspect, Los Pailes steam vents in Rincon de La Vieja.

Family of howler monkeys rests during midday heat in Santa Rosa Park.

Santa Rosa: Costa Rica's first park was established to protect the site of Costa Rica's battle with William Walker and his men that preserved the country's independence. It also includes the Playas Naranjo, a 7 mile walk each way to a beautiful beach on which leatherback turtles nest, and Nancite, several miles farther north where huge arribadas of Pacific Ridley turtles nest. The park extends north to Bahia Santa Elena, including former lands of Nicaraguan dictator, Somoza, with beautiful white sand beaches, some an easy walk from roads leading into area, much dry forest wildlife. From the Interamerican Highway north of the park's main entrance, turn left to Cuajiniquil. December through April are best months for camping and road conditions.

In 1987 the land between the formerly separated parts was added by President Arias. It includes the airstrip allegedly used by the CIA to supply the contras. Putting that land into a national park seems a typically Costa Rican solution to the problem!

Guanacaste: Extends from the existing park eastward to the top of the cordillera, providing room for species, including birds and butterflies, which migrate up and downslope during the year. Campesinos are being trained as rangers, giving them work as the land reverts from cattle pasture to tropical forest. Several research stations usually have rustic accommodations available with advance notice. Call the conservation unit headquarters in Santa Rosa Park for information, 69-5598. Access is easy since the Interamerican Hwy. skirts the park.

Besides the national parks, there are the biological reserves, such as

Carara and Tapantí, parts of which you can visit by permit only or with a guided nature group. Geotur and Costa Rica Expeditions run day trips to Carara, and the latter also has tours to Tapantí. These quiet places with limited trails have much more wildlife than you'll see, but with guides, you can enjoy an exciting experience.

What a lot to explore! The wilderness aspects of these parks and heavy growth in most places can give you a much greater respect for short distances! But there's so much to see and marvel at, even if you just sit quietly in camp and wait to see what walks, crawls or flies past.

Pelicans roost in island trees between crashing dives for fish.

The rainforest goes to market—logs from the southern zone on the Interamerican Highway.

SO YOU'D LIKE TO HELP

Costa Rica, as a developing nation, welcomes your help if you want to contribute to its progress as well as simply enjoy it. Besides the knowledge that you have helped, this gives you a chance to meet some wonderful people you otherwise would have missed.

Costa Rica's national parks need international support as they've only been established recently and are still being increased. The nation has been unable to build needed facilities or even to buy all the private land within them—in some cases a large proportion of the park. To protect the wildlife and plants for which the parks were established, more rangers are needed, with equipment to do the job. When I visited one park, the only jeep needed repairs, there was no fuel for the patrol boat, and the only pair of binoculars had lenses too mildewed to see through. Besides out-numbering the rangers, the poachers were better equipped.

Besides Peace Corps volunteers assigned to individual parks, the **Servicio Parques Nacionales** has its own volunteer program, open to volunteers who can live very simply and work at needed projects including trail building. The office is on the ground floor of the park system headquarters at Calle 25, Ave. 8/10. For information, in English if you need it, call 23-6963.

The **Fundación de Parques Nacionales**, Apdo. 236, 1002 San Jose, (Tel.23-8437 and 33-0003) was established to raise money for the parks, to set priorities for its use in the park system, and to assure that donated funds are spent for that purpose. Its office is on the second floor of the edificio cristal, Ave 1, Calle 1/3. Donations can be made to be used where the foundation sees greatest need or for particular units of the system. Here's one use for the money you couldn't change back to dollars on leaving or as a meaningful gift you don't have to pack for nature-loving friends at home.

Tax-deductible donations can be made from within the United States specifically for the Costa Rican Parks to:

World Wildlife Fund .... **The Nature Conservancy**
1255 23rd St. NW .... 1815 North Lynn St.
Washington, DC 20009 .... Arlington, VA 22209

Fundación Neotrópica (same office, address, and phone as Fundación de Parques Nacionales above) works both within and outside parks to protect the environment. They have specific projects such as helping rural people develop markets for products harvested from rainforest without clearcutting the forest, promoting reforestation, etc. Many authorities feel the only way to protect the forest and its animals from people who are only trying to feed their families is to develop cooperative projects. Drawing boundary lines on maps doesn't guarantee protection.

While **Monteverde Cloud Forest Reserve** isn't a park and is run instead by the Tropical Science Center, its needs are similar. The **Monteverde Conservation League**, Apdo. 10165, 1000 San Jose, raises funds to buy land adjacent to the present reserve on both east and west that is essential breeding habitat for the bare-necked umbrella bird and resplendent quetzal as well as the jaguar and many other species. You can get an idea how far your dollars will go from current land prices here. An acre of rainforest with stream frontage is worth about $50 That's all it takes to give permanent protection to the quetzal's home. The League has agreements with some farmers to buy their land, but must raise the money before the land is deforested or sold.

The Children's Rainforest, is an international project started in Sweden, and now includes children, schools, and adults buying land adjacent to the Monteverde Cloud Forest to enlarge the habitat. Large donations are credited to tracts often named as memorials. Donations can be made to the Monteverde Conservation League, the World Wildlife Fund, or The Nature Conservancy, designated for the "International Children's Rainforest Program".

Waiting for the bus in Bebedero, a village near Palo Verde National Park, I asked the man beside me where the children went to school after they finished 6th grade here. "Some go to stay with relatives in Cañas and some ride the bus every day. It costs a lot of money and they have to take their lunch. The ride is an hour each way. Most of them can't go." He didn't mention school uniforms, another cost. I asked if Bebedero had a library so those who stayed home could continue to read. "No, the nearest library is in Cañas, too."

Beside me on the curb a barefoot ten year-old girl turned the pages of this book, reading a few English words and looking at the pictures of her country. "Ah, los canales. Que linda!"

Village libraries in towns with no high schools are the only way Costa Ricans can continue education past the 6th grade if they can't afford to live elsewhere to go to school. There are presently 95 libraries outside San Jose though the country needs hundreds more. Most of these have very few books, all of which must be read in the library. Libraries are critical in a democracy where everyone votes and must understand what he's voting for. Sra. Oduber, wife of the former president, made these her concern and helped get the system as far as it is.

To be sure that funds and books could be donated for this cause and spent accordingly, I met with staff at the National Library in San Jose and learned how the donations should be directed. To donate funds or books (new or used, Spanish preferred), address:

Sra. Vera Violeta Salazar Mora,
Directora, Dirección Bibliotecas Públicas,
Apdo. 10.008,
San Jose, Costa Rica, Central America.
(Phone 36-1828)

You can specify (especificar): "Para comprar de libros de las Bibliotecas Públicas."

In San Jose can go to the National Library across from the National Park on the hill and ask for this department. (The National Library building is closed for 1991 and possibly longer due to earthquake repair. the department is operating from another building in San Jose until the repairs are completed.) Sra. Salazar says that with such specification the money will not be spent in San Jose nor will it be used to simply build more concrete somewhere. If you'd like to help democracy in Latin America, here's a personal way to do it.

I hope someday all villages without libraries will at least have a few shelves of library books in the school where any villager can read them and where students will then have more books available.

People wishing to **volunteer to teach** English in Costa Rican schools can write to the Ministerio de Educación, Departamento de Inglés, 1000 San Jose, Costa Rica. This program is starting as we go to press. Rural schools especially need help in most subject areas as they sometimes can get only high school graduates as teachers.

Retired executives can help Costa Rica and other developing nations by sharing their managerial skills through **International Executive Service Corps**, P. O. Box 10005, Stamford, CT 06904 in the U.S. or **C.E.S.O.**, Suite 200, 1867 Yonge Street, Toronto, Ontario, Canada M4S 1Y5 in Canada. The program is effective in Costa Rica, and our readers have enjoyed participating.

The **Peace Corps** is very active in Costa Rica and includes retired couples with experience and skills Costa Rica needs. I've some truly radiant people who've volunteered in public health, libraries, and schools.

Costa Rica is a great vacation land for those who want to relax. It's also an inspiring place with welcoming people for those who want to help others.

Split-leaf philodendron being raised in forest for export. The sprinkler system, fed by a creek, is bamboo with perforations!

SOURCES OF INFORMATION

To call or send fax from outside Costa Rica, use country code 506 before numbers given.

TOUR AGENCIES

T.A.M
Calle 1, Ave. ctl./1
Apdo. 1864-1000
San Jose
Phone 23-5111

Swiss Travel Service
Lobby of Hotel Corobici
Apdo. 7-1970,
1000 San Jose
Phone 31-4055

Orchid Travel
Apdo. 812-1011 Y Griega
San Jose
Phone 38-3586

Panorama Tours
Calle 9, Ave. ctl./1
Apdo. 7.323,
1000 San Jose
Phone 33-0233

Rio Colorado Lodge
Apdo. 5094,
1000 San Jose
Phone 32-4063,32-8610
US: (800) 243-9777
FAX: 31-5987Fishing, canal trips, dove hunting

Agencia de Viajes Atlántico
Apdo. 1078 Centro Colón
1007 San Jose
Phone 32-2732, 32-8888
Canales trips

Typical Tours
Ave. 4, Calle 24/26
Apdo. 842-1000
San Jose
Phone 21-3158

Fiesta Tours
Ave. 1, Calle 5/7
Apdo. 8-4320,
1000 San Jose
Phone 23-3433

Agencia de Viajes Miki
Calle 20 sur, Paseo Colón
Apdo. 328-1007 Centro Colón
Phone 33-0613, 21-3681

Interviajes
Calle 3, Ave. 4 Heredia
Apdo. 296-3000
Heredia
Phone 38-1212
Scenic reasonably priced tours for Costa Ricans and visitors

Agencia de Viajes Las Olas
Hotel Jacó Beach
Apdo. 962,
1000 San Jose
Phone 61-1250, 32-4811

Guanacaste Tours
Apdo. 55-5000
Liberia, Gste.
Phone 66-0306, FAX 66-0307
Tours to beaches, national parks.

Nature Tours

Calypso Tours
Apdo. 6941,
1000 San Jose
Phone 33-3617
FAX:33-0401
Boat tours, Gulf of Nicoya

Geotur
Apdo. 469 Y Griega
10ll San Jose
Phone 34-1867
Day nature tours in
  parks, biological preserves.

Costa Rica Expeditions
Calle ctl., Ave. 3
Apdo. 6941,
1000 San Jose
Phone 22-0333, 57-0766
FAX 57-1665
Nature tours, raft trips,.
lodges at Tortuguero,
Monteverde, Corcovado

Costa Rica Sun Tours
Ave. 7, Calle 3/5
Apdo. 1195
1250 Escazú
Phone 55-2011, 55-2112
FAX 55-3529
Eco-Center agency for own
Tiskita, Arenal Observ. & many
nature tours, lodges.

Horizontes
Calle 28, Ave. 1/3
Apdo. 1780-1002
San Jose
Phone 21-1594, 22-2022
FAX 55-4513
Marenco Biol. Station

Rios Tropicales
Paseo Colon, adj. Mercedes Benz
Apdo. 472-1200
San Jose
Phone 33-6455
FAX 55-4354
Raft trips, sea kayaking

Aqua Sport
Apdo. 100
Playas de Coco
Guanacaste
Phone 67-0050
Diving tours, rentals air

Diving Safaris, Inc.
P. O. Box 425-2010 Zapote
San Jose
Phone 24-0033
Boat tours, diving rentals, air

Rara Avis
Apdo. 8105-1000
San Jose
Phone 53-0844
FAX 21-2314
Rainforest preserve,
lodges

Papagayo Excursions
Playa Tamarindo
Carretera San Jose-Santa Cruz
Tamarindo, Guanacaste
Phone 68-0652, 32-6854
FAX 68-0859, 55-3355
Turtle nesting, estuary cruises

See descriptions of Nature Tours & Lodges throughout Costa Rica, page 80

EMBASSIES & CONSULATES IN/NEAR SAN JOSE

Nation	Address	Telephone
Argentina	Ave. ctl., Calle 27	21-6869
Austria	Calle 2, Ave. 2	23-2822
Belgium	Los Yoses	25-0351
Brazil	Calle 4, Ave. ctl.	33-1544
Britain	Paseo Colón, Calle 38/40	21-5566
Canada	Calle 3, Ave. ctl.	23-0446
Colombia	Ave. 5, Calle 5	21-0725
Chile	Bo. Dent	24-4243
China	Los Yoses	24-8180
Ecuador	Calle 1, Ave. 5	23-6281
El Salvador	Calle 5, Ave. ctl.,Los Yoses	25-5887
France	Carret. Curridabat	22-1149
Germany	Ave 3, Calle 36	21-5811
Greece	Guayabos	25-9413
Guatemala	Calle 24/28, Ave. 1	33-5283
Holland	Calle 1, Ave. 2	22-7355
Honduras	Calle 1, Ave. 5	22-2145
Italy	Calle 29, Ave. 8/10	24-6575
Japan	Rohrmoser	32-1255
Korea	Calle 2, Ave. 2	33-1056
Mexico	Calle 5, Ave. 1/3	33-8874
Nicaragua	Barrio California	33-9225
Panama	San Pedro	25-3401
Peru	Calle 4, Ave. ctl.	22-5644
Spain	Calle 30/32, Paseo Colón	22-1933
Switzerland	Calle 5, Ave. 3/5	21-4829
U.S.S.R.	Curridabat	25-5780
U.S.A.	Pavas	20-3939
Uruguay	Calle 2, Ave. 1	23-2512
Venezuela	Los Yoses	25-8810

Call or visit in the morning, as afternoon hours vary. To write the U.S. Embassy in Costa Rica, the quickest and easiest way is United States Embassy in Costa Rica, APO Miami, FL 34020. Letters travel by pouch from there.

COSTA RICAN CONSULATES

CANADA

614 Centre A. Street N.W.	1155 Dorchester Blvd. W.
Calgary, Alberta	Suite 2902, Montreal
7 Lia Crescent Don Mills	P. Q. Canada H3B 2L3
Toronto, Ontario, Canada	(514) 866-8159
1520 Alberni Street	(514) 866-0442
Vancouver, B.C	

UNITED STATES—Consulates General (For the address of local consu-

Jurisdiction	Address lates, call consulate gen'l.)
Washington, D.C., Maryland,	**1825 Connecticut Ave.NW, Ste. 3211**
West Virginia, Virginia	**Washington, D. C. 20009**
	(202) 234-2945
New York, Pennsylvania,	**80 Wall Street, Suite 1117**
Connecticut, Delaware,	New York, NY 10005
New Jersey, Massachusetts	(212) 425-4620
Rhode Island, Maine,	
Vermont, New Hampshire,	
Rhode Island	
California, Oregon,	**3540 Wilshire Blvd. , Suite 404**
Washington, Montana,	Los Angeles, CA 90010
Colorado, Wyoming, Idaho,	(213) 380-7915
Nevada, Utah, Arizona,	(213) 380-7925
Alaska, Hawaii	FAX (213) 380-5639
Florida, Georgia, North and	**28 W. Flagler St., Suite 806**
South Carolina	Miami, FL 33130
	(305) 377-4242
Louisiana, Alabama,	**World Trade Ctr. Bldg.,2 Canal St.**
Mississippi, Tennessee,	New Orleans, LA 70130
Kentucky, Arkansas	(504) 525-5445
Texas, Oklahoma, Kansas	**3000 Wilcrest, Suite 145**
New Mexico	Houston, TX 77042
	(713) 266-0484
Illinois, Michigan, Ohio,	**8 S. Michigan Ave., Suite 1312**
Indiana, Wisconsin,	Chicago, IL 60603
Minnesota, Missouri, North	(312) 787-3323
Dakota, South Dakota,	
Nebraska, Iowa	

RECOMMENDED READING

Guidebooks, international, with Costa Rica section:

Central America on a Shoestring, by Geoff Crowther, Lonely Planet Publications, Australia. Covers extremely basic hotels as well as better ones. Bus and transportation information. 1992.

Mexico & Central American Handbook, Trade & Travel Publication Ltd., England (distributed in the U.S. by Rand McNally). Information for the budget traveler. 1991.

Guidebooks, Costa Rica:

Costa Rica, A Natural Destination, by Ree Strange Sheck. Emphasizes national parks. John Muir Publications.

The New Key to Costa Rica, by Beatrice Blake and Anne Becher, Editoria Texto Ltda., Costa Rica. Guidebook which emphasizes living in Costa Rica.

Costa Rica by Paul Glassman, Passport Press, 1989. General guide.

The Rivers of Costa Rica, Gallo and Mayfield. Photos, maps, tables.

Costa Rican Life:

The Costa Ricans, by Richard, Karen, and Mavis Biesanz, Waveland Press, Prospect Heights, IL. Very well done social history and description of the Costa Rican people.

What Happen—A Folk History of Costa Rica's Talamanca Coast, by Paula Palmer, Ecodesarrollos, Costa Rica Oral history by coastal residents.

Natural Science: Any of these published in the U.S. is far less expensive in the U.S. or Canada and is worth getting before you leave home.

A Guide to the Birds of Costa Rica, by Gary Stiles and Alexander Skutch. Cornell University Press. (800) 666-2211 to order with credit cards. Com-plete guide with detailed plates for identifying birds. Paperback and hard cover.

A Field Guide to Mexican Birds and Adjacent Central America, by Roger Tory Peterson, Houghton-Mifflin.

A Guide to the Birds of Panama, by Robert Ridgely, Princeton University Press.

Butterflies of Costa Rica by Philip DeVries, Princeton University Press. 50 color plates. 327 p.

A Neotropical Companion, by John C. Kricher, Princeton University Press, 1989. More than an introduction to tropical animals, insects and plants; information with charm and humor.

Life Above the Jungle Floor, Donald Perry. Simon & Schuster. Narrative of research life in rainforest canopy.

Costa Rica: Country Environmental Profile—A Field Study, available in bookstores or at the Tropical Science Center, San Jose. Excellent in-depth study of environmental issues in Costa Rica.

Costa Rican Natural History, edited by Daniel H. Janzen, University of Chicago Press. Thorough discussion of the geography, climate, flora, and fauna of Costa Rica.

Costa Rica National Parks, by Mario Boza INCAFO, Spain. Chapter on each of Costa Rica's national parks, beautiful photographs.

Audio tape: *It's a Jungle In There*, sounds of the tropical rainforest. Recorded in stereo at Monteverde and La Selva. 60 minutes of birds, monkeys, tropical downpour, etc. Earl Vickers, 236 W. Portal Ave., #140, San Francisco, CA 94127. $10. (Add $2 for overseas mail.) Part of profits goes to Children's Rainforest.

SUPPLIERS

Mosquito and no-see-um nets for bed and person—Campmor, P.O. Box 997, Paramus, NJ 07653-0997. 1-800-526-4784.

Ear plugs—for sleeping. Yellow foam ones are comfortable and mute sounds you may not be used to, (the cantina down the street at 2 a.m.) Available at hardware and chainsaw stores, gun shops.

"Chigarid"—for instant, permanent relief of chigger (kills the mite), mosquito, and tick bites. C & C Labs, P.O. Box 7779, Dallas, TX 75209 (214) 748-7953. In drugstores in U.S. Middle West and South., or order from company for retail price, about $3 in 1991, plus shipping.

USEFUL ADDRESSES

(To telephone or fax to Costa Rica, dial 011 for the international lines from U.S., then 506, Costa Rica's country code, from anywhere.)

Instituto Costarricense de Turismo
Apdo. 777
San Jose, Costa Rica
Phone 23-1733
Airport off. 42-1820
(open till 9 p.m.)

ICT Office of Tourist
Information
Plaza de la Cultura
Calle 5, Ave. ctl./2
Open Monday–Friday,
8:00 a.m. to 4:30 p.m.

Costa Rican Tourist Board
1101 Brickell Ave.
BIV Tower, Suite 801
Miami, FL 33131
Phone (305) 358-2150
(800) 327-70333

The Tico Times
P. O. Box 4632
San Jose, Costa Rica
(located: Ave. 8, Calle 15)
Phone 22-8952, 22-0044
FAX 33-6378

ASCONA
Apdo. 83790
1000 San Jose
Costa Rica
Phone 33-3188
(conservation association)

TICA Bus
Calle 9, Ave. 4
San Jose
Phone 21-8954

National Park Service
Calle 25, Ave. 8/10
San Jose, Costa Rica
Phone 23-6963, 33-5473

Fundacion de Parques Nacionales
Apdo. 236
1002 San Jose, Costa Rica
Phone 22-4921, 23-8437

Tropical Science Center
Calle 1, Ave. 2
(2 blks s. of Metr. Cathedral)
San Jose, Costa Rica
Phone 22-6241

World Wildlife Fund
1601 Connecticut Ave.
Washington, D. C. 20009
(202) 387-0800

As
R
Apc
San
Ave.
Phon
8:30-3

Langu
(many
INTEN
Apdo. 8
San Jose
Phone 25-6009, 24-6353

North American-Costa Rican
    Cultural Center
Apdo. 1489
San Jose
Phone 25-9433

Instituto Internacional Forester
75 m s. of Automercado Los Yoses
San Jose
Phone 25-1649

Instituto Universal de Idioma
Apdo. 164
San Jose, Costa Rica
Phone 23-9662

Conversa
Apdo. 17 Centro Colón
San Jose, Costa Rica
Phone 21-7649, 33-2418

American Institute for
    Language & Culture
Apdo. 200
1001 San Jose, Costa Rica
Phone 25-4313

ICAI (culture & language courses)
Apdo. 10302
San Jose
Phone 33-8571, FAX 21-5238

The Nature Conserva
International Prog
1785 Massachus
Washington
(703) 841-

Sources

Youth Hostels:
Costa Rican Youth Hostels
Ave. Ctl., Calles 29/31
24-4085

USEFUL WORDS AND PHRASES

abanico=fan
abierto=open
agua=water
agua caliente=hot water
aire (con, sin)=air conditioning
alto=stop
Apartado(Apdo.)=post office
  box
apartotel=apartment hotel
almuerzo=lunch

alto=high
amable=kind
aquí=here
arroz=rice
avenida=avenue
ayer=yesterday
azúcar=sugar
azul=blue

bajo=low
baño (con, sin)=bath
barato=cheap
blanco=white
bolsa=bag
bueno=good
buenos días=hello

cabina=cabin
café=coffee
calle=street
cambio=change (money)
carne=meat
caro=expensive

casado=basic meal
cafe negro=black coffee
cena=supper
cerrado=closed
cerveza=beer
claro=light
comer=eat
comida=meal, dinner
comprar=to buy
con leche=coffee with
  cream
correo=post office
cuánto cuesta=what does it cost
cuarto=room
cuarto silencio=quiet room
cuenta=restaurant or hotel
  check

derecha=right
desayuno=breakfast
deseo=I want
dificil=difficult
dolor=pain
domingo=Sunday
dónde está=where is
dueño=owner

ensalada=salad
entrada=entrance
escuela=school
esta noche=tonight
estacion, no estacion=parking
estampillas=stamps
este=east

fácil=easy
farmacia=drug store
finca=ranch
frijoles=beans
frito=fried

gerente=manager
gracias=thank you
grande=big, large
gris=gray

habla inglés=do you speak
  English?
Hable usted más despacio, por
  favor=please speak more slowly
hasta luego (adiós)=goodbye
hay, no hay=there is, there isn't
helado=ice cream
hermosa=beautiful
hoy=today
huevo=egg

iglesia=church
impuesto=tax (e.g., on hotel
  bills)
izquierda=left

jamón=ham
jueves=Thursday

leche=milk
lechuga=lettuce
llave=key
lado=side
limpio=clean
lluvia=rain
lunes=Monday

malo=bad
mañana=tomorrow, morning
martes=Tuesday
médico=doctor

mercado=market
mi cuenta, por favor=I
  wish my bill please
miércoles=Wednesday
muy=very

naranjo=orange
negro=black
necesito=I need
noche=night
norte=north

oeste=west
oficina=office
oscuro=dark

pan=bread
paragua=umbrella
  (man's)
pension=inexpensive hotel,
  but doesn't indicate meals served
papas=potatoes
pequeño=small
pescado=fish
pimienta=pepper
piña=pineapple
piscina=swimming pool
playa=beach
poco=little
pollo=chicken
por favor=please
pulpería=small grocery store

que-what, who
Qué hora es?-What time is it?
queso=cheese
quiere usted=do you want
que quiere usted?=what do
  you want?
quiero=I want, I wish

rápido=fast

recto=straight ahead
rojo=red

sábado=Saturday
sal=salt
salida=exit
semana=week
sombrilla=umbrella(woman's)
sucio=dirty
sud-south

tarde=late, afternoon
tarjeta de crédito=credit card
temprano=early
tico (tica)=Costa Rican
    term for themselves
tiene=you(he, she) have/has
tostadas=toast
tipico=typical

ventana=window
verde=green
viernes=Friday

Numbers

uno=1	diez y ocho=18	seiscientos=600
dos=2	diez y nueve=19	setecientos=700
tres=3	veinte=20	ochocientos=800
cuatro=4	veintiuno=21	novecientos=900
cinco=5	veintidós=22	mil=1000
seis=6	treinta=30	dos mil=2000
siete=7	cuarenta=40	
ocho=8	cincuenta=50	
nueve=9	sesenta=60	
diez=10	setenta=70	
once=11	ochenta=80	
doce=12	noventa=90	
trece=13	cien=100	
catorce=14	doscientos=200	
quince=15	trescientos=300	
diez y seis=16	cuatrocientos=400	
diez y siete=17	quinientos=500	

THE AUTHOR

Ellen Searby has traveled in 38 countries and 47 of the United States by jet, her two-seat plane, car, bicycle, canoe, raft, and on foot. She earned a B.A. in biology and an M.A. in geography from Stanford. She lived in Alaska and worked on the Alaska state ferries from 1975 to 1990, first as a U.S. Forest Service shipboard naturalist answering thousands of travelers' questions, and then as a member of the ferry crew. Using her knowledge of travelers' needs, she writes and publishes *Alaska's Inside Passage Traveler*, an annually updated guide to Alaska's ferries and the Inside Passage.

When she came to Costa Rica on a much-needed vacation, people who saw her Alaska book persuaded her to write a book for Costa Rican visitors, clearly explaining the choices they have in sights, activities and facilities. She returned to do the research, and the result is *The Costa Rica Traveler*. She continues her field research and photography in Costa Rica, enjoying Costa Rican friendliness with her combined work and play.

Ellen Searby is married to retired forestry pilot, Henry Jori. In 1990 she retired from the Alaska ferry to full-time writing and publishing, now living on the family farm in the northern California redwoods.

Index

Index

Flash!

As we go to press for each printing even within the life of the edition, this section is rewritten with last minute information we think you may need, as well as conditions we expect will change rapidly. If information here differs from that in another part of the book, go with what's here. This section expands as needed into the Notes pages presently following.

On April 22. 1991 Costa Rica was jolted by a Richter 7.4 earthquake centered southwest of Puerto Limón in the Valle de Estrella near the Caribbean Coast. The Cocos and Caribbean tectonic plates shoved, with Costa Rica's eastern coast raised 1.5 meters! This quake was stronger than the Mexican quake in 1983 or the 1989 quake in California.

Puerto Limón was badly damaged. The Internacional Hotel downtown collapsed and the Hotel Las Olas near Portete had major damage. The city was without electricity, telephones, and running water for days. The hospital and many other buildings were seriously damaged. Small houses, including many built up on poles, were knocked off their foundations. At Moín two oil tanks at Costa Rica's oil refinery burned and the rising land left the harbor shallow and the southern kilometer of the canal dry!

From Siquirres east to the coast and south into Panama, almost all road and train bridges collapsed and roads cracked deep and wide. For days the only way to reach Puerto Limón or the southeastern villages was by air or boat, hindering relief and delivery of supplies from other countries. Talamancan Indian villages were isolated for weeks.

While San Jose was shaken and windows and plaster were broken, damage was minor.

Driving to Limón is now possible, but the water system is still not all working. The road south to Cahuita, Puerto Viejo, and the Panamanian border has reopened with temporary one-way bridges. Cahuita lost six houses with other buildings damaged; Puerto Viejo lost twenty-four. August floods washed out some new bridges and again cut off the southeasern region for several days.

Some tours are running on the canales to Tortuguero using the lower Reventazón River to enter the canal at Parismina and go north from there. The canal south of Parismina is being dredged. Parismina Tarpon Rancho was severely damaged when the quake liquified the soil under it. Rio Parismina Lodge, across the canal, is open.

While this quake was devastating in southeastern Costa Rica, travelers should note that most of the country, including most beaches and national parks, wasn't damaged and is still a great travel destination. I expect most quake damage to be repaired by the 1991-92 high tourist season, so have chosen to leave descriptions of the southeast in the main book text unchanged while updating the facilities usable by tourists in this Flash section at each printing. When you're ready to go, ask your tour agent or the ICT office in San Jose for the latest as to what is open in the southeast.

The National Theater, Costa Rica's architectural treasure, was damaged in a succession of 1990 earthquakes until it had to be closed for repairs during 1991 and 1992. Foreign governments, foundations, companies and private citizens are donating the millions of colones needed. Interested tourists can donate in the lobby. You can enjoy one of the daily tours through the lovely first and second floors (small admission fee). Performances by drama and dance groups and the National Symphony are being given in the Teatro Melico Salazar on Avenida 2.

Costa Rica's rate of inflation and rate of currency devaluation against the U.S. dollar are both averaging over 20% annually in 1991. The exchange is about 132 colones per U.S. dollar, with small devaluations weekly. The economic uncertainty as well as an increased demand for hotel rooms has led many hotels to raise their prices even when the prices are quoted in dollars. For your convenience, here's a short conversion table at 140 colones per U. S. dollar, which the exchange is expected to reach in 1991:

$								
$	1	=	140	colones	10	colones	=	$ .07
	5	=	700		50		=	.36
	10	=	1400		100		=	.71
	20	=	2800		500		=	3.57
$	100	=	14,000	colones	1000	colones	=	$7.14

In 1991 there is a cholera epidemic in Peru with some cases reported in Columbia, Guatemala, and Mexico. While none has been found in Costa Rica at presstime, authorities are concerned and are tightly screening people entering from those areas. Since cholera is believed spread by eating raw shellfish as well as by drinking polluted water, even in Costa Rica you are encouraged to avoid these and, if you're housekeeping, to wash vegetables in water to which you've added a small amount of bleach. Carrying a canteen or water bottle and iodine solution allows you to treat drinking and toothbrushing water if you will be camping, driving, hiking, or staying where you don't trust the water.Wash your hands before eating. I carry hand soap or packaged wipes for convenience.

I would appreciate any comments or information you're willing to pass along after your trip. Many of you have been very helpful to other travelers as well as to me, reporting corrections and changes as well as your experiences when hotels and tours agencies have changed management. This book is updated regularly, and useful tips can be added when we reprint. I apologize for not having time to help plan trips or answer questions unless we meet in Costa Rica or at my slide shows. Several thousand readers outnumber me and the 24 hour day.

Last minute note! After we went to press, we learned that the ICT's toll-free phone number, 800-327-7033, is now answered by GTE in Texas where they will take your address and send you a brochure with some information and listings for getting more. If you have questions, you can call the tourism office in San Jose, Costa Rica, 011-506-23-8423. Travel agents have access to computerized information through **American Airlines** and **LACSA**.

Pan American flies to Costa Rica and offers connections in Miami for its flights from Paris.

Costa Rica is a wonderful place with some of the world's finest people. I hope you'll come and explore it—and have as great a time in this peaceful country as I have!

Readers who would like a **free update flyer** (Flyer #3-1) after December 15, 1991 are welcome to write to Windham Bay Press, Box 1198, Occidental, CA 95465 and request it.

Notes

Notes

Notes

Windham Bay Press

Guidebooks for independent travelers who want to **See More and Spend Less!** Great photos! Clear maps. Fun to read! Easy to use! Perfect gifts.

The Costa Rica Traveler, Getting Around in Costa Rica by Ellen Searby. 3rd edition, 1991.

Tells all you need to know to explore a warm and friendly spot in the Central American sun—how to get there, what to bring, how to explore on your own, when you'll see more with a naturalist guide. Lists nature lodges plus 300 hotels personally inspected, with their prices and facilities (even whether the desk staff speaks English)!

The Costa Rica Traveler tells where you'll find wildlife and where to go for the particular birds, monkeys or sea turtles you want to see. A calendar shows fishing seasons, turtle and bird nesting, Costa Rican holidays, and other special activities you may want to plan for.

If you're thinking of retiring in Costa Rica, investing or volunteering there, **The Costa Rica Traveler** has tips, addresses and phone numbers *you need*. **Publishers Weekly Travel Bestseller** for warm destinations in Spring 1990 and 1991!

Readers and reviewers say: "I've been going to Costa Rica for 18 years, but your book is the best!"

"**The Costa Rica Traveler,** by Ellen Searby, veteran travel writer with a demanding eye for value and frequently updates her excellent guide, which carefully rates hotels and takes you off the beaten track." *The Tico Times*, "For the armchair traveler, this book is a great read. For the Costa Rica bound—it's a must!"*Marlin Magazine*

Tropical Beaches And So Much More!

ISBN 0-942297-04-0. 304 pages, maps, over 100 photos. US$14.95

Costa Rica Road Map

Most complete map of Costa Rica we have seen, newly published in Canada, text in English.

* 8 miles to the inch.
* Shows all beaches, mountains, parks and biological reserves.
* Shows all roads where you can drive even a 4-wheel drive, and all towns big and tiny.
* Shows which towns have service stations!
* Colors and type show mountain ranges and an incredible amount of information clearly.
* Map is about 30 x 30 inches, easy to handle in car or bus.
* **Essential for planning your trip and for exploring Costa Rica by car or bus.** Fine for slide and VCR shows when you come back. $7.95.

A Guide To The Birds of Costa Rica, By Stiles and Skutch
• The *only* complete bird guide to Costa Rica—includes 52 pages color.
• Makes bird identification easy—most of the time!
• Highly readable, durable for years of field use, paperback.
• Essential for any birder in Costa Rica!
Published by Cornell University Press. US $34.95.
(Plus shipping. See schedule on order blank.)

Special Costa Rica Set—everything the birder needs but his binoculars!
• The Costa Rica Traveler, 3rd edition
• Costa Rica Road Map
• A Guide to Birds of Costa Rica
One copy of each of the above sent together to same address. US$57.00.
See very special shipping rate for the set—save $4 to $8.

All New 2nd Edition in December 1991!

The Vancouver Island Traveler, Guide to the Freshest,
Friendliest Place on Earth, by Linda Daniel
Cool and forested from nature, but warm and friendly from its welcoming people, Vancouver Island offers you sightseeing and shopping in Victoria, world class fishing, golfing beside the shore, sea kayaking, beach and mountain hiking, caving, diving, bicycling, camping beside lakes and ocean, and simply relaxing!

Canada's Vancouver Island is just a short ferry or plane ride from Seattle or Vancouver. The perfect place to travel with children, it's clean and has lots for them to do. Distances are short so you don't have to keep them for long in car or RV.

The Vancouver Island Traveler gives you all the information you need to plan an exciting or relaxing getaway trip doing what you like best. Hotels, hostels, campgrounds and restaurants are listed, with Daniel's recommendations, even her choices for tea shops in Victoria!
"Finally a detailed guide book" for the island. *The Province*, Vancouver, B.C.
Safe, Friendly, Nearby!
ISBN 0-942297-05-9. 224 pages, maps, over 90 great photos, US$12.95.

Alaska's Inside Passage Traveler, See More, Spend Less. 14th
edition. By Ellen Searby
Alaska's Inside Passage Traveler is the authority for using one of the world's last great travel bargains, the Alaska ferry fleet.
Ferries go through "narrows" close to both shores where you can see wildlife on the beach and eagles in their nests. Ferries stop at all the ports, rather than selected ones. Best of all, you can get off at any port, stay as long

as you wish, and catch another ship. You can bring your car or RV, a bicycle, or a kayak. You can reserve a stateroom, or sleep inexpensively on the solarium deck.

Alaska's Inside Passage Traveler tells you all you need to know to make the most of the ferry way to see the Inside Passage and its towns. Hotels, hostels and campgrounds are listed with their rates. Searby gives suggestions for traveling with chldren or pets, driving an RV in Southeast Alaska and on the ferry, senior rates, and how to enjoy the wilderness here safely.

Author Ellen Searby worked 15 years on the ferries, first as a U.S. Forest Service naturalist and then as a member of the crew.

Readers and reviewers say: "This is the insider's guide to the Inside Passage. If Searby doesn't know it, no one does."

"A must for Alaska travelers." "These books are absolutely the most informative and worth-while." "The book is just what we were hoping for." ISBN 0-942297-06-7. 208 p., maps, 90+ photos. US$12.95

Zip Close Bubble Bags!

Save your gear in rainforest or desert! Keep your cameras, lenses and binoculars clean and dry in the field! Pad such fragile and valuable items from each other in your day pack while you hike, kayak, cycle, or even ride a trotting horse!

No More Rattles in Your Pack!

Author Ellen Searby brings her cameras home in good shape from months of field use by keeping each in a separate bag in her pack. "It's great to be able to reach in and grab one for a quick shot of a monkey, leaving the others in their bags. I give the bags to my naturalist friends, too."

Heavy duty inner and outer layers of plastic with a layer of airtight bubbles between. Washable, reusable many trips. Roomy 10x12" holds camera or binoculars. #G-1, $2.50 each.

All of the books listed here are available in bookstores, especially those specializing in travel. Stores can order them for you or you can order from Windham Bay Press
Box 1198
Occidental, CA 95465   U.S.A.
(707) 823-7150
You are welcome to send for our latest catalog.
We hope you have a wonderful trip and look forward to your next one!

Our books are available from stores throughout North America, or order from Windham Bay Press.

Order Form (all prices in US $)
Windham Bay Press, Box 1198, Occidental, CA 95465 U.S.A. Phone & Fax:
(707) 823-7150

Qty.	Item	Price	Amount
_____	Costa Rica Traveler, 3rd ed.,	14.95	_____
_____	Costa Rica Road Map,	7.95	_____
_____	Guide to the Birds of Costa Rica	34.95	_____
_____	Special Costa Rica Set (all of above)	57.00	_____
_____	Alaska's Inside Passage Traveler,	12.95	_____
_____	Vancouver Island Traveler (after Nov. 1991)	12.95	_____
_____	Zip Close Bubble Bag	2.50	_____

Subtotal $ _____

Sales tax 7 1/2% on orders for CA addresses $ _____

Shipping, see schedule below: $ _____

(**Books**—Traveler guides: US surface $1.50 first book, .50 ea. add'l. Air $3 first book, .50 ea. add'l. book. Canada surface $2.50, Air $4. Air to Latin America $5, Europe, $7, Asia $10. **Birds of Costa Rica**—US surface $2, Air $4.25. Canada surface $2.25, air $5.25. Latin America, $8.50. Europe $15. All others $19. **Maps & Bags**—U.S., $1 ea. Canada $1.25 ea., All other countries $2 ea. **Costa Rica Set** U.S. surface FREE, air $4. Canada Surface $1.50, air $4.)

Total $ _____

(Please enclose check payable though US bank or US or Canadian postal money order in US $.)

Ordered by

Address

Ship to (if different address)

Prices and postage rates good through January 31, 1992. After that date, please request new catalog.